AF710695

The Taxation of Corporations and Shareholders

International Tax Program
Harvard Law School
Cambridge, Massachusetts

K
4544
N67
1982
LAW LIBRARY
GOLDEN GATE UNIVERSITY

The Taxation of Corporations and Shareholders

Martin Norr

KLUWER LAW AND TAXATION PUBLISHERS

Deventer/Netherlands

Antwerp · Boston · London · Frankfurt

Typographical Design: Pieter J. van der Sman
Cover Design: Bert Arts

Copyright © 1982

By the President and Fellows of Harvard College

All rights reserved. No part of this publication may be reproduced, stored in a retrieval system, or transmitted in any form or by any means, mechanical, photocopying, recording, or otherwise, without the prior written permission of the copyright owner.

First published by Kluwer Law and Taxation Publishers, Deventer, Netherlands
D/1981/2664/38 (Belgium)

ISBN 90 6544 015 1 (The Netherlands)
ISBN 90 6321 083 3 (Belgium)

Library of Congress Cataloging in Publication Data
Norr, Martin.
The taxation of corporations and shareholders.
On page opposite t.p.: International Tax Program, Harvard Law School.
Bibliography: p. 199
Includes index.
1. Corporations—Taxation. 2. Dividends—Taxation. I. Harvard University. International Tax Program. II. Title.
K4544.N67 343.05'26 81-15641
ISBN 90-6544-015-1 342.3526 AACR2

PRINTED IN THE NETHERLANDS

Contents

Foreword

This monograph is principally the work of the late Martin Norr. He completed a draft of the entire monograph but had not yet revised it when he died in late 1972. At that time, the integration of corporate and shareholder taxation was just beginning to become of widespread interest in the United States. With the increasing interest thereafter, the International Tax Program began to revise his manuscript, making as few changes as possible in the original draft. We had the benefit of criticism and analysis from Professor Richard M. Bird of the University of Toronto, now Director of the Institute of Policy Analysis there. In addition, Mr. Mitsuo Sato of the Ministry of Finance in Japan gave freely of his time in carefully suggesting changes throughout the manuscript. The present version of Chapter 3 owes a great deal to his additions and suggestions. Thanks are also due to Professor Hugh J. Ault of Boston College Law School for the Appendix, containing his description of the German integration system that became effective in 1977, which was first published in *Law & Policy in International Business.*

Mr. Norr's interest in the subject of corporate and shareholder taxation developed while he was writing the International Tax Program's World Tax Series volume *Taxation in France*, published in 1966. The integration of French taxes on corporations and shareholders took place just after that volume was finished, but had been under discussion in France for some time before then. Despite the large amount of literature generated on the topic in the United States during the past ten years, Mr. Norr's insights into the practicality of integration still remain fresh and useful. In particular, Chapter 7, which deals with international aspects of the subject, highlights a series of difficulties that continue to confound experts today. Those who are particularly concerned that the problems of integration in the international context are the most important ones to solve before the United States again considers adopting integration will find support for that view in this volume.

When Mr. Norr wrote the first draft of this monograph, it was intended to be part of the Tax Technique Handbook series that the International Tax Program publishes. It outgrew that format, however, and is being issued as a separate monograph. Although some of the features of the handbook format are present, the 100-page limit has been exceeded. In addition, an extensive research bibliography has been added which covers not only the works cited in the monograph, but also other English-language materials on integration published through early 1981.

That this monograph now becomes available is principally the result of the efforts of Professor Elisabeth A. Owens, Director of Research at the International Tax Program. Under her direction, Christopher A. Klem updated the manuscript to 1977 during his third year at Harvard Law School and the succeeding months when he began law practice with the firm of Ropes & Gray in Boston. Special credit is due to Martha S. Cooley, Editorial Assistant, and Gretchen A. Hovemeyer, Editorial and Publishing Director, who copyedited the manuscript and prepared it for publication.

The International Tax Program was founded in 1952 in response to a resolution of the United Nations Economic and Social Council and with the aid of a substantial grant from the Ford Foundation. After the first dozen years, the Ford Foundation grant steadily decreased. At the present time, the largest source of foundation support is the Lincoln Institute of Land Policy at Cambridge, Massachusetts. Other direct financial support for the Program's research activity dealing with the developed countries or relations between the developed and the developing countries is provided by the international business community through the Program's Liaison Committee. Indirect support is provided by foreign governments, the United Nations Development Program, and the United States Agency for International Development, all of which grant scholarship and fellowship aid to the foreign officials who study at the Program each year. For further information about the International Tax Program, its current publications, and its training activities, please write to the International Tax Program, Pound Hall, Harvard Law School, Cambridge, Massachusetts 02138, USA.

Oliver Oldman

Learned Hand Professor of Law
and Director of the
International Tax Program,
Harvard Law School

1
Purpose, Scope, and Definitions

1/A. Introduction

1/A.1. In General

This book deals with "perhaps the single most complex technical question in income taxation"[1]: the taxation of corporate-source income to corporations and to their shareholders. On the assumption that an individual income tax is already in use, the analysis begins by considering the arguments for and against the enactment of a corporation income tax in addition. It concludes that the arguments in favor of a corporation income tax are stronger than the arguments against and therefore assumes that such a tax is also adopted.

Proceeding on this basis, the study next considers the effect of the coexistence of a corporation income tax and an individual income tax, particularly on the portion of a corporation's profits which is distributed to its shareholders as dividends. Generally, corporate profits will first be taxed at the corporate level, and any dividends paid out of those profits will then be taxed, in addition, at the shareholder level. Some countries provide no relief from this two-tier taxation of distributed profits. From time to time, however, other countries have adopted one technique or another for relating the corporation and the individual income taxes to each other. Usually, the tax at one level is adjusted to take at least partial account of the tax at the other level.

1. Bird and Oldman (eds.), *Readings on Taxation in Developing Countries* (1st ed.) 167. To the same effect, see Thom, "The Individual and the Family in Tax Reform," in Canadian Tax Foundation, *Report of the Proceedings of the Twenty-Second Tax Conference* 14, 20: "Probably the most difficult and intractable problems of tax law are those relating to the taxation of the corporation and its shareholders."

Fiscal history since World War II demonstrates that neither those countries which have denied an adjustment nor those which have offered an adjustment are entirely satisfied with their solutions to the problem. Certain countries that are at comparable levels of development have used different techniques to relate the corporation and the individual income taxes and have then demonstrated their dissatisfaction with those techniques by adopting other techniques. Certain other countries at the same level of development have at one time seen no need whatsoever to relate the two taxes and at another time taken the opposite position. Such fiscally advanced countries as France, Germany, the United Kingdom, the United States, the Netherlands, Sweden, and Canada, for example, have in recent years made or proposed significant changes in their systems of taxing corporate-source income to corporations and shareholders. On the basis of their experience, some of the countries that made changes in one direction reversed their decisions not long afterward. Others found that particular tax techniques adopted as temporary measures were in their national interest and made them permanent. If nothing more, the variability of past experience demonstrates the difficulty of arriving at satisfactory tax techniques in this complex area. For a developing country, the problems of corporate and shareholder taxation may be even more puzzling than they are for a developed country.

The perfect system of taxing corporations, or of relating the corporation and the individual income taxes to each other, has so far eluded the ingenuity of tax specialists. Except in some very elementary areas, therefore, this study does not attempt to provide definitive answers to the questions that it discusses. Instead, it explores a range of alternative answers and indicates the technical difficulties that experience has shown each alternative to involve. For the most part, the alternatives analyzed are those which are in use today in countries with different legal systems and at different stages of development.[2]

The purpose of this study is to provide the materials essential for an informed choice, not to set forth an ideal solution. If France, Germany, Japan, and the United States, for example, offer different solutions to the problems of corporate and shareholder taxation, it seems probable that no single solution is suitable for all countries.[3]

2. See United Nations, Economic and Social Council, Fiscal Commission, *Corporate Tax Problems* 4: "... extensive illustration by actual examples ... is an essential technique in this type of research."

3. The original draft of this book was written in 1972, when each of the countries mentioned did offer a different solution. Now, however, Germany falls into the same class as Japan, which provides relief at both the corporate and the shareholder levels. Although the descriptions of the tax laws in effect in various countries have been brought up to date as of 1977 to the extent possible, Germany's change in the treatment of corporations and shareholders,

1/A.2. The Political Factor

The absence of definitive answers to virtually all of the questions discussed in this study may be due to an intangible factor that, as a practical matter, often accounts for the solutions adopted by various countries from time to time—the political factor.[4] It is not unreasonable for reasonable people to differ on matters of corporate and shareholder taxation, and they often do so. No one can show that a government that offers distribution relief to shareholders is clearly wrong. Similarly, no one can show that a government that denies distribution relief is clearly wrong.

If one solution to the problem of corporate and shareholder taxation appears to have no more merit than another, the choice may be made on the basis of political inclinations and tendencies, generally unstated and undefined. For example, it is no accident that in the United States, it was a Republican Administration (under President Eisenhower) which provided a degree of distribution relief to shareholders (through a dividends-received deduction) and a Democratic Administration (under President Kennedy) which withdrew this relief. In the United Kingdom, similarly, it is no accident that it was a Labour Government which in 1965 abandoned a system of distribution relief well over 100 years old and that it was a Conservative Government which again provided distribution relief to shareholders in 1973. In none of these cases can it be said that the political party involved was unreasonable or clearly wrong.

The political factors cannot be quantified. Nevertheless, this study would lack candor and realism if it failed to recognize that political factors may control the choice among alternatives when no one alternative can be shown to be plainly right or plainly wrong.

This study is designed primarily for the guidance of developing countries. It is hoped, nevertheless, that it will be of benefit to developed countries as well. Recent experience demonstrates that even the governments and the taxpayers of countries with mature and sophisticated tax systems have found their solutions to the problems of taxing corporations and shareholders unsatisfactory and have therefore adopted, or are looking for, new solutions.

which took place in 1977, is not reflected in the text because the pre-1977 German system was used throughout the original draft to exemplify a highly developed split-rate integration system, and the 1977 change in German law does not affect the validity of the author's analysis of that system. The current German treatment is described briefly in the Appendix.

4. "Tax history is intimately tied to general history, and undoubtedly to economic history, but also, and even more than one might have thought, to political history"; translation from Ardant, 1 *Histoire de l'impôt* 9.

1/B. Scope and Organization

Once such key words as "corporation," "shareholder," and "dividend" have been defined, the first problem discussed in this study is the basic tax treatment of the corporation itself. One possibility, which is often considered but rarely pursued, is to disregard the corporation as an entity for tax purposes and tax its profits pro rata (under the individual income tax, for example) to the persons who hold the shares of the corporation. Another possibility is to tax the corporation's profits directly to the corporation as an entity separate from its shareholders.

If, as is generally the case, this inquiry leads to a decision to tax the corporation as an entity separate from its shareholders, consideration must then be given to the tax treatment of profits distributed as dividends to shareholders. Should these distributions be taxed to the shareholders, and if so, how? Should the distributions be taxed to the recipients on the same basis as other items of income (wages or interest, for example), with no adjustment made for the fact that the profits from which the dividends are paid have (at least in principle) already been taxed at the corporate level? Or should there be some link between the tax on the corporation's profits and the tax on the shareholder's dividends? For example, should the tax on the shareholder's dividend be adjusted to take account of the tax previously imposed on the profits in the hands of the corporation? If an adjustment is deemed desirable, where should it be made? For example, should the tax at the corporate level be reduced in some way on the portion of the corporation's profits which is paid out to shareholders as dividends? Or should the tax at the shareholder level be adjusted by providing special treatment for the dividend in the shareholder's hands? Or should the adjustment be made partly at one level and partly at the other? If some adjustment is thought necessary, the techniques available and the problems inherent in each must be examined.

The process of adjusting the tax at one level to take account of the tax that has been or may be imposed at the other level is generally referred to as the "integration of corporation and individual income taxes." This process will ordinarily be called "integration" in this book.

After discussing the arguments for and against integration, the study considers the level (corporate or shareholder) at which integration should be provided. The following chapter analyzes the various legal techniques by which integration may be provided at the corporate level. The next chapter analyzes the techniques by which integration may be provided at the shareholder level. Each of these chapters considers only domestic aspects. The final chapter of the book deals with the international aspects of integration: the impact, for example, of particular systems of integration on investment abroad and on investment by nonresidents.[5]

1/C. Definitions

1/C.1. Corporation and Shareholder: In General

The corporation is "the central economic institution of modern society."[6] As an economy develops, therefore, and particularly as industrialization proceeds, the use of the corporation as a form of business organization increases. Indeed, industrialization seems almost inevitably to be marked by an increase in the number and the importance of corporations.[7]

Quite apart from tax factors, the corporate form of organization offers advantages to medium- and large-scale industry and commerce which make its use normal, almost inevitable, in those sectors. For small-scale enterprises, the advantages of the corporate form are less pronounced; even in the most highly developed countries, such alternative forms of business organization as the individual proprietorship and the partnership continue to be widely used, for example, in farming, retailing, handicrafts, and the service trades. Even in those sectors, however, an entrepreneur or an artisan may find such advantages in the use of the corporate form that he may deem it advisable to organize his enterprise in that form.

The advantages of the corporate form may become evident from an examination of what is meant by a "corporation." In this work, a corporation is defined as a business organization formed by one or more persons for the purpose of carrying on a profit-making activity.[8] The organization is formed under authority given by a general or a special legislative enactment; it operates under a charter, articles, or statutes drafted and filed with a public authority, in accordance with that enactment.

5. The last chapter of this book relates only to the international aspects of integration, not to the international aspects of income taxation in general.

6. Mason, "Corporation," 3 *International Encyclopedia of the Social Sciences* 396 (1968).

7. Mason (ed.), *The Corporation in Modern Society* 1:

> ... something very like the modern corporation is the inevitable product of an industrializing society, whether that society follows a capitalist or a socialist trend of development. .... Given the technologically determined need for a large stock of capital, the managerial requirements set by the problem of administering the efforts of many men, and the area of discretion demanded for the effective conduct of an entrepreneurial function, the corporation, or a reasonable facsimile thereof, is the only answer.

8. This study relates only to corporations organized for profit. Religious, municipal, nonprofit, charitable, and similar corporations are not considered.

For virtually all purposes, the legislative enactment endows any corporation that is properly formed under its terms with a legal personality separate from that of the persons who own shares in the corporation. Under the governing enactment, in short, the corporation is a separate legal entity. Because it is an entity distinct from its shareholders, the corporation continues in existence regardless of changes (by sale, gift, or death, for example) among the persons who from time to time may own its shares. As a separate and continuing entity, the corporation has the right to do business, to own property, to assume obligations, and to sue and be sued in its own name.

Limited liability is perhaps the most important consequence of the corporation's being an entity separate from its shareholders. Except in special circumstances, the shareholders are not liable for the debts, torts, or contracts of the corporation; their liability is limited to the amount of their capital contributions.[9] Limited liability, in turn, permits the corporation to assemble from a number of shareholders the amounts of capital that it may need for its operations. In contributing capital to the corporate enterprise, or in acquiring shares from a contributor, the shareholder does not put his personal fortune at risk. Ordinarily, creditors and other persons doing business with the corporation must rely on the credit of the corporation as such rather than on the credit of any person holding shares in the corporation.

Limited liability is a key feature of the corporate form of organization. Limited liability makes it more feasible to aggregate into a single enterprise capital from several or many sources. The fact that many persons may own interests in the corporation calls attention to yet another characteristic of the corporate form of organization: centralized management.

In a widely held corporation, it is impracticable, even impossible, to poll all shareholders before the decisions involved in the normal operation of the firm can be made. For this reason, the legislative act governing the formation of corporations requires that the shareholders officially designate representatives whose responsibility is to provide the enterprise with centralized and continuing management and direction.[10] The titles of these representatives, who may or may not be shareholders as well, vary from one legal system to another; in the United States and the United Kingdom,

9. Fletcher, 13A *Cyclopedia of the Law of Private Corporations* (perm. ed.) §6213.

10. In a closely held corporation, however, the shareholders often participate actively in management, and many of the formalities called for by the corporation law may be ignored. As a practical matter, a closely held corporation may be managed in the same way as a general or a simple partnership. The law, nevertheless, calls for observance of the formalities, including the official designation of management representatives with authority to act for the corporation. Some of the differences between widely held and closely held corporations are discussed in section 1/C.2 below.

they are called "directors" and will be referred to as such in this book. The directors, in turn, hire and supervise the officers of the corporation, who are directly in charge of the corporation's day-to-day operations.

Within broad limits, the directors' authority over the affairs of the corporation includes almost total authority to retain within the corporation, or distribute to the shareholders, all or part of the corporation's earnings. This is true even in a country in which the authority to approve or disapprove dividend declarations proposed by the directors belongs, at least nominally, to the shareholders. The authority of the shareholders to approve or disapprove dividend proposals generally does not include the authority to compel payment of a dividend; that lies in the reasonable business discretion of the directors.

Given the existence of limited liability and centralized management, the shares or beneficial interests in the corporation can be transferred by the holders without jeopardizing the continuity of the enterprise. The separate legal existence of the corporation ordinarily continues notwithstanding the death, disability, or withdrawal of a shareholder.

A corporation cannot exist, however, without at least the minimum number of shareholders or stockholders required by the law governing the formation of corporations. The function of the shareholder is to provide the basic stock of fixed or permanent capital needed by the corporation; as distinguished from loan capital, share capital need not be repaid during the lifetime of the corporation. In return for his capital contribution, each contributor receives a pro rata "share" in the ownership of the corporation; hence the term "shareholder."[11] In other words, the shares represent equal fractional parts of the total share capital of the corporation. Whether a particular shareholder owns one share or thousands of shares depends on the total number of shares issued by the corporation and the relative size of his capital contribution. The shareholder owns an interest in the corporation, but not in the corporation's assets or liabilities; the corporation, as a legal entity separate from its shareholders, interposes itself between the shareholder and the corporation's assets and liabilities.

As a practical matter, the capital contributed to a corporation by its shareholders must often be supplemented by debt or loan capital borrowed from individuals or financial institutions; sometimes these lenders are also shareholders. A supplier of debt or loan capital ranks as a creditor of the corporation, whereas a shareholder as such does not. The shareholder's

11. In the past, corporations were often known in English as "joint-stock companies," and the shares in them were called "stock" or "shares of stock." The owner was, and often still is, called a "stockholder," rather than a "shareholder." In French and other languages, however, the word *stock* means the stock of goods held by a business as inventory. To avoid confusion, this book will ordinarily use the words "share" and "shareholder," rather than the words "stock" and "stockholder."

position as a pro rata owner of an interest in the corporation is therefore different from the position of a creditor. A creditor is generally entitled, on a specified date, to the repayment of the principal of his loan and to the payment of interest at a predetermined rate that is designed to compensate him for the "hire" of his money. A shareholder, however, is not entitled to "repayment" of his capital contribution by the corporation, though he may sell all or some of his shares to a third party. Nor is the shareholder entitled to be paid by the corporation for the use of his money at a fixed rate.[12] From time to time, however, he may be entitled to a "dividend."

For purposes of this study, a "dividend" is defined as the amount of the corporation's earnings and profits which the directors (or other appropriate organs of the corporation) periodically determine shall be divided pro rata among the shareholders. Only distributions formally declared as dividends by a corporation's directors are included in this definition and will be considered dividends in this study. Many jurisdictions tax a "concealed dividend," such as excessive rent paid by a corporation to a shareholder for the use of property owned by him, in the same manner as a dividend proper. Nevertheless, distributions that are not formally designated as dividends are outside the scope of this study.[13]

Except in very unusual circumstances, a shareholder has a claim on a corporation's earnings and profits only when and to the extent that a distribution therefrom has been formally declared as a dividend. Whether or not to declare a dividend and the size of the dividend are almost entirely within the discretion of the corporation's directors.

Neither corporate law nor good business practice requires that all corporate profits be distributed to shareholders as dividends.[14] In fact, a full current distribution of corporate profits to shareholders is definitely not typical. Most corporations generally retain a significant portion of their profits for use in the normal conduct of their business activities or for growth and expansion. The proportion retained varies from country to country, from corporation to corporation, and even from time to time in the life of a particular corporation. Nevertheless, the retention by business

12. There is a minor exception to this rule. Some shares, called "preferred" shares, entitle the holder to a fixed rate of dividend, which the corporation must pay before it distributes dividends to the holders of ordinary or "common" shares. Preferred shareholders are not entitled, however, to any share in the profits beyond the fixed rate.

13. On the deductibility of business expenses and the tax treatment of disbursements not properly deductible as such, see Popkin, *The Deduction for Business Expenses and Losses.*

14. On the contrary, the corporation laws of many countries require a corporation to retain some portion of its earnings in a "legal reserve" for the added protection of its creditors. Retention may be required, for example, until the legal reserve amounts to 20% of the corporation's share capital.

corporations of a very considerable portion of their earnings is the almost universal pattern, a pattern grounded both in business practice and in the legal authority of corporate directors over the declaration of dividends.

The phenomenon of retention is a major factor, perhaps the most important single factor, in determining how corporations are taxed, as will be shown in Chapter 2. Throughout this book, therefore, a distinction will constantly be drawn between "retained profits" and "distributed profits." Tax provisions whose purpose or effect is to induce a greater degree of distribution will often be referred to under the rubric "distribution relief."

A shareholder who buys common shares in a corporation seeks financial gains of two separate varieties; which variety is the more important varies from country to country and from shareholder to shareholder. First, the shareholder hopes that the corporation will earn a profit and that the value of his shares will increase as a result. In other words, he seeks capital appreciation. Second, the shareholder hopes that the corporation's profits will be large enough to permit the periodic distribution of dividends. In other words, he also seeks a current return on his capital.[15]

A shareholder does not have the rights of a creditor, but he does have a right, not possessed by a creditor, to share pro rata in such profits as may be distributed by the corporation. He also has a hope, again not possessed by a creditor, that the corporation's success will result in an increase in the value of his investment. But because the interests of a shareholder are subordinate to those of a creditor (in the event, for example, that the corporation fails to prosper), the shareholder's risk of loss is generally greater than that of a creditor. In the event, for example, of the dissolution or the liquidation of the corporation, either forced or voluntary, the corporation's shareholders are subordinate to the corporation's lenders and other creditors.

1/C.2. The Widely Held Versus the Closely Held Corporation

As a matter of both law and practice, virtually all corporations today exhibit the basic characteristics of separate personality and limited liability. As a practical matter, however, corporations are not homogeneous; they differ from one another in various respects.

One obvious difference is in the size and the scope of their operations. A

15. If the corporation is a closely held corporation, the shareholder may have another aim: to obtain employment as an officer, a director, or an employee so that he is entitled both to a salary and to the perquisites of the position desired (a company car, expense allowances or reimbursements, and so forth). An aim of this sort can rarely be realized by acquiring shares in a widely held corporation.

corporation in the oil, automobile, or computer industry, for example, may have operations all over the world; it may require hundreds of millions of dollars in capital, employ hundreds of thousands of persons, have hundreds of thousands of shareholders scattered all over the globe, enjoy a sales volume larger than the gross national product of many of the nations of the world, and report annual profits in the millions or even billions of dollars. Some of the shareholders of such a corporation will also be officers, directors, or employees of the corporation, but the great majority of them will have no connection with the corporation except as shareholders. They will not serve as directors, officers, or employees, for example, or participate in management except to the extent that they vote (usually by proxy) at annual meetings.

At the other extreme is a corporation that operates a grocery store, a gasoline station, or a repair service in a small town; it may have a capital measured in the hundreds or thousands of dollars, a sales volume of only a few dollars a day, and no shareholders outside the family circle. In some countries, such as the United States, a corporation may be formed with only a single shareholder. Other countries, such as France, require some minimum number of shareholders; as a practical matter, these shareholders are often members of, or representatives of, a single family unit or of several families.

Both as a practical matter and in terms of tax consequences, the most important of the differences among corporations may be the number of shareholders and the range of share ownership. These differences, which can be summarized by the two phrases "widely held" and "closely held," often affect the decisions of legislators and others on the matters of tax policy considered in this study. In many countries, these differences account to some extent for variations in the tax treatment of the two types of corporation.

A widely held corporation, such as the first corporation described above, may have several hundred, several thousand, or even several hundreds of thousands of shareholders, most of whom are strangers to one another and many of whom are geographically distant from the head office of the corporation. The shares of the corporation may be listed for trading on an organized stock exchange or "bourse" or, even in the absence of such an exchange or of a formal listing, may be traded regularly in a less formal way on an "over-the-counter" market. In the United States, for example, there are no more than several thousand corporations whose shares are listed and traded on the New York Stock Exchange and on similar but smaller exchanges in Boston, Philadelphia, and other major cities. But there may be as many as fifty thousand corporations whose shares, though not formally listed on any exchange, are bought and sold regularly through brokers or other financial intermediaries.

Most of the shareholders of a widely held corporation will be strangers to its management and to one another, and centralized management is therefore essential. Polling the hundreds or thousands of shareholders for their views on the questions that must be answered in the daily operation of the corporation is not practicable. Even such important questions as whether to enter a new line of business, whether to make a contract in the millions with a new supplier or a new customer, whether to spend millions on a new plant at home or abroad, and whether to borrow money in amounts that may run to two or three hundreds of millions of dollars cannot be taken up with the shareholders, but must be decided by the directors of the corporation, or by officers or employees designated by them. Moreover, most of the shareholders will lack the experience and the knowledge required in making an informed decision. The average shareholder of a widely held corporation is necessarily remote from management. The pioneering work of Professors Berle and Means in the 1930s demonstrated how completely ownership and control are separated in a widely held corporation.[16] To argue that such an enterprise is like a partnership is to ignore reality.

Closely held corporations, which are far more numerous than widely held corporations, are a different matter. Typically, the shareholders participate actively in the management and day-to-day operations of the corporation, or are relatives or friends of active participants. Most closely held corporations are family corporations. The shareholders are not strangers to management or to one another. Ownership and control are not separate, but go hand in hand. In principle, the shares of a closely held corporation are transferable; however, as a practical matter, such shares, like partnership interests, lack marketability and are rarely transferred for consideration. For all practical purposes, a closely held corporation does resemble a partnership. The essential difference between a closely held corporation and a partnership is that the participants in the corporation, though operating the firm as they would a partnership, have chosen the corporate form of organization in order to enjoy the benefits of limited liability.

Because corporations fall into two distinct categories, the widely held and the closely held, the existence of two different views of the corporation is not surprising. In one view, the corporation is a fiction of law. It is no different from the individuals who compose it, but simply a legal convenience enabling those individuals to band together in order to carry on a profit-making activity; it is in no essential respect different from a partnership. This view was not held, however, by the legislators who made the existence of corporations possible by enacting either general or special

16. Berle and Means, *The Modern Corporation and Private Property*.

corporate laws. Nor was it held by the courts, which had to deal with the financial relations between corporations and their shareholders. A classic statement by Lord Justice Lindley put the matter this way[17]:

> A sale by a person to a corporation of which he is a member is not, either in form or in substance, a sale by a person to himself. To hold that it is, would be to ignore the principle which lies at the root of the legal idea of a corporate body, and that idea is that the corporate body is distinct from the persons composing it.

To deny the separateness of the corporation from the persons who compose it is to negate the very reason for the corporation's existence. Nevertheless, there were reasonable men in England, for example, in the late 18th and early 19th centuries (before the Limited Liability Act of 1855 confirmed the separateness of a corporation from its members by absolving the members from liability for the debts of the corporation) who viewed the corporation as no more than a legal convenience.

The early view that the corporation was essentially like a partnership or a family had relevance for most of the corporations that were created long before the adoption of the Joint Stock Companies Act (1844), when no distinction was drawn between incorporated and unincorporated companies.[18] The view still has relevance for most of the closely held, family corporations that exist today. The closely held corporation, even in the modern world, does bear a close resemblance to a partnership, and it must therefore always be kept in mind that the participants have deliberately chosen the corporate form of organization in order to obtain the benefits of limited liability.

The view of the corporation as a fiction, a legal convenience that disguises what is essentially a partnership, has little, if any, relevance, however, for such corporations as General Motors, British Petroleum, Pechiney, and Bayer, which are only a few examples of the many widely held corporations of different national origins which exist in the world today. Professor van den Tempel points out that for modern, widely held corporations, the old view of the corporation is simply "obsolete."[19] He adds:

> Modern industrial development has meant that notably the public share company, of which the shares are quoted on the stock exchange, when seen from an economic and social point of view has an existence of its own, independent of that of its shareholders.

17. *Farrar* v. *Farrars, Limited,* 40 Ch. D. 409–410 (1888).

18. Réamonn, *The Philosophy of the Corporate Tax* 37, 38.

19. Van den Tempel, *Corporation Tax and Individual Income Tax in the European Communities* 8.

In other words, the widely held corporation does enjoy an independent personality, and it has rights and duties separate from those of its members. Moreover, this separate legal personality has practical economic consequences that no one can ignore; it makes of the widely held corporation an entity possessing economic autonomy distinct from its shareholders and capable of acting in its own interest. Unlike the closely held corporation, the widely held corporation cannot reasonably be thought to resemble a partnership.

It may be appropriate to apply a uniform system of taxation to all corporations, both widely held and closely held; many countries do. Yet some of the tension and flux in the tax treatment of corporate-source income may be attributable to the existence of two categories of corporation; in some circumstances, a tax structure that is appropriate for one category may be inappropriate for the other. Whenever any particular technique for taxing corporate-source income is under discussion, it may therefore be helpful to see whether that technique suits both widely held and closely held corporations. A system that is appropriate for widely held corporations, for example, may need adjustment if it is also to be suitable for closely held corporations. By the same token, a system that is appropriate for closely held, family corporations may be outmoded and ill-suited to widely held corporations.

1/C.3. Quasi Corporations

For the benefit of small-scale enterprises, the legal systems of many countries provide for the existence not only of corporations proper, but also of various forms of business organization which resemble corporations proper in important respects. These forms of organization, which are particularly useful to closely held firms, include "limited liability companies" (in French, *sociétés à responsabilité limitée*; in Spanish, *sociedades a responsabilidad limitada*). Such firms are exactly like corporations in that each of them is a legal entity separate from its participants and the participants enjoy limited liability. They differ from corporations in that public participation is generally limited; there may be a ceiling on the number of participants allowed (20 or 50, for example) or on the amount of share capital employed. In addition, there are usually restrictions on the extent to which the shares or interests in the enterprise are transferable.

Because these forms of organization have the features of limited liability and separate legal personality which mark corporations proper, many of the countries in which such organizations exist subject them to the same tax rules as corporations proper. In the interests of simplicity, this study will ordinarily refer only to corporations, but that term should be understood to include not just corporations proper, but also "quasi corporations"—that is, forms of business organization whose attributes (notably limited liability and separate legal personality) are enough like those of corporations proper that whatever tax system is provided for the latter is also extended to the former.

2

The Corporation Income Tax: Arguments For and Against

2/A. The Need To Tax Corporate Profits

If a country levies a tax on the income of individuals, what tax treatment should it apply to the profits of business corporations? This is the first question discussed in this study.

Virtually every country that levies an individual income tax, and in which the corporate form of business organization is at all common, also levies a corporation income tax, which is collected annually from business corporations on the basis of their current profits. The essential reason for imposing a tax on the profits of corporations is a practical one—the need to protect the individual income tax.

In a country that levies an individual income tax, a person who does not incorporate his business enterprise is required to pay the individual income tax on the profits from his individual proprietorship. If that country does not also levy a tax on the profits of business enterprises organized as corporations, the same individual has the alternative of organizing his enterprise in the form of a corporation and can therefore escape the current imposition of the individual income tax on the profits of the business.

This alternative is related to the phenomenon of retention. It was pointed out in Chapter 1 that few corporations currently distribute all or most of their profits as dividends to shareholders; most corporations retain a significant portion (perhaps one half) of their profits in their own hands. Indeed, the retention by business corporations of a substantial part of their profits is an almost universal pattern. If some way were not found to tax these profits as earned, an intolerable fiscal discrimination against unincorporated business would result. The earnings of an unincorporated business (an individual proprietorship, for example) would be subjected, as earned, to the individual income tax in the hands of the owner, whereas the earnings of an incorporated business would escape taxation as long as they were retained in the hands of the corporation. In addition to this discrimination, the failure to levy a tax on corporate profits would result in the government's being deprived of tax revenue from a major portion of the business sector. Even those who view the corporation income tax as defective in principle find that, as a practical matter, it is an appropriate "device for ... bringing retained earnings into the reach of the income tax."[1]

The problem of retention may be viewed in still another way: retained corporate profits may be regarded as the savings of shareholders. Since other kinds of income saved by shareholders are subjected to taxation, there appears to be no reason for savings that take the form of retained corporate profits to go tax-free. Both equity and the revenue needs of the government demand that there be no exemption for the savings of an individual whose investments take the form of shares in a corporation that does not make prompt and complete distributions of its profits. That these profits might be distributed later and subjected to taxation in the shareholders' hands at that time is no answer; until such time as a dividend is actually distributed, the shareholder will enjoy the benefits of tax deferral. If other types of personal savings are taxed as earned, then savings that take the form of undistributed corporate profits must also be taxed currently.

In short, any country that taxes the income of individuals must find some method of taxing the profits of business corporations. This is true whatever the size of the corporation and the number of shareholders involved. The following sections of this chapter discuss alternative methods of taxing corporate profits.

2/B. Disregard of the Corporate Entity for Tax Purposes

2/B.1. In General

Two opposing views of the corporation were mentioned in Chapter 1. One regards the corporation less as an entity than as a fiction of the law, a form of organization which enables a group of individuals to band together, by contract, in order to carry on a profit-making activity jointly. The other

1. Musgrave, "Taxation of Corporations," in Canadian Tax Foundation, *Report of the Proceedings of the Twenty-Second Tax Conference* 124, 126. Musgrave states elsewhere that unless taxes are collected from corporations, "retained earnings escape personal income tax until realization or death." "The Carter Commission Report," 1 *Canadian Journal of Economics* 159, 164 (1968).

view recognizes that the corporation is a creature of the law, but emphasizes that the corporation is an entity separate from its owner or owners for virtually all legal purposes and that it may have an economic autonomy and a taxable capacity of its own.[2]

These conflicting views affect tax policy. The view that the corporation is "a form of contractual co-operation, by means of which the joint shareholders run an enterprise," has recently been called "obsolete," at least as far as publicly held corporations are concerned.[3] Obsolete or not, however, this view of the corporation persists in many minds. Those who adhere to this view may conclude that the profits of the corporation should be regarded as the income of the shareholders for tax purposes, and that if it is necessary to tax these profits, some way should be found to disregard the corporate entity and to tax the profits to the shareholders under the individual income tax. Moreover, the rates of the individual income tax are usually, though not invariably, progressive; they are therefore generally thought to reflect the views of society about the equitable allocation of income tax burdens. This circumstance reinforces the view of many that corporate profits should be taxed, insofar as practicable, to shareholders under the individual income tax. The following subsection will consider methods by which this might be done and the arguments for and against these methods.

2/B.2. Taxation of Corporate Profits Directly to Shareholders: The Partnership Method

One possible method of taxing corporate profits is simply to disregard any distinction between retained profits and distributed profits and to tax all of the corporation's profits, whether or not physically distributed, to the shareholders in proportion to their interests in the corporation. This method would simply disregard the existence of the corporate entity for tax purposes. Whether the corporation's profits are retained by the corporation or paid out to shareholders, they would be imputed to the shareholders and taxed directly to them. In short, the shareholder's individual income tax rate would be applied to his aliquot share of the corporation's profits in the year in which the profits were earned. If profits retained by the corporation but already taxed to the shareholders as earned

2. "The policy question is whether it is more meaningful to regard the corporation as a quasi-independent economic unit or as only an aggregation of individual investors who are essentially similar to partners." Goode, *The Corporation Income Tax* 5.

3. Van den Tempel, *Corporation Tax and Individual Income Tax in the European Communities* 8.

are later distributed physically to the shareholders, no additional income tax would be due from the shareholders.

This method of taxing the profits of a corporation to its shareholders is often referred to as the "partnership method" because it is the method commonly used by the United States, Great Britain, France, Sweden, and many other countries to tax the profits of ordinary partnerships. Those countries do not regard a partnership as an entity for income tax purposes; instead, the partnership's profits, whether retained by the firm or distributed to the partners, are taxed to the partners. Another name for this treatment is "fiscal transparency"; the tax authorities "look through" the partnership to its owners and tax them directly on their shares of the firm's profits.[4]

If the partnership method were used to tax corporations, retained earnings would be taxed to the shareholders in exactly the same manner as dividends are; that is, they would be subject to the progressive rates of the individual income tax. In other words, the partnership method would bring all corporate earnings, including those retained by the corporation, within the immediate reach of the individual income tax imposed on the shareholders.

In some countries, the partnership method is available on an optional basis to closely held corporations (for example, corporations with ten or fewer shareholders). Moreover, in certain special circumstances, corporate earnings may be taxed directly to the shareholders of closely held corporations in order to counter tax avoidance on a national or an international scale.[5] The fact is, however, that no developed country uses the partnership method as its regular method of taxing ordinary business corporations. The method is not imposed either on closely held or on widely held corporations. Nor, as far as it is known, has any developing country chosen to impose the partnership method of taxation on corporations. The arguments against the compulsory application of the partnership method to corporations are essentially practical ones. It is argued that to tax corporate profits, retained as well as distributed, directly to shareholders is administratively impracticable, at least in the case of widely

4. The treatment that partnerships receive for tax purposes simply parallels their treatment for other legal purposes. For example, if a partnership is not an entity separate enough from its partners to give its partners the benefits of limited liability, then the partners are liable to the government for tax on their share of the partnership's profits, just as they are liable to creditors for debts of the partnership. By the same token, if a partnership is conferred legal personality by company laws, as is the case in some countries (Japan, for example), its profits are taxed to the entity itself, not to the partners. For the tax treatment of partnerships in various countries, including developing countries, see Sato, "The Tax Treatment of Partnerships" (unpublished, 1 May 1973).

5. See, for example, WTS: *United States*, 11/3.4 ("Provisions Controlling Use of Foreign Corporations and Other Foreign Entities for Tax Avoidance Purposes").

held corporations. Even though applying the partnership method to closely held corporations may be just as feasible as applying it to ordinary partnerships, other reasons exist for not requiring its use in their case.

For a corporation that has a considerable number of shareholders, some of whom hold their shares not through the entire tax year but only for varying portions of a year, the problem of determining each shareholder's aliquot share of taxable corporate profits (or deductible losses) may be difficult. The shareholders of a widely held corporation may number 5,000, 10,000, 25,000, or more; since at least some of these shareholders will buy and sell their shares during the course of the year, fixing each shareholder's aliquot share in the corporation's taxable profits will be more difficult than fixing each partner's share in a partnership's taxable profits. As a general rule, partnerships have only a small number of partners, and the ownership of partnership interests is relatively stable. The existence of bearer shares, common in many countries, compounds the difficulty of determining each shareholder's aliquot share of a corporation's profits. So does the complexity of certain corporate capital structures—the use, for example, of cumulative preference, of participating or similar shares, or of income bonds, with a prior claim on corporate earnings—and the existence of intercorporate shareholdings. If the corporation is a widely held corporation, the tax administration's routine adjustments in the amount of corporate income after audit would presumably require retroactive adjustments in the taxable income of hundreds or thousands of shareholders.

The weight of opinion agrees with Professors Shoup, Surrey, Oldman, and their colleagues, who concluded in a study of Venezuela that the partnership method "presents probably insuperable difficulties in administration. This is certainly so for large corporations."[6] Similarly, Professor Goode stressed the "formidable administrative difficulties" that the partnership method would involve, at least for all corporations other than those "that resemble true partnerships in the simplicity of their capital structure and the small number of their owners."[7]

Some economists have argued that solutions to the practical and administrative difficulties of the compulsory partnership method might be found if more thought were devoted to them.[8] As matters stand, however, the administrative burdens of compulsory imputation are generally considered to outweigh the advantages of the system—at least for widely held

6. Shoup *et al.*, *The Fiscal System of Venezuela* 116.

7. Goode, *The Corporation Income Tax* 184, 186.

8. Holland, "Stockholder Differential Taxation and Tax Relief," in United States, Congress, House of Representatives, Committee on Ways and Means, 3 *Tax Revision Compendium* 1551, 1572; Musgrave, "Growth With Equity," 53 *American Economic Review, Papers and Proceedings* 323, 330 (1963).

corporations.[9] Furthermore, no developed country relies on the compulsory imputation of the profits of ordinary corporations to their shareholders as its normal method of taxing those profits. In the case of developing countries, even those tax advisory missions which acknowledge the theoretical advantages of the partnership method do not recommend that it be enacted into law.[10]

In support of the practical arguments against compulsory imputation, other arguments have been advanced, but none is very weighty. It is said that to tax shareholders on undistributed corporate profits by imputation fails to give the proper attention to the concept of realization. As a general rule, income tax systems tax individuals only on realized income, that is, on income physically received by them or readily available to them. Yet even if it is conceded for the sake of argument that the profits of a corporation are the income of its shareholders who are entitled to ratable shares of those profits in the event of distribution, it may still be argued that at best that income is only unrealized income. The very fact of retention means that undistributed profits remain at the risk of the business; as a practical matter, they may not ever be distributed and may therefore never be realized in possession and enjoyment by the shareholders. To tax shareholders on their aliquot shares of a corporation's undistributed profits is therefore regarded by some as inequitable. It is also argued that it may be a burden on some shareholders to require them to use other resources to pay tax on sums which are deemed to be income but which are not physically available to them.

Most of these arguments could also be made against the ordinary method of taxing partnership profits to partners. In the partnership case, however, they are generally thought to be unconvincing, probably because partners are far fewer in number than shareholders and, as a practical matter, may have a closer relationship to their partnerships than most shareholders do to their corporations. In Professor Goode's phrase, the use of the partnership method depends on the view that shareholders, as individual investors, are "essentially similar to partners." In fact and in law, however, shareholders (at least in those corporations which are not closely held) are not essentially similar to partners. In their relation to management, for example, and in the extent of their liability for the acts of management, shareholders are essentially dissimilar to partners. It would therefore seem that the compulsory application of the partnership method to corporations,

9. See Canada, Royal Commission on Taxation, 4 *Report of the Royal Commission on Taxation* 49; McLure, "Integration of the Personal and Corporate Income Taxes: The Missing Element in Recent Tax Reform Proposals," 88 *Harvard Law Review* 532, 563–564 (1975).

10. As a matter of tax relief for small business, however, it is often recommended that closely held corporations be given the option of electing the partnership method whenever that method would be to their fiscal advantage.

which would involve the imputation to shareholders of retained as well as distributed corporate profits, is not practicable.

Yet for a closely held corporation (with no more than five or ten shareholders, for example), the partnership method of taxation would appear to be as practicable as it is for a partnership. Why then is it not imposed on closely held corporations? The reason appears to be the progressivity of the rate structure of the individual income tax. The imposition of progressive individual rates, rather than the usually flat corporate rate, on each shareholder's aliquot part of the corporation's profits (retained as well as distributed) would in many cases increase the tax burden of the shareholders of closely held family corporations. It may, of course, be argued that even though it results in a heavier tax burden, the application of progressive rates to the shareholder's aliquot share of corporate profits is justified on equity grounds. That is, it serves to maintain equality in tax treatment between sole proprietors or partners and the shareholders of closely held corporations. However, a major practical difficulty of applying the partnership approach to closely held corporations is deciding how to draw a line of demarcation between corporations whose shareholders are to be subject to progressive taxation and those whose shareholders are not to be. The line must necessarily be arbitrary. As a result, some countries make the partnership method available *on an optional basis* to closely held corporations as a measure of small-business relief. In practice, the option is exercised only if its effect will be a reduction in tax. In those countries in which the partnership method is available for closely held corporations, its use is voluntary, not compulsory.[11] The partnership method is not required of closely held corporations (generally, small family-owned corporations) for fear that its application might increase their tax burden.

In summary, applying the partnership method of taxation to corporations is attractive at least in theory as a way of bringing all corporate earnings, retained as well as distributed, within the scope of the individual income tax. Yet, as far as it is known, no country in the world actually uses the partnership method as its regular method of taxing corporate income. In the case of widely held corporations, the method is not used, nor is it recommended by tax advisory missions, because of its administrative problems. In the case of closely held corporations, the partnership method may be made available on an optional basis in certain instances, but requiring its use in all instances is considered impracticable because it would sometimes result in a heavier tax burden for closely held cor-

11. To counter tax avoidance, the application of the partnership method may be made compulsory for certain special categories of closely held corporations (for example, foreign personal holding companies or controlled tax haven corporations under U.S. law).

porations that are small and family-owned. Moreover, it is difficult to draw a line between the corporations for which heavier taxation is perhaps justified on equity grounds and those for which it is not.

2/C. Compulsory Distribution of Corporate Profits to Shareholders

If the retention of corporate profits by corporations is the phenomenon underlying the search for a means of taxing corporate profits and if it is not practicable to disregard retention by imputing corporate profits to the shareholders, another possibility exists. The tax problems arising from retention could be avoided simply by *requiring* corporations to distribute their profits to their shareholders.

A country's corporate law or tax law, or both, could provide, for example, that within a reasonable time after the end of each fiscal year, every business corporation must make an actual physical distribution of its profits to its shareholders. In the ordinary case, these distributions would then be subject to tax in the shareholder's hands. As far as the individual income tax is concerned, the corporate entity would, in effect, cease to be a buffer between the profits of the corporation and the corporation's shareholders. This solution to the problem of retention would make all of the corporation's profits income to the shareholders and would also give the shareholders the funds with which to pay tax on that income. No tax on corporations as such would be needed in order to protect the individual income tax. If after a compulsory full distribution of its profits, a corporation needed funds to meet the requirements of its business operations, it would have to obtain those funds from outside sources—from lenders in the form of loan capital, for example, or from shareholders in the form of additional equity capital.

From time to time, attempts have been made to encourage distribution by subjecting retained profits to a heavier tax burden than distributed profits. Sometimes, indeed, the tax penalty for retention has been so heavy that, at least in the popular mind, it was regarded as equivalent to compulsory distribution. Great Britain's Finance Act of 1965, for example, provided that if certain "close companies" failed to distribute at least 60% of their profits to their shareholders, any shortfall would be subjected to the individual income tax rates in the companies' hands; this treatment was sometimes referred to as "compulsory distribution." Putting a tax price on corporate retentions, even a high price, is one thing, but prohibiting such retentions is another. Holding companies and other special varieties of corporation aside, the arguments against compulsory distribution are so strong that no nation, as far as it is known, requires ordinary business corporations to make current physical distributions of their profits to their shareholders.

In the case of a closely held corporation, it might not be impracticable after a full distribution of profits for the corporation to obtain from its shareholders the funds needed to carry on the business. Nevertheless, even for closely held corporations, a requirement that all current profits be distributed is generally thought to be too radical an interference with corporate management to be tolerable under normal circumstances. It may be argued that decisions about retention or distribution should be left to the discretion of the corporation's directors, who are responsible for maintaining the corporation's finances at a level appropriate to the reasonable business needs of the corporation. Moreover, as a practical matter, even though a corporation has earned profits, they may not be physically available for distribution; they may have been reinvested, for example, in inventory or in fixed assets, such as buildings and machinery.

For widely held corporations, the periodic need to request that shareholders reinvest all or part of their dividend receipts would create a heavy administrative burden. As a result, the compulsory physical distribution of the profits of ordinary business corporations is almost never given serious consideration. In order to protect creditors, many countries go in the opposite direction, requiring corporations to retain some portion of their profits in a "legal reserve" until the reserve has reached some stated proportion of the share capital. And to ensure that funds are available for reinvestment, some countries may offer tax incentives to the retention of profits.

2/D. Taxation of Corporate Profits to the Corporation as an Entity

2/D.1. In General

If the phenomenon of retention calls for a tax on corporate profits and if neither compulsory imputation nor compulsory distribution of those profits to shareholders is practicable in the case of the ordinary business corporation, the alternative is to tax the profits directly to the corporation as a taxable entity separate from its shareholders. Indeed, this is the practice in virtually every country in which corporations exist.

This section will discuss various methods of taxing corporate profits to the corporation as a separate entity. Whether and how the tax on the profits earned by the corporation should be integrated with the tax on the recipients of dividends paid from those profits are discussed in Chapters 3, 4, 5, and 6.

2/D.2. Imposition of the Individual Income Tax

One method of taxing the profits of a business corporation to the corporation as an entity is simply to subject the entity's profits to the same tax and the same rates that are applied to the incomes of individuals. This method has the virtue of simplicity: all income recipients, whether individual or corporate, are treated in the same manner for tax purposes. A country that imposes an individual income tax at progressive rates ranging, for example, from 5% to 40% will apply exactly the same rate schedule to corporations, each of which will be treated as a separate entity for this purpose.

The major objection to this system centers around the rate schedule. Although some countries provide a mild degree of progression in their corporate rate schedules (usually as an incentive to small businesses), it is generally felt that the sharper degree of progression applied to individual incomes under most individual income tax laws should not be imposed on corporate profits in the hands of corporations. Moreover, although it is not impossible for an upper-bracket individual to avoid the full rigors of progression by spreading his income among several taxpayers (his children, for example), such income splitting is difficult to accomplish unless the individual actually parts with his interest in the principal giving rise to the income. In contrast, splitting a corporation into a number of smaller corporations that are beneficially owned by the same interests as the original corporation is relatively easy. Since the profits of each of the smaller corporations will fall into a lower bracket than those of the original corporation, such splitting allows a corporation to escape the full effect of the progressive rates of the individual income tax.

The application to a corporation's profits of the same progressive rates that are levied on the incomes of individuals gives rise to another problem. How should dividends distributed from these profits be treated in the shareholders' hands? To apply double progression to corporate-source income (that is, to tax profits to the corporation at progressive rates and then to apply the same progressive rates to dividends in the shareholders' hands) is generally thought to put an excessive burden on corporate-source income. The usual solution adopted by the few countries that apply progressive individual rates to corporate profits is to exempt dividends from tax in the hands of the shareholders. This treatment may, however, sharply reduce the impact of progression for the individual. If an individual spreads his investments among a number of corporations that are in relatively low brackets and receives from them distributions that are exempt from tax in his hands, the effective rate of his corporate-source income will be lower than its total might be thought to justify.

Moreover, some economists argue that the imposition of a progressive tax on corporate profits may discourage corporate growth by penalizing the efforts of corporations to improve their business efficiency.[12] The more a corporation earns, the heavier its tax burden will be. Consequently, corporations may find that their efforts are much less rewarding than they would be under a flat-rate tax. The net result, it is argued, will be a loss to the economy as a whole. This point may be especially important in a developing country, whose tax policy is often oriented more toward economic growth than toward equity or the redistribution of income and wealth.

Apart from the problems raised by progression and the ease with which a business entity may be split into separate units in order to avoid the full weight of progression, the arguments against applying the individual income tax to the corporation as an entity carry little weight. It is said, for example, that because the individual income tax usually provides for the exemption of some minimum subsistence level of income or offers family allowances, dependency exemptions, and the like, the tax is inappropriate for corporations. Such problems can easily be solved by the legislative draftsman, however.

Nonetheless, the problems raised by progression are such that virtually no country in which the individual income tax is more than mildly progressive and in which corporations control a significant part of the business sector taxes corporate profits by treating the corporation as a separate entity and subjecting it to the progressive rates of the individual income tax. Only a handful of developing countries in which the corporate sector is not yet important (in Central America, for example) use this method of taxing corporate profits.

If the individual income tax is levied at a flat rate, however, or at only mildly progressive rates, the arguments against applying the same rate schedule to individuals and to corporations as entities lose their force. In Sweden, for example, the rates of the *national* income tax applied to individuals are sharply progressive. These progressive rates are not applied to corporations; instead, corporations are subjected to a flat-rate national tax of 40%. The rate of the *local* income tax is flat, however (averaging about 24%), and it applies equally to corporations and to individuals.

Unless the income tax on individuals is levied at a flat rate, it is generally

12. For example, see Prest, "Corporate Income Taxation in Latin America," in Joint Tax Program of the Organization of American States, Inter-American Development Bank, and Economic Commission for Latin America, *Fiscal Policy for Economic Growth in Latin America* 234.

thought inappropriate to apply the individual income tax to corporations. Yet it might well be appropriate to adopt the highest rate from a progressive schedule of individual tax rates as the flat rate applicable to corporate earnings. In this way, the incentive for high-income individuals to incorporate their businesses solely in order to protect their earnings from the highest personal rates through corporate retentions is eliminated. Moreover, under some of the forms of integration discussed below, this equality in rates may serve as an impetus toward a desired distribution of corporate earnings.[13]

2/D.3. Imposition of a General Business Income Tax

Another possible method of taxing corporate profits is to subject corporations to an income tax that is also levied, at the same rate, on other business enterprises. Under such a system, income from business activity is taxed to each business enterprise at a uniform rate, whether the enterprise carrying on the activity is an individual proprietorship, a partnership, or a corporation.

In countries using flat-rate schedular income taxes, for example, corporations may be taxed at the same rate and according to the same rules as other business firms (such as individual proprietorships and partnerships). Under a schedular system, income from different sources is taxed under different "schedules" and at different rates. Income from employment may be taxed at one rate, income from capital at another rate, income from business at a third rate, and so on; the rates are almost invariably flat, rather than progressive.

Until 1948, for example, France followed a schedular system; it included a general business income tax, which was levied on the income of all business enterprises regardless of their form (*impôt sur les bénéfices industriels et commerciaux*). Whether earned by the largest corporation in the country or by the smallest individual proprietorship, income from business was taxed at a uniform rate (24%).[14] In its 1948 tax reform, however, France abandoned this system and adopted a separate corporation income tax (*impôt sur les sociétés*), under which corporations were treated for tax purposes (1) as entities separate from their shareholders and (2) as entities different from unincorporated businesses.

Underlying France's adoption of a separate corporation income tax was the argument that to continue to use a general business income tax (applicable at a uniform rate to incorporated and unincorporated enter-

13. See the discussion in section 3/D.2b.

14. Dividends were subject to a second level of taxation under another schedular tax (*impôt sur le revenu des valeurs mobilières*).

prises) was to overlook the fact that a corporate system is different from a system based on individual entrepreneurs. Modern industrial techniques, it was said, can for the most part be availed of only by enterprises that are able to assemble capital from a number of contributors; the institution of shares with limited liability permits corporations to make such assemblages of capital. In France, therefore, it was argued that the economic power and the taxable capacity of corporations increased more than proportionately to the capital available to them. The development and modernization of the French economy had been marked by a change from a "family economy" to a "corporation economy." The traditional practice of taxing individual proprietorships and partnerships (both essentially family enterprises) at the same rate that was applied to France's largest corporations failed to take account of the new economic power and taxable capacity of corporations and of the advantages of doing business in the corporate form.

Again, the matter of rates was particularly important. The general business income tax had created very few problems as long as its rates were relatively low. As government revenue needs rose after World War II, however, higher rates were imposed, and it was argued that a level of taxation feasible for corporations would be excessively burdensome for small individual proprietorships.

The French tax reform of 1948 therefore abandoned the general business income tax, which fell equally on corporations and other forms of business enterprise. In its place, France adopted a corporation income tax (*impôt sur les sociétés*), which applied at a flat rate only to the profits of corporations and similar business organizations with limited liability. The profits of individual proprietorships and partnerships were taxed to the proprietors and partners under an individual income tax, which was levied at progressive rates beginning at a level far lower than the corporate rate. Within a few years, the rate of the French corporation income tax reached 50%, which was far higher than the effective rates of the individual income tax imposed on most individual proprietors and partners.

As revenue needs and tax rates rise, the arguments against taxing corporate profits by means of a business income tax that applies equally to all enterprises, regardless of form, become weighty. Virtually all countries in which corporations are numerous and important have abandoned the general business income tax as a source of national government revenue.[15]

15. A number of countries impose a business license tax (similar to the French *patente*) on all business enterprises, regardless of their form of organization. In some countries, this tax may have an income component, but most business license taxes are not based on actual or net income. Instead, payroll, floor space, the value of assets, and other presumed indicia of profitability are the typical elements of the tax base; the tax is due even from an enterprise that shows a loss. In a large proportion of the countries that impose such a tax, the yield goes to the local, rather than the national, government.

2/D.4. Imposition of a Corporation Income Tax

a. In General

If corporations cannot be permitted to operate as tax-free shelters for business profits, and if the various methods of taxing corporate profits which were discussed in the preceding three sections are not practicable, what alternative remains?

Countries in whose economy corporations are significant have answered this question by treating corporations for tax purposes as entities (1) separate from their shareholders and (2) different from such other business organizations as individual proprietorships and partnerships. This treatment has two tax consequences. As the result of the view that corporations are entities separate from their shareholders, corporate profits, whether retained by the corporations or distributed to their shareholders, are taxed in the first instance directly to the corporations, not to their shareholders. As the result of the view that corporations are different from individual proprietorships and partnerships, the tax levied on corporate profits is a tax separate (at least in terms of its rate) from the tax levied on the income of those other forms of business organization. This separate tax—which is imposed on corporations as distinguished from unincorporated firms, which is collected from corporations as distinguished from their shareholders, and which is calculated on the basis of corporate profits—will generally be referred to hereinafter as the "corporation income tax."

In countries that impose a corporation income tax, any portion of a corporation's profits which is distributed to the shareholders is generally subject to the individual income tax in the hands of individual shareholders. In many of these countries, but not all, there is some degree of integration between the corporation income tax and the individual income tax; that is, with respect to distributed profits, there is some reduction either in the corporation income tax or in the individual income tax (or, sometimes, in both), which is designed to take account of the imposition of the other tax. The arguments for and against integration, and the methods of integration commonly used, are discussed in later chapters of this book. The remainder of this chapter will discuss the arguments for and against the corporation income tax, without regard to the degree of integration that may be provided for distributed profits, and without regard to special concessions that may be provided for closely held corporations.

b. Arguments for the Corporation Income Tax

The basic argument for imposing a corporation income tax is the practical argument that arises from the retention of earnings by corporations. If corporations cannot be required to make current physical distributions of all of their profits, if corporations habitually retain a significant portion of their profits, and if a compulsory imputation of retained profits to shareholders is not practicable, the collection directly from the corporation of a tax based on its profits is necessary in order to protect the integrity of the individual income tax. If there were no corporation income tax, the insulation of retained earnings from income taxation would permit corporations to be used as havens for accumulating tax-free savings. This argument in support of a corporation income tax is sometimes called the "compensation argument": the corporation income tax compensates the government for the revenue lost by virtue of the fact that corporate profits are not subject to the individual income tax as long as they are not distributed to shareholders.

In the most comprehensive tax study of recent years, Canada's Royal Commission on Taxation (the Carter Commission) confessed that it could find "no grounds in principle for taxing corporations." Nevertheless, the Commission recommended the imposition of a corporation income tax partly because the absence of such a tax "would permit massive and unwarranted postponement of personal income tax."[16]

The argument that a corporation income tax is necessary in order to prevent corporations from being used as shelters from the individual income tax appears, however, to support only a corporation income tax on *retained* earnings. What, then, is the argument for collecting from corporations a tax whose base includes *distributed* earnings as well?

Again, the argument is essentially a practical one: the argument of "fiscal expediency." Since the underlying purpose of the tax system is to collect revenue, this argument has weight. Corporations are easy to identify, to locate, and to tax. Their accounting methods are generally better than those of individual taxpayers, and a tax on corporate income is therefore within the administrative competence of most countries. In many countries, corporations carry on so large a proportion of the business activity of the nation that a tax on the income of a few score or a few hundred corporations may bring in more revenue than a tax on the incomes of hundreds of thousands of individuals.

Even a moderate tax on corporate income is likely to yield a considerable amount of revenue. Experience shows that a corporation income tax is "an elastic and highly productive source of revenue ... highly responsive to the secular growth of national production as well as to cyclical fluctuations in activity."[17] The "most persuasive" argument in support of the

16. Canada, Royal Commission on Taxation, 4 *Report of the Royal Commission on Taxation* 4, 5.

17. Goode, "Corporation Income Tax Rates," in United States, Congress, House of Representatives, Committee on Ways and Means, 3 *Tax Revision Compendium* 2280.

corporation income tax, the United Nations Fiscal Commission concluded, "has been its revenue yield"; "for the tax administrator, ... the corporation is an ideal object of taxation."[18]

The political factor supports this conclusion. There are fewer corporations and shareholders than individual citizens, and shareholders may be less inclined to resist corporation taxes or tax increases than to resist individual taxes or tax increases. As the Shoup Mission described it, the corporation income tax is "politically popular, easy to administer, and productive of substantial revenues."[19]

In addition, it is argued that if domestic corporations have foreign shareholders, the country must collect from those corporations a tax based on their profits (whether retained or distributed) in order to obtain its share of the income earned in the country but attributable to the nonresident shareholders. The Canadian Royal Commission, for example, concluded that, whatever the other considerations, a corporation income tax is "necessary in any event in order to tax the income of [corporations and similar] intermediaries which is attributable to nonresidents."[20]

Nonresidents usually invest in a country via the corporate form of organization in order to gain the advantages of limited liability and to insulate themselves from liability to local creditors and employees. The fact that dividends paid to nonresident shareholders are ordinarily subject to withholding at the source does not alter the need to impose a tax on domestic corporations that have foreign shareholders. Treaties and international practice limit the rate at which tax is withheld. In addition, withholding is inadequate because it applies only to distributed profits, which may amount to only a fraction of a corporation's total profits.[21]

Another practical argument for the corporation income tax, an argument

18. United Nations, Economic and Social Council, Fiscal Commission, *Comparative Approach to National and International Corporate Tax Problems* 19, 31.

19. U.S. Tax Mission to Japan (Shoup Mission), 1 *Report on Japanese Taxation* 105.

20. Canada, Royal Commission on Taxation, 3 *Report of the Royal Commission on Taxation* 52. The argument is often reinforced by a reference to the foreign tax credit system used in the United States and an increasing number of other capital-exporting countries; see, for example, Canada, Royal Commission on Taxation, 2 *Report of the Royal Commission on Taxation* 203. Given the existence of a credit for foreign taxes, the failure of a capital-importing country to tax the income of foreign-owned corporations would merely benefit the treasury of the capital-exporting country rather than the latter's shareholders. This argument has validity if a foreign firm operates in a capital-importing country through a branch, but is generally of less weight if the foreign firm is operating in the capital-importing country through a subsidiary.

21. Professor Richard A. Musgrave stresses the need to ensure adequate taxation of profits going to nonresident shareholders as a reason for use of the corporation income tax. "The Carter Commission Report," 1 *Canadian Journal of Economics* 158, 164 (1968). This argument may be particularly important in developing countries, where major corporations may be owned in large part by foreign interests.

that gains weight as corporations become more significant in an economy, is that for a tax collected from corporations on the basis of their profits to exist side by side with a tax collected from individuals on the basis of their incomes contributes to a desirable diversification of revenue sources. Moreover, the existence of a corporation income tax adds to the flexibility of tax policy. As revenue needs or economic needs vary, the makers of tax policy may raise or lower one set of rates—corporate or individual—without affecting the other. Similarly, incentives and other special provisions may be enacted or withdrawn for one tax in circumstances in which such action might be inappropriate for the other.

Even a country in which the corporate sector is as yet relatively small may find it advantageous to enact a corporation income tax. This tax would provide the country with a revenue source that would keep pace with the growth of national production, particularly within the corporate sector, as development proceeds. As an accompaniment to a progressive individual income tax, moreover, even a flat-rate corporation income tax may make the tax structure as a whole somewhat more progressive. Shareholders generally have more wealth and larger incomes than nonshareholders. As Professor Samuelson puts it,[22] to the extent that the corporation income tax is not shifted but actually reduces dividends,

> it is progressive, since most dollars available for dividends accrue to people of more than median income. (Although it is true that many poor widows and orphans own some shares of stock, still the total that they own is not a large fraction of all stock shares).

Moreover, most of the nations of the world already use a corporation income tax. The growing internationalization of economic life suggests that the minority of countries that do not yet use the tax must consider the wisdom of harmonizing their tax systems with those of the majority.

In support of these essentially pragmatic arguments for a corporation income tax, various theoretical arguments may be made. None is particularly weighty. Corporations receive significant benefits from society, it is argued; these benefits are sufficient to warrant a tax on corporate profits which is separate and distinct from any tax that may be due from the shareholders on the distributed portion of those profits. Related to the "benefit" argument is the "social costs" argument: corporations both enjoy the benefits of public spending (on security or education, for example) and impose burdens on the public (traffic or pollution, for example). Such costs and benefits may justify taxes on business in general, but they have little bearing on corporations in particular. Moreover, there may be little or no

22. Samuelson, *Economics* (10th ed.) 166. For a more detailed analysis of the redistributive effects of a corporation income tax, see Goode, *The Corporation Income Tax*, Chapter 5.

correlation between the profits earned by corporations and the benefits received or burdens imposed by them.

Because the legal and economic separateness of the business corporation (including its right to do business and hold property in its own name and its privilege of limited liability) derives from the government, some argue that the government is entitled in return to tax the corporation's profits. This "privilege" argument carries little weight today. The argument was developed at a time when incorporation was granted only by a special act of the legislature; its force has been reduced by the adoption of general or "free" corporation laws that make incorporation a right rather than a privilege. Moreover, there would seem to be little correlation between the value of the right or privilege of incorporation and the amount of a corporation's profits. To the extent that the right or privilege of incorporation has a value for which the government may be entitled to collect a fee, a more appropriate method of collection might be a stamp, registration, or similar tax on the act of incorporation.

In conclusion, those who favor the corporation income tax emphasize the legal separateness of the corporation, rather than the view of the corporation as a mere association of individuals banded together in a profit-making activity. The tax treatment of partnerships parallels their nontax treatment; similarly, under a corporation income tax, the tax treatment of corporations parallels their nontax treatment. For other legal purposes (creditors' rights and tort liability, for example), the corporation enjoys (indeed, insists on) an independent legal personality and has its own rights and duties, separate from those of its members; why not also for purposes of tax law? The separate legal personality of the corporation has, moreover, practical economic consequences; it makes the corporation (particularly the large, widely held corporation) a separate entity that has economic autonomy, is distinct from its shareholders, makes its own decisions, and is capable of acting in its own interests.

The profits earned by a corporation belong to the corporation, which has control over those profits and which, within broad limits, may retain or distribute them as its management deems appropriate. The income of this separate entity enjoys a separate existence that warrants its being taxed separately from the incomes of its members. Moreover, it is argued, the income of the corporation has a collective taxable capacity that parallels its economic autonomy. This taxable capacity, which is independent of the capacity of the members or shareholders, has a separate economic force sufficient to justify the separate taxation of corporate income.[23]

23. These arguments may not apply with full force to a closely held (generally small) corporation, in which ownership and management are ordinarily in the same hands. For this reason, certain countries whose general practice is to tax corporations as entities separate from their shareholders provide special tax concessions for closely held corporations.

In the practical world in which tax administrators and policy makers must operate, corporations constitute "social and economic entities with their own character and pattern of behavior."[24] The corporation income tax is usually defended on the ground that it is necessary to protect the individual income tax. Without derogating from that argument, it may also be argued that the power and position of the modern corporation justify a tax on the profits of the corporate enterprise as such. In defense of the corporation income tax, Dr. Colm wrote[25]:

> It is difficult to see why the government should be justified in taxing incomes received by individuals but not in taxing the yield of production before it has been distributed to the individual agents of production. . . ..
>
> Not as a substitute but as a supplement, there is need and justification for taxes which give the government a share of income right at the source. It is hard to see why the total income from production should first be distributed and then taxed and why some part of the yield should not be taxed before it is distributed to individuals.

That is, the corporation income tax is a way "to provide adequate recognition under the tax system of the economic importance of corporations as prime income recipients in a high-level economy."[26]

c. Arguments Against the Corporation Income Tax

Although all developed countries and most developing countries collect a corporation income tax, there are arguments against such a tax. The main argument relates to the distributed component of corporate profits. Virtually every country using a progressive individual income tax includes dividends in the taxable income of shareholders; regardless of any relief offered through integration, no sufficient reason exists to exempt this particular variety of income from the income tax levied on other varieties of individual income. It is argued, though, that the combined impact of two taxes—one tax at the corporate level on the corporation's profits and a second tax at the shareholder level on the distributed portion of those profits—places a tax burden on the corporate-source income of individuals which is disproportionate to the burden imposed on individual income from other sources, such as wages and interest. As a general rule, moreover,

24. Colm, "The Corporation and the Corporate Income Tax in the American Economy," 44 *American Economic Review, Papers and Proceedings* 486, 488 (1954).
25. Colm, "The Corporation and the Corporate Income Tax in the American Economy," 44 *American Economic Review, Papers and Proceedings* 486, 495–496 (1954).
26. Slitor, "The Corporate Income Tax: A Re-Evaluation," 5 *National Tax Journal* 289, 302 (1952).

there is no such two-tier taxation of the profits of other forms of business organization. The profits of an enterprise organized in the form of an individual proprietorship or a partnership are ordinarily subject to taxation at one level only. No tax is levied on the profits of such an enterprise as an entity. Instead, the profits of the enterprise, whether retained or distributed, are taxed only under the individual income tax: the proprietor himself is taxed or the partners themselves are taxed on a pro rata basis.

The following example illustrates how the two-tier taxation of corporate-source income (without integration) may operate in a typical case. The results will differ in other cases, depending on the rate and the distribution patterns assumed.[27]

Example

Individual *A* in the 40% bracket of the individual income tax operates a grocery store as an individual proprietorship. The grocery earns a profit of $100 before tax. *A*'s tax on his business income is therefore $40, and his after-tax income is $60.

The country in which the store is located imposes a corporation income tax at the rate of 30%; this tax and the individual income tax are not integrated. *A* forms a corporation to operate the grocery, and he is the sole shareholder. The corporation income tax on the grocery's profit is $30, and $70 remain as after-tax profit. If the corporation pays the full amount of this profit to its shareholder, *A*, as a dividend, *A* will receive $70, on which the individual income tax at 40%, or $28, is payable. The total tax on *A*'s corporate-source income is $58: $30 at the corporate level and $28 at the individual level. This amount is $18 more than the total tax of $40 payable if *A* had not incorporated the business.

As a result, it is argued, the corporation income tax puts an excessive burden on corporate-source income, discriminates against the corporate sector, and hampers the use of the corporation as the most modern and efficient form of business organization. According to this argument, moreover, the line of demarcation between business enterprises operating in the corporate form and those operating as individual proprietorships or partnerships is arbitrary. Hence, if there is to be tax discrimination among business enterprises, a more significant line of demarcation might be between large, publicly held corporations, on the one hand, and all other business organizations, including small, privately held corporations, on the other.

27. In the interests of simplicity, this study will generally assume in its examples that the pertinent corporation law allows the formation of corporations with a single shareholder. Some countries do not recognize the validity of single-shareholder corporations and require a minimum number of shareholders, such as seven. Even in these countries, however, the use of relatives, employees, or other associates to hold nominal amounts of stock may permit the organization of what are essentially single-shareholder corporations.

As far as large-scale, widely held business corporations are concerned, the argument of discrimination against the corporate form of organization may carry little weight. For reasons unrelated to taxation, such businesses can scarecely be conducted except in the corporate form, and their major competitors are likely to be other large corporations subject to the same tax regime.

For the small-scale business operation, the problem of tax discrimination against the corporate form may be real, though perhaps exaggerated. Many small enterprises (for example, small retailers and artisans) have little need for the corporate form of organization and are not likely to use it in any event. To what extent the corporation tax discriminates against the use of the corporate form of organization depends, moreover, on the relationship between the rates of this tax and the rates of the individual income tax. If the rates of the corporation income tax (especially as affected by relief provided for small businesses) are below the rates of the individual income tax imposed on the individual entrepreneur, the result may be a tax incentive to the individual to incorporate his business and to retain earnings within the corporation, where they would be sheltered from the individual income tax. In addition, as a practical matter, the corporate form may offer tax advantages to the small entrepreneur that compensate for the burden of the corporation income tax. These advantages stem chiefly from his ability to deduct his own compensation and certain other expenses from corporate income subject to tax. Far from finding that the corporation income tax is invariably a burden on small, closely held corporations (even with a 50% rate on corporate income), France, for example, found it appropriate several years ago to adopt tax measures deliberately designed to discourage the use of the corporate form of organization by such firms.[28]

In any event, the argument that the corporation income tax discriminates against the use of the corporate form by small enterprises can be met by making adjustments in the structure of the tax which would take account of the special problems of small firms. At the cost of some complexity, many systems of corporation income tax provide such adjustments by making available some variety of small-business relief. In addition, because the major argument against the corporation income tax centers around the added burden on the *distributed* component of corporate profits, many countries seek to reduce that burden by providing some degree of integration between the corporation and individual income taxes.

Opponents of the corporation income tax sometimes object also to its

28. Japan, too, has found that the imposition of a corporation income tax is not necessarily a burden on small corporations; the fact that certain deductions were available to corporations caused businesses to rush to incorporate despite the theoretical burden of the corporation income tax. See Uematsu, "Computation of Income in Japanese Income Tax Administration: A Study in the Adjustment of Theory to Reality," in von Mehren (ed.), *Law in Japan* 567, 608.

effect on the *retained* component of corporate profits. The collection from corporations of a tax that is based on their profits is said to be objectionable because it reduces the amount of retained earnings available to corporations for growth and expansion. This effect is said to be particularly hard on small, closely held corporations that have less access to outside capital than large, publicly held corporations and hence are more dependent on retained earnings.[29]

The impact of the corporation income tax on retained earnings may be particularly significant in developing countries, where capital may be scarce and the small, growing corporation the most dynamic vehicle for industrial development. For industrial enterprises, the corporate form of organization may be a necessity; for industry, the partnership form may be inappropriate even if it offers tax advantages.

As with other tax questions, the problem of alternatives arises. The objection that the corporation income tax burdens the retained earnings of growing corporations must be weighed against the fact that an alternative source of revenue may be equally injurious to the corporate sector. As far as the burden on retained earnings is concerned, moreover, the argument against the corporation income tax depends primarily on the rate of the tax and its relationship to the rates of the individual income tax. If the rate of tax on the retained earnings of corporations is not significantly higher than the average rate of tax on the incomes of individuals who own corporations, the burden on the retained component may be no greater than the burden of tax on other income.

Furthermore, to counter the argument that the corporation income tax unduly reduces retained earnings, it is not necessary to abandon the tax entirely. Intermediate solutions are available. For example, many countries provide retention allowances for retained profits, particularly those reinvested in the development of the business. If it is thought that the corporation income tax bears excessively on the retained earnings of small corporations, the remedy may be some form of small-business relief within the structure of the tax rather than the abandonment of the tax as a revenue source. The complete exemption of retained earnings from any tax

29. Butters and Lintner, *Effect of Federal Taxes on Growing Enterprises* 49. See also Miller, "The Corporation Income Tax and Corporate Financial Policies," in Commission on Money and Credit, *Stabilization Policies* 381, 430, n. 38. Professor Miller concludes that even apart from tax factors, "the rational choice" for most corporations is to rely as heavily as possible on retained earnings.

Van den Tempel asserts that the private corporation often has "no choice other than retention of profit, because self-financing forms practically the only source of capital for modernization and expansion." *Corporation Tax and Individual Income Tax in the European Communities* 17.

at the corporate level is objectionable because it offers too easy a refuge from the individual income tax.

In addition to the arguments that the corporation income tax places an excessive burden on corporate-source income, discriminates against the corporation as a form of business organization, and depletes the supply of capital available to corporations for growth and expansion, there are other arguments that may be made against the tax. None is very weighty. One argument holds that because the corporation income tax falls on net profits rather than on, say, gross receipts or value added, it encourages wasteful corporate expenditures that are largely of a sumptuary or luxury character and benefit corporate owners or executives. That this problem exists is clear; however, it will exist under any form of tax that seeks to reach the net profits of business enterprises. The cure would seem to lie in the drafting of legislative rules governing business deductions and in the tight administration of those rules, rather than in the abandonment of a tax resource that may be thought appropriate for other reasons.[30]

The corporation income tax is also said to encourage debt financing rather than equity financing because (under most systems, but not all) interest is ordinarily deductible for tax purposes, whereas dividends are ordinarily not deductible. There is scant empirical evidence to support this argument except in the case of closely held corporations, which may resort to "thin capitalization"—the financing of corporations by an unrealistically small equity base, supplemented by loans that are more or less permanent and are made by the same persons who own the equity capital in substantially the same proportions. Again, the problem may be met by solutions other than the abandonment of the corporation income tax. One solution is the adoption of integration devices that tend to equalize the tax treatment of dividends and interest (see Chapter 4). Another solution is the use of rules limiting abusive interest deductions on loans from shareholders, particularly in the case of closely held corporations. This problem emphasizes the fact that corporations are not homogeneous; arguments that carry weight in the case of a closely held corporation may be irrelevant if applied to a large, publicly held corporation.

Although the corporation income tax is considered to be relatively simple to administer and to be within the administrative competence even of developing countries, it nevertheless brings some administrative complexities in its train. As the corporate sector expands and as both taxpayers and tax administrators grow more sophisticated, it may become necessary to provide rules dealing with (1) affiliated corporations, holding companies,

30. The deductibility of sumptuary and personal expenditures of business enterprises under a net income tax is discussed in Popkin, *The Deduction for Business Expenses and Losses.*

intercorporate dividends, and the like; (2) corporate reorganizations, including mergers and liquidations; and (3) the excessive retention of earnings by corporations (especially closely held or family corporations) in order to avoid personal income taxation.

Finally, the relationship between the rates of the corporation income tax and those of the individual income tax is stressed by those critics of the corporation income tax who regard corporate profits more as the profits of the individual owners of the corporation than as the profits of an entity separate from those owners. Any given rate of corporation income tax is likely to be higher than the rate applicable to some shareholders and lower than the rate applicable to others; in either case, it may be regarded as inequitable. A corporation income tax system that does not take into account the shareholders' income level discriminates particularly against low-income shareholders, whose marginal income tax rate is presumably lower than the corporation income tax rate; in the extreme case, a shareholder's rate may be zero. Some countries seek to meet this difficulty by adopting a method of integration which—at least with respect to the distributed component of corporate profits—puts the emphasis on the individual income tax and treats the corporation income tax on that component as a total or a partial prepayment of the individual's tax (see Chapters 3, 4, and 5).

2/E. Conclusion

Several arguments for and against the corporation income tax have been summarized in the preceding sections. Those who oppose the tax may be said to adhere to the view that shareholders are "essentially similar to partners." Those who defend the tax assert that such a view, perhaps valid in the era of the "family economy," is obsolete in the era of the "corporate economy" and that today's shareholders are not essentially similar to partners but are persons who, for their own convenience, have deliberately chosen a status different from that of partners. Corporations are not homogeneous, and perhaps there can never be a single answer to the question whether a corporation is an entity different from a partnership and separate from its shareholders or nothing more than a large partnership. While the debate about the true nature of the corporation however, goes on, lawmakers and tax administrators must make decisions and raise revenue. Legislators in most nations of the world have found it expedient to impose a corporation income tax with such exemptions, exceptions, and variations as seem to be in the national interest. In 1968, the *International Encyclopedia of the Social Sciences* reported[31]:

> The taxation of the income of corporations has come to be one of the major sources of fiscal revenue in most countries. . . .. This widespread and heavy reliance on the corporation income tax testifies to its administrative feasibility and political popularity.

The practical arguments in support of the corporation income tax—its revenue potential, its relative ease of administration, and its utility in protecting the individual income tax—are such that the overwhelming majority of legislatures and tax policy makers of the world have chosen to adopt a corporation income tax. Professor Shoup and his colleagues sum up the matter in this way[32]:

> There is . . . an increasing trend toward regarding the corporation as a separate entity from whom income tax may be obtained in addition to the tax on shareholders' dividends. The relative ease of collection of corporate taxes, the dominant role of corporations in business life, the separation of management from shareholders, are all factors in this trend.

This increasing acceptance of the corporation income tax "suggests that legislators and the public regard the tax as an equitable, not merely an expedient, way of raising revenue."[33]

The burden of proof is heavy, then, on those who assert that the almost universal practice of levying a corporation income tax is wrong. At the same time, many (but not all) of the legislators and policy makers who have adopted the corporation income tax have taken account of the force of some of the arguments against this tax by adopting either or both of two relief methods. To meet the argument that the corporation income tax places an excessive burden on corporate-source income, many countries provide some integration of corporation and individual income taxes. To meet the argument that the corporation income tax weighs particularly heavily on small corporations, some countries include small-business relief in their corporation income tax structures.

31. Harberger, "Corporation Income Taxes," 15 *International Encyclopedia of the Social Sciences* 538 (1968). Professor Harberger adds that the tax is less important in the developing countries than in the developed, but that "this is due mainly to the fact that the corporate sector itself is less important, rather than to a failure of the developing countries to levy the tax at all or to a tendency on their part to impose the tax at significantly lower rates than those applied by the more advanced countries." Professor Harberger shows that of all the major countries, Japan places the heaviest reliance on the corporation income tax.

32. Shoup *et al.*, *The Fiscal System of Venezuela* 116.

33. Goode, *The Corporation Income Tax* 203.

3

Integration of Corporation and Individual Income Taxes: Arguments For and Against

This chapter incorporates substantial revisions suggested by Mitsuo Sato of the Japanese Ministry of Finance

3/A. Integration Defined

Most countries levy an individual income tax whose tax base includes dividends (distributions to shareholders paid out of corporate profits). As a general rule, these countries at the same time treat corporations for tax purposes as entities separate from their shareholders and levy a corporation income tax under which corporate profits are taxed to corporations as they are earned. The term "integration" relates to the reciprocal relationship between the corporation income tax and the individual income tax. As commonly used in the context of taxation, integration refers to a variety of tax techniques that, while different in form, have a common aim: the elimination or the reduction of the "extra" burden of the corporation income tax on distributed profits.

In this sense, integration is a limited process, because it involves only the distributed component of corporate profits. The word "integration" is sometimes used in a broader sense to pertain to the tax treatment of the retained, as well as the distributed, component of corporate profits; in that broader sense, integration refers to tax techniques that seek to make the total amount of corporate profits, whether retained or distributed, subject only to the progressive rates of the individual income tax levied on the shareholders. Total or full integration of this sort can be achieved by the "partnership method" discussed in Chapter 2. According to this method, each shareholder is taxed under the individual income tax on his imputed aliquot share of the corporation's profits (retained as well as distributed).

Virtually the same result may also be achieved by the approach proposed in Canada by the Carter Commission.[1] Under this proposal, corporations were to be taxed at a uniform rate of 50%, whereas shareholders were to be subject to the individual income tax on both dividends received and the share of undistributed profits which the corporation at its option chose to allocate to them. That is, both the dividends received and the share of allocated retained earnings were to be included in the individual income tax base of shareholders. To offset this treatment, however, shareholders were to be entitled to a full credit of the corporation income tax against the individual income tax due on dividends and the allocated share of corporate retentions, both of which were to be grossed up by the amount of the corporation income tax. To the extent that this credit exceeded the amount of the individual income tax (as would have often been the case, given the proposed top marginal rate of 50% for the latter), it was to be refunded to the shareholder. The equality between the uniform corporate rate and the top marginal individual rate was thought to provide considerable incentive for the corporation either to distribute or to allocate all of its earnings, since high-income shareholders would have nothing to gain (in terms of taxes) by corporate retention without allocation, whereas low-income shareholders would actively seek distribution or allocation because of the refund they would receive. Under this approach, all corporate profits would be subject to taxation at progressive individual income tax rates, and the corporation income tax would amount to no more than a means of withholding the individual income tax.

This proposal was not implemented in the subsequent legislative process in Canada, however. For the reasons discussed in Chapter 2, it is assumed here that both the "partnership method" and a full integration approach such as that recommended by the Carter Commission are impracticable as normal methods of taxing corporations and shareholders.[2] Therefore, "integration" will generally refer here to a system that covers only the distributed part of corporate profits and not to a system that is comprehensive enough to cover retained as well as distributed profits. The latter

1. See Canada, Royal Commission on Taxation, 4 *Report of the Royal Commission on Taxation* 3–98. For the fate of the Commission's recommendation in the subsequent legislative process in Canada, see Bucovetsky and Bird, "Tax Reform in Canada: A Progress Report," 25 *National Tax Journal* 15 (1972).

2. McLure, however, concludes that "even though a number of important details remain for clarification, in comparison to alternative methods for achieving full integration of the corporate and personal taxes, the general approach advocated by the Carter Commission has the crucial advantage of administrative feasibility." McLure, "Integration of the Personal and Corporate Income Taxes: The Missing Element in Recent Tax Reform Proposals," 88 *Harvard Law Review* 532, 573 (1975).

type of system will be referred to as "full" integration, as distinguished from "ordinary" integration.

In this limited sense, integration may be defined as the use of a tax structure that includes both a corporation income tax (which taxes profits to corporations as earned) and an individual income tax (which taxes dividends from such profits to shareholders as distributed), but in which there is either (1) some adjustment of the corporation income tax at the corporate level to take account of the fact that dividends are subject to the individual income tax at the shareholder level or (2) some adjustment of the individual income tax at the shareholder level to take account of the fact that corporate dividends are paid out of corporate income that has already borne a tax at the corporate level.[3]

This chapter will first describe the "extra" burden of the corporation income tax on distributed profits; the arguments for and against integration will then be discussed in the light of that analysis and various tax policy considerations. Although the analysis and the arguments will turn mainly on the definition of integration developed above, there will be some references to "full" integration, as distinguished from "ordinary" integration.

3/B. Measuring the Additional Burden of the Corporation Income Tax

The use of a tax structure that includes both a corporation income tax on corporate profits as earned and an individual income tax that is comprehensive enough to apply to corporate profits distributed to shareholders as dividends is sometimes described as "economic double taxation." Although the phrase itself has been said to have "nothing to do with the desirability or undesirability of the phenomenon"[4], it nevertheless may be considered to involve a value judgment and, indeed, to carry pejorative implications. In effect, the phrase denies that corporations are separate from shareholders and assumes that the income of the corporation is the income of its shareholders. It is only on this assumption that the charge of "double taxation" can have meaning.

In an effort to avoid value judgments and to minimize any pejorative implications, this study will generally describe a system involving (1) taxation, under a corporation income tax, of corporate profits to cor-

3. Some countries (Japan, for example) make adjustments at both the corporate and the shareholder level (see Chapters 4 and 6).

4. Van den Tempel, *Corporation Tax and Individual Income Tax in the European Communities* 10. The Musgraves use the term "an absolute corporation tax" to refer to this tax regime. Musgrave and Musgrave, *Public Finance in Theory and Practice* 271, 272.

porations as earned and (2) taxation, under an individual income tax, of dividends as received by shareholders as "two-tier taxation of corporate-source income."

One of the purposes of integration is to eliminate or reduce the "extra" taxation of that portion of corporate profits which is distributed to shareholders as dividends. The amount of extra taxation is the difference between the combined tax paid on corporate-source income (the total of the corporation and individual income taxes) and the tax due on the same amount of income, under the individual income tax, from an unincorporated business that is not subject to the corporation income tax.

Table 1 shows the amount of the additional burden of the corporation income tax on the assumption that the corporation income tax rate is 30% and the individual income tax is progressive with four brackets—0%, 10%, 20%, and 40%. It is also assumed that the corporation distributes all of its after-tax income.

Table 1 demonstrates that one result of the use of an unintegrated corporation-individual income tax structure, in a country that levies a progressive individual income tax, is that the additional burden on shareholders of the two-tier system is not the same for all income brackets. The additional burden of the corporation income tax *decreases* as the rate of the individual income tax on the shareholder *increases.* Column 7 shows that the additional burden of the corporation income tax on a shareholder whose income is so small that he is in the zero rate bracket is 30 units. This shareholder would have paid no individual income tax on the 100 units of dividend income which he would have received in the absence of the corporation income tax. The additional burden on the shareholder whose income is so large that he is in the top, 40% bracket is only 18 units, which is the difference between the combined tax burden of 58 units and the 40 units which he would have paid as the individual income tax on the 100 units of dividend income that he would have received in the absence of the corporation income tax.

There appears to be considerable agreement among the nations of the world on the question whether corporation and individual income taxes should be integrated. Many countries' tax structures do provide at least partial integration of their corporation and individual income taxes. There is no such agreement, however, on the question of how integration should be achieved. Techniques of integration in use today vary widely from one country to the next, and a 1970 survey stresses "the extraordinary anarchy of the systems now in force."[5] Even neighboring countries at comparable

5. Cardyn, "General Report: The Multiple Burden on Dividends and Shares by Taxation on Income and Capital of Both Corporations and Shareholders," 55a *Cahiers de droit fiscal international* I/39 (1970).

TABLE 1: *Additional Burden of the Corporation Income Tax on Full Distribution of After-Tax Corporate Income to Shareholders**

Shareholder Marginal Individual Income Tax Rate (1)	Corporate Income Before Tax (2)	Corporation Tax at 30% (3)	Dividend Received by Shareholders (4)	Shareholders' Individual Income Tax (5)	Total Tax (6)	Additional Burden of Corporate Income Tax (7)
0%	100	30	70	0	30	30
10%	100	30	70	7	37	27
20%	100	30	70	14	44	24
40%	100	30	70	28	58	18

*This table has been adapted from Table 5-5 in Pechman, *Federal Tax Policy* (rev. ed.) 141. The following formula may be used to find the additional burden of an unintegrated corporation income tax (where C is the corporation income tax rate, and M is the individual shareholder's marginal rate): $C(1-M)$. See Shoup, *Public Finance* 315.

stages of economic development (France and Germany, for example) have used systems very different in form. Particular circumstances in particular countries presumably dictate the choice of one method of integration over another. As will be seen in the next three chapters, different methods of integration may have different results in their impact on both corporations and shareholders.

3/C. Analysis of the Effect on Dividend Distribution

3/C.1. In General

The integration of the corporation and individual income taxes has been adopted in various countries because of its advantages relative to those of other systems of taxing corporations and shareholders. Although the empirical data are far from complete, it is reasonable to believe that the different methods of taxing corporations and shareholders have different impacts on corporate and shareholder behaviors. Whatever the political influence on a tax system may be, it is generally desirable for a tax policy to have solid analytical grounds. Before the arguments for and against integration are discussed, a brief analysis will therefore be undertaken here.

A crucial difference between the alternative systems of taxing corporate-source income seems to be their differential effect on corporate decisions regarding the disposition of profits earned—more specifically, the differential effect on the dividend-payout ratio. In order to consider the implications, economic and other, of the different methods of taxing corporations and shareholders, it is essential to have some knowledge of how these methods affect the corporate behavior of profit distribution.

3/C.2. Analysis

Before analyzing the differential effects on dividend payout of the different methods of taxing corporations and shareholders, we must define these methods. They may be classified into three major types according to whether, and to what extent, the corporation income tax and the individual income tax are integrated. At one extreme, a corporation is recognized as a separate entity distinct from its shareholders and is therefore taxed in its own capacity. According to this view, the corporation income tax and the individual income tax are imposed independently of each other, and there is no recognition of the fact that distributed corporate profits are taxed both when earned by the corporation and when received by the shareholder. As was noted above, this system is described in this study as the "two-tier taxation of corporate-source income."

At the other extreme, a corporation is considered to be no more than the aggregate of its shareholders. The corporation income tax, including the portion levied on undistributed profits, is therefore treated as a withholding tax to be fully credited by the shareholders against the individual income tax due on their imputed shares of corporate profits. As an alternative, the separate corporation tax is eliminated completely, and shareholders are taxed on their imputed shares of corporate profits, whether or not these profits are distributed as dividends (the partnership method). With this approach, the corporation income tax and the individual income tax on shareholders may be said to be fully integrated (the full integration method).

Between these two extremes, there are two intermediate systems in common use in industrial countries which partially integrate the corporation and individual income taxes by providing relief for corporate distributions of profits at either the corporate or the shareholder level. Relief (or adjustment) at the corporate level usually takes the form of a lower tax rate on corporate distributions than on retained profits (the split-rate system). Relief (or adjustment) at the shareholder level is normally provided by a credit for part of the corporation income tax against the individual income tax due on dividends received by shareholders (the dividends-received credit system). These two systems, together with their variations and extreme forms, will be discussed in detail in Chapters 5 and 6.

The question to be answered here is what are the differential effects on corporate dividend behavior of these different systems of taxing corporate-source income? In order to answer this question, the reaction of corporate managers to the taxation of corporate-source income must be analyzed. Two different hypotheses may be used for this analysis. One hypothesis is that corporate managers, in making a decision about how much corporate earnings to distribute to shareholders, concentrate on the corporation income tax, completely disregarding the individual income tax that is due on dividends received by shareholders. The other hypothesis is that, in making such a decision, corporate managers take account of both the corporation income tax and the individual income tax due on dividends.

If the first hypothesis is accepted, the above question may be answered very easily. All of the alternative systems except the split-rate system are neutral with regard to the distribution and the retention of corporate profits. They neither encourage nor discourage corporate distributions, because the corporation income tax does not vary with the payout ratio and only the corporation income tax matters to corporate managers. Thus, because of their uniform tax rates on the entire amount of corporate profits, the two-tier system, the dividends-received credit system, and the full integration system do not interfere with corporate decisions about profit distributions, regardless of whether or not relief is subsequently provided at the shareholder level. A capital gains tax is also irrelevant because such a tax is normally imposed on shareholders, rather than corporations.

The split-rate system, in contrast, is not neutral with regard to the distribution and the retention of corporate earnings. Because its tax rate on the distributed portion of corporate profits is lower than that on the retained portion, this system makes the tax burden of the corporation dependent on the payout ratio. If the corporation distributes nothing, its corporation income tax is maximized, whereas if it distributes all of its after-tax profits, its corporation income tax is minimized.[6] For this reason, the system influences corporate decision making. Moreover, corporate managers may face the problem of a trade-off between the tax saving and the retention of profits for reinvestment. If stock dividends are subject to the lower tax rate, corporate managers may partly reconcile such conflcting interests.

However clear the answer may be, the validity of the hypothesis itself must be questioned. Is it true that corporate managers consider only the corporation income tax in deciding how much of the corporation's profits to distribute? In the light of actual corporate and shareholder behavior, this hypothesis does not appear to be very realistic. The separation of ownership and management in the widely held corporation does not mean that the manager can disregard shareholders' interests. A fast-growing firm must be attentive to the market evaluation of its stocks. Although it may be true that for well-established firms, retained earnings are a more important source of financing, this does not mean that the managers of such firms may completely ignore the interests of shareholders. If corporate dividend policy is influenced not only by the interests of the corporation itself but also by those of the shareholders, then the second hypothesis may be said to be more realistic than the first: that is, corporate managers take into account both the corporation income tax and the individual income tax in deciding how much profit to distribute.

In all of the systems except the full integration system, the total tax

6. Under some existing split-rate systems, the tax on distributed profits must itself be paid from retained earnings bearing the higher tax. This results in the so-called "shadow effect." For example, assume that split rates of 50% for retained earnings and 25% for distributed earnings are to be applied to a corporation's income and that the corporation distributes all of its income. The total tax on the corporate income is 33.3%, not 25%, since the amount retained to pay the tax on the amount distributed is itself taxed at 50%. The new German tax law, effective 1 January 1977, eliminated the "shadow effect" by declaring that amounts used to pay taxes on distributed earnings would not be treated as retained earnings.

burden depends upon the payout of dividends, but the way in which it does so differs between systems. Under the two-tier system, one unit of additional dividends always results in an increase in the total tax burden which is equal to the marginal tax rate of the shareholder (M). In the case of the integration systems (the split-rate system and the dividends-received credit system), the situation is different. Whether and to what extent the integration systems increase the total tax burden as the dividend payout increases depends on the relationship between the marginal individual tax rate (M) and the rate of distribution relief. In the split-rate system, the rate of distribution relief is the difference between the corporation tax rate on retentions (tr) and the corporation tax rate on distributions (td); in the dividends-received credit system, it is the rate of the dividends-received credit (S). As long as the marginal individual tax rate (M) is lower than the rate of distribution relief (either $tr - td$ or S), any increase in dividend payouts *decreases* the total tax burden by the amount corresponding to the difference between the two rates: $M - (tr - td)$, or $M - S$. If the marginal tax rate is higher than the rate of distribution relief, any increase in dividend payouts *increases* the total tax burden by the amount corresponding to the difference between the two rates. Under the full integration system, the total tax burden is not a function of dividend payouts.

A few illustrations may suffice to explain this point. Assume that the marginal individual tax rate is 30%, that the corporation tax rate is 50%, and that the rate of distribution relief is $33\frac{1}{3}$%.[7] The two-tier system increases the total tax burden by 0.3 units for each additional unit of dividends. The split-rate system and the dividends-received credit system, in contrast, decrease the total tax burden by 0.033 units (0.333 – 0.300) for each additional unit of dividends. The full integration system neither increases nor decreases the total tax burden, which is fixed at a level calculated by applying the marginal individual tax rate to the entire amount of corporate profits, whether retained or distributed.

If the marginal individual tax rate is 50% instead of 30% and if the other rates are the same as assumed above, a one-unit increase in distributions results in a 0.5-unit increase in the total tax burden under the two-tier system, and a 0.166-unit increase (0.500 – 0.333) in the total tax burden

7. According to this last assumption, under the split-rate system, the retained part of corporate profits is taxed at 50% (tr) and the distributed part at 16-2/3% (td). In the case of the dividends-received credit, the cash dividend is grossed up by 50% and the shareholder is entitled to a tax credit of the same amount, that is, 50% of the cash dividend. For example, if the shareholder receives 100 units of dividends and these dividends are grossed up by 50 units, then the amount of grossed-up dividends is 150 units, and the shareholder is given a credit of 50 units against his individual income tax due on the grossed-up dividends. The rate of the tax credit for the grossed-up dividends, shown as S, is therefore 33-1/3%. Note that in both cases, the integration is only partial in that the extra burden of the corporate tax on distributed profits still exists, but to a lesser extent.

under the integration systems. Again, a change in distributions does not alter the total tax burden under the full integration system.

Some tentative answers to the question of corporate dividend behavior posed at the outset may be drawn from the analysis above. First, the two-tier system of taxation discourages the distribution of profits by increasing the total tax burden as dividend payouts increase. In other words, the system is not neutral with regard to the retention and the distribution of corporate profits; it favors retention and disfavors distribution. The degree to which it discourages distribution depends simply on the level of the shareholder's marginal tax rate. If this level is generally low, the discouraging effect may not be great, but if it is generally high, the effect may be substantial.

Second, the two integration systems may encourage the distribution of corporate profits, but the degree of encouragement depends crucially on the relationship between the shareholder's marginal income tax rate and the rate of distribution relief. As long as the marginal tax rate (M) does not exceed the corporate rate differential ($tr - td$) or the dividend credit rate (S), an additional distribution reduces the total tax burden. The saving in the total tax is zero at the point at which M equals ($tr - td$) or S; beyond that point, the total tax burden increases as the profit distribution increases. If the marginal tax rate applied to the average shareholder is high, the distribution relief offered under the integration systems may discourage rather than encourage the payout of dividends.

Third, the two systems of integrating the corporation and individual income taxes have the same effect of encouraging (or discouraging) profit distributions if the rate of distribution relief is equal between the two systems.[8] This holds even if the corporation income tax rates under the two systems are different, because the saving in the total tax burden depends on the relationship between the shareholder's marginal tax rate and the rate of distribution relief, not on the absolute level of the corporation tax rate.

Finally, only one of the systems is neutral with respect to the retention and the distribution of corporate earnings. The two-tier system always discourages distribution; the integration systems encourage or discourage distribution depending upon the relative level of the shareholder's marginal tax rate and the rate of distribution relief. Complete neutrality is achieved only by the full integration system, under which the total tax burden does not change with the payout of dividends but is directly determined by the marginal tax rate of the shareholder.

So far, the effect of a capital gains tax has been ignored, but some type of capital gains tax exists in many countries. The effect of a capital gains

8. Of course, the shareholder's marginal tax rate (M) must be the same under the two systems.

tax is therefore introduced in the analysis here. For purposes of simplicity, capital gains are assumed to accrue only from retained corporate profits, to be taxed on an accrual basis, and to be subject to the same tax rate as other income.[9] The differential effects of the alternative systems on dividend payout are not at all the same if a capital gains tax is imposed. First, the two-tier system now neither encourages nor discourages profit distributions; it becomes completely neutral with regard to the retention and distribution of corporate profits. Neutrality exists because undistributed profits are now taxed as earned in the form of shareholders' capital gains, and there is no tax advantage in using a corporation as a "tax shelter" to avoid individual income taxes on corporate-source income. Under this system, shareholders and corporate managers may be indifferent to the payout ratio. This analysis may support the conventional argument that the preferential treatment of capital gains has encouraged the retention of corporate profits.

Second, the integration systems now always encourage distribution. Corporate managers may save the total amount of tax by increasing distributions as much as possible. The reason is that retained corporate profits are taxed as capital gains at a normal individual income tax rate, whereas distributed corporate profits benefit from distribution relief at either the corporate or the shareholder level. If the relief provided for distributions were also granted to retentions (that is, to capital gains), this discriminatory effect would undoubtedly disappear, and the integration systems would be quite neutral with respect to retention and distribution. The revenue loss aside, such a system appears to be unlikely, however, because granting such relief to capital gains would contradict a basic objective of integration—to encourage the distribution of profits. One of the policy implications of this analysis may be that the taxation of capital gains should be tightened, rather than relaxed, if integration is really intended to encourage dividend payout.

Finally, under the full integration system, retained profits are taxed currently to the shareholder through a procedure called "allocation." There is therefore no need to add a capital gains tax to the system so far as gains from profit retentions are concerned.[10] Complete neutrality may be maintained.

One further reflection on corporate behavior may be necessary. Although the second hypothesis upon which the analysis relies seems more reasonable than the first and permits a more realistic analysis, corporate

9. In reality, capital gains accrue from other factors: corporate growth potential and changes in market interest rates. Also, in practice, capital gains are taxed on a realization basis, not on an accrual basis.

10. Of course, capital gains accruing from other sources (so-called "good-will" gains) may be taxed.

managers may not, in fact, give equal attention to the two taxes at the different levels. The primary concern of the managers might be a tax payable by the corporation itself, and the tax consequences for shareholders might be of secondary importance to them. This consideration may require a modification of the earlier proposition that if the rate of distribution relief is the same under both integration systems, then the two systems are identical in their effects of encouraging or discouraging the distribution of corporate profits. The managers might be expected to react more sharply to changes in the corporation income tax than to changes in the total tax, including the individual income tax, due on dividends received by shareholders. Because it directly affects the corporation income tax, a split-rate system with distribution relief identical to that of a dividends-received credit system may be a more direct stimulus to distribution than the latter system, under which the corporation income tax does not vary with the payout ratio and the total tax varies with the credit given to the shareholder.

3/C.3. Summary

Certain conclusions may be drawn from the preceding discussion. First, the two-tier taxation system tends, more than the other systems, to discourage the distribution and encourage the retention of corporate profits. This effect depends on the level of the shareholder's marginal individual income tax rate. The higher the marginal rate, the greater the discouragement of profit distributions. In theory, this discrimination against distribution may be neutralized by full taxation of capital gains on an accrual basis. In practice, however, capital gains taxation is not complete enough to offset the discriminatory effect. The empirical evidence in the United States seems to support these conclusions.[11]

Second, the two systems of integration may stimulate dividend payout, but this effect depends on the relationship between the rate of distribution relief and the shareholder's marginal income tax rate. If the marginal rate is higher than the rate of distribution relief, the total tax burden (the corporation income tax and the individual income tax due on dividends) increases as the dividend payout increases. If the middle- and low-income shareholders are insensitive to the tax consequences and the high-income shareholders exert more influence on corporate dividend policy, the systems may not be very effective in encouraging the distribution of profits. In the absence of empirical data, this hypothesis cannot be tested. In any

11. Brittain, *Corporate Dividend Policy*, Chapter IV.

case, the strengthening of capital gains taxation may reinforce the effect of encouraging distribution.

Third, the split-rate system might have a more stimulating effect on distribution than a dividends-received credit system offering comparable distribution relief, because corporate managers are probably more attentive to the corporation income tax than to the total tax burden, including the individual income tax due on dividends received by shareholders. However, the experiences of Germany[12] and Japan[13] appear to suggest that the split-rate system's effect of encouraging profit distributions has not been significant, though it is not easy to isolate the impact of the tax factor from the impact of other factors influencing corporate dividend policy.

Finally, the only method of achieving complete neutrality with respect to the retention and the distribution of corporate profits is the full integration system (and the partnership method). Under this system, the entire amount of corporate profits is taxed at the marginal income tax rate of the shareholder and the total tax burden on corporate-source profits therefore does not change with the distribution (or the retention) of such profits. Two major qualifications to this statement are that all of the retained earnings must be "allocated" to the shareholders and that all of the shareholders, whether or not resident in the country of the corporation paying the dividends, must be entitled to the benefit of full integration. The latter point is discussed in Chapter 7, which deals with the international aspects of corporate and shareholder taxation.[14]

3/D. Arguments for Integration

3/D.1. Equity and Redistribution

Generally speaking, the arguments for integration reflect the arguments against the corporation income tax (see Chapter 2). Those who favor integration tend to emphasize the view that the corporation is a legal

12. See van den Tempel, *Corporation and Individual Income Tax in the European Communities* 16; Kaldor, "The Economic Effects of Alternative Systems of Corporation Tax," in United Kingdom, Parliament, House of Commons, *Report From the Select Committee on Corporation Tax* 248, 254. But see Häuser, "West Germany," in National Bureau of Economic Research, *Foreign Tax Policies and Economic Growth* 97, 137, reporting a substantial increase in dividend payouts in the early years in which the split-rate system was in operation.

13. Brittain, *Corporate Dividend Policy* 196.

14. This summary has compared the results to be expected from the various tax systems. It is quite another matter, however, to estimate the effects of a change from one system to another. The early stimulative or discouraging effects on dividend distribution may well be dissipated as the economy adjusts to the new system.

fiction, a form of organization that is essentially similar to a partnership and is not properly taxable except in the same way as partnerships. According to this view, a corporation, at least for tax purposes, is hardly an entity separate from its shareholders.[15]

To the extent that is the case, corporate-source income suffers a heavier tax burden than income from other sources; corporate profits are taxed to the corporation as earned and again to the shareholders when distributed. Income from other sources (wages or interest, for example) is not subject to two-tier taxation. Equity requires, however, that all income, whatever its source, bear a uniform burden of taxation; hence, the argument is that if the tax burden on dividend income is heavier than the tax burden on other income, the tax structure is inequitable. The proponents of integration generally recognize the practical need to impose a corporation income tax, but they assert that integration is necessary in order to reduce or eliminate the unfair and discriminatory burden that the corporation income tax imposes on the distributed portion of corporate profits. In other words, integration is needed to restore equity to the tax structure.

Moreover, its proponents argue that integration serves another objective of individual income taxation. To the extent that an integration system stimulates the distribution of corporate profits, more corporate-source income is brought within the reach of the progressive individual income tax. Progressivity and, hence, the redistributive effect of the individual income tax is strengthened by integration. Although the integration systems may not always encourage the distribution of profits (according to the analysis in the preceding section), they should constitute an essential aspect of progressive income taxation insofar as they mitigate the heavy pressure to retain profits in the corporation which emerges under a two-tier taxation system.

This line of thinking leads to the argument that a full integration system, rather than the ordinary integration systems, is the best way to achieve these two objectives of progressive income taxation. Under this system, the entire amount of corporate profits, whether distributed or retained, is subject to the individual income tax; here, the corporation income tax is no more than a withholding tax to be credited by shareholders against the individual income taxes due on distributions and allocated retentions. Corporate-source income is therefore taxed in exactly the same way in which income from other sources is taxed. Moreover, not only the distributed part but also the retained part of corporate profits is brought within the reach of progressive taxation. Equity and redistributive requirements are thus best met.

15. See Goode, *The Corporation Income Tax* 182: "The underlying rationale of integration of corporate and individual income taxes is the belief that the corporation as such is not a suitable taxable subject."

Yet this system has never been adopted by any country as its regular method of taxing corporate-source income. The major reasons for this may be the administrative difficulties involved in its implementation, the revenue losses engendered by its adoption, and the unsettled problem of the shifting of the corporation income tax. The last problem will be discussed in the next section.

3/D.2. Economic Efficiency

a. Neutrality Among Forms of Business Organization

Integration is also defended from the point of view of economic efficiency. Taxation is said to involve an "excess burden" if it places a burden on the economy which is separate from, and in addition to, the revenue that it raises. For instance, if there were no separate tax on corporate-source profits, an enterprise would choose the form of business organization most suitable to it—be it a corporation, a partnership, or a sole proprietorship. If, however, a separate tax on corporate-source profits is introduced, the enterprise must take into account the tax factor in deciding what form of business organization it should adopt. Considering the heavier tax burden that would result from the choice of the corporate form, the enterprise may choose the partnership form even if the corporate form is better suited to its business needs. The loss in economic efficiency resulting from the choice of a less efficient form of business organization is an excess burden involved in the taxation of corporate-source income.

From the standpoint of economic efficiency, then, the tax system should be as nearly neutral as possible in its impact on different forms of business organization. The two-tier taxation system, however, is not neutral in this regard. It discriminates against the corporation as a form of business organization by taxing twice the distributed component of corporate profits—once when earned and again when distributed. Under most tax systems, noncorporate business profits, such as those of partnerships and sole proprietorships, are subject only to the individual income tax. The integration of the corporation and individual income taxes is therefore needed to make the tax structure more neutral among forms of business organization and to reduce the excess burden involved in the tax system. Under the integration systems, the distributed component of corporate profits is relieved, at least in part, from the two-tier system of taxation because of the relief given to distributions at either the corporate or the shareholder level.

Again, the ideal method of achieving neutrality within the tax system is the full integration system rather than the ordinary integration systems.

Under the full integration system, the corporation income tax is in effect removed, and the entire amount of corporate profits, whether retained or distributed, is subjected to the individual income tax in the same manner as other noncorporate business profits; hence, there is no discrimination against the corporate form of doing business. This point may be particularly important for small businesses, because it is the small enterprise that may suffer from this discrimination against the corporate form of organization. In the case of large, widely held corporations, nontax requirements (such as the need for a broad mobilization of capital funds) may overwhelm tax considerations, and these large enterprises must in any case choose the corporate form of organization. Small enterprises, however, may be prevented by tax barriers from choosing the corporate form even though they may need its advantages. It is argued that in order to remove the tax obstacles to the use of the corporate form by small businesses, full integration should be made available to small corporations (which are ordinarily closely held) even if it is denied to large, widely held corporations. This argument appears to have some force. As a general rule, the United States, for example, makes no provision for the integration of the corporation and the individual income taxes; there is no relief from the burden of the corporation income tax in the case of the widely held corporation. But the United States has recognized that there may be merit in the argument that, in the case of small, closely held corporations, the corporation income tax may be discriminatory. The U.S. tax code therefore gives the closely held corporation (that is, one with no more than ten shareholders) an option to elect full integration by choosing to be taxed under the partnership method.[16]

b. Efficient Allocation of Capital Funds

Proponents of integration argue that the two-tier system of taxation operates to encourage undue retention of earnings by corporations. As shown by the analysis in the preceding section, the higher the shareholder's marginal income tax rate, the greater the encouragement given to the retention of corporate profits. Theoretically, this effect on corporate behavior may be mitigated by tightening the taxation of capital gains. In most countries, however, the capital gains tax is not complete enough to offset the positive impact of two-tier taxation on the retention of profits. Tax-induced retentions, the argument runs, may lead to a less efficient allocation of capital resources among corporations. In other words, large

16. The U.S. option was adopted in 1958, as part of the so-called "small business" legislation of that year. See WTS: *United States*, 9A/7.

and mature firms, which can enjoy large profit retentions, tend to be less attentive to the profitability of investment and tend to make less efficient investments. In contrast, new and growing enterprises, which must rely on the issuance of new shares as a means of financing, may be ignored in the capital market because the amount of funds in the market is less than it would be if retention were not encouraged. "Survival of the fattest" instead of "survival of the fittest" may thus prevail, and the net result may be less efficient investments by the corporate sector as a whole.[17]

To the extent that integration encourages distribution, it is defended from the viewpoint of allocative efficiency. By removing barriers to the distribution of corporate earnings, integration serves to improve the functioning of a capital market. More profits are paid out to shareholders and reinvested through the "market test," which, at least theoretically, ensures that capital resources are used in the most efficient manner.[18] As shown by the analysis in the preceding section, the greater the distribution relief (and the lower the marginal income tax rate of the shareholder), the greater may be this advantage of the integration systems. Although there is no clear evidence that the adoption of integration has had a major impact on corporate distribution policy, the proponents of integration argue that integration is nonetheless necessary in order to achieve a more efficient allocation of capital resources.

This argument assumes, however, that the country in question has developed to the point where the existence of an underwriting network or of other financial institutions makes reinvestment practicable for the ordinary shareholder. Often, however, such institutions do not exist, particularly in most developing countries.[19]

17. As a representative argument along these lines, see Chown, *The Reform of Corporation Tax* 11–14.

18. The increase in dividend outlays is also said to make share investment more attractive to more persons and, hence, to aid the development of a capital market. As an example, Germany introduced integration in 1953 "in order to encourage corporate distributions as a means of reviving the then dormant capital market." WTS: *Germany* (2d ed.), 11/5.8b3, n. 279. Israel, also, has long provided partial integration by a system of taxes on corporate profits which results in a rate at the corporate level which is lower for distributed than for retained profits; "the purpose of the law is to encourage distribution of profits by companies." Joulus and Klimowsky, "National Report, Israel: The Multiple Burden on Dividends and Shares by Taxation on Income and Capital by Both Corporations and Shareholders," 55a *Cahiers de droit fiscal international* II/171, II/173 (1970).

19. Communauté Économique Européene, Commission, *Le Développement d'un marché européen des capitaux* 233.

3/D.3. Transitional Measures for Developing Countries

Another argument for integration also relates to the developing countries. Few developing countries exempt corporations from tax. Some, however, exempt dividends from tax in the hands of individual shareholders. In the course of modernizing and improving their tax structures, countries in the latter group may wish to treat dividends as taxable income. To move in one step from the full exemption of dividends to the full taxation of dividends may be too abrupt, however, to be politically acceptable. The transition to a new tax treatment for dividends (or for corporations, for that matter) may be eased by the adoption, at the same time, of some method of integration. As will be shown in more detail below, integration is a form of tax reduction; it can be used, therefore, to alleviate the burden of a new or higher tax on corporations or shareholders.[20] If revenue needs increase at a later time, after the new or higher tax has become established, the country can review the advisability of its integration system in the light of then-current circumstances.

There is another side to the use of integration as a transitional device. A nation that adopts integration as a temporary measure may find that the old rule that temporary taxes tend to become permanent taxes has a corollary: temporary tax concessions tend to become permanent tax concessions.

3/E. Arguments Against Integration

3/E.1. The Problem of Shifting

Two conflicting views of the corporation were noted in Chapter 1. The proponents of integration tend to reject the view that the corporation is an entity separate from its shareholders. By the same token, the opponents of integration tend to regard the corporation as an entity separate from its shareholders. In the light of the latter view, it is appropriate to tax the two separately. If corporation and shareholder are separate for other purposes, there is no need to integrate them for tax purposes. A tax on one is not a tax on the other.

In any event, the case for integration depends on the assumption that the

20. Tax missions to developing countries generally recommend against integration. As an exception, the Shoup Mission to Venezuela recommended some form of integration. At the time of the recommendation, Venezuela did not tax dividends to shareholders; the recommendation of integration was coupled with a recommendation that dividends be subjected to taxation. Integration would therefore have eased the transition to the new system. See Shoup *et al.*, *The Fiscal System of Venezuela* 111; see also Oldman, "Tax Reform in El Salvador," 6 *Inter-American Law Review* 379 (1964).

burden of the corporation income tax falls on the corporation and thus on the shareholders as the persons ultimately entitled to the corporation's profits. There is no firm conclusion about the validity of this assumption, however.[21] As far as is known, the burden of the corporation income tax may be shifted in whole or in part to consumers (by way of sales prices), to employees (by way of wages), or to suppliers (by way of purchase prices). To the extent that the tax is shifted, there is no "double taxation" of corporate-source income and no need for integration on equity grounds.

Professor Richard Musgrave, a leading authority on the shifting and incidence of the corporation income tax, is of the view that there is probably "a high degree of shifting." He adds, "to the extent that the corporation tax is passed on, profits are not reduced; and if profits are not reduced, no extra tax is imposed on dividends, and dividend relief [by way of integration] is inappropriate."[22]

3/E.2. Economic Growth

a. Encouragement of Retention

Different methods of taxing corporate-source income must also be viewed from the standpoint of economic growth, because corporate savings are, in many countries, a primary source of private saving and investment. Economic growth depends to a large extent on the level of private saving and investment. The taxation of corporate profits, in contrast, limits the investment that otherwise would be undertaken, by reducing the funds available for investment. In this way, any system of taxing corporate profits suppresses corporate investment. These systems of taxation may

21. Discussing "the thorny problem of tax incidence," Professor Samuelson asserts: "Economists are not yet in agreement on final results. Some think the corporate income tax falls mostly on the consumer; some argue it falls mostly on stockholders or capitalists." Samuelson, *Economics* (10th ed.) 175, 176. See also Pechman, *Federal Tax Policy* (rev. ed.) 111: "There is no more controversial issue in taxation than the question: *Who bears the corporation income tax*? On this question, economists and businessmen alike differ among themselves..... Unfortunately, economics has not yet provided a scientific basis for accepting or rejecting one side or the other." Dr. Pechman quotes some representative views and summarizes the evidence for each.

22. Musgrave, "Taxation of Corporations," in Canadian Tax Foundation, *Report of the Proceedings of the Twenty-Second Tax Conference* 124, 135. To take a concrete example, the Musgrave Commission on Tax Reform in Colombia recommended against integration for Colombia in part because "the proposition that double taxation exists rests on the assumption that the tax is in fact borne by profits and not shifted to the consumer or wage earner, but there can be no certainty that this assumption is valid." Musgrave and Gillis, *Fiscal Reform for Colombia* 81.

have an additional effect on corporate saving and investment, however, through their encouragement or discouragement of profit distributions.

In this respect, the opponents of integration may accept the validity of a proposition put forth by its proponents, but may draw a different conclusion from that proposition. One argument for integration, discussed above, asserts that an unintegrated corporation and individual income tax structure is bad because it penalizes dividends and thereby encourages the retention of earnings. Those who oppose integration may assert that even if one grants that an unintegrated system encourages retention rather than distribution, it does not follow that this result is bad; depending on the economic circumstances of the country in question, the retention of earnings by corporations may contribute more to growth and development than the distribution of those earnings to shareholders.[23]

For some, the distribution of earnings is preferred to retention on grounds of economic efficiency (as was argued above). As Dr. Slitor states with reference to Colombia, the argument is that integration will increase dividends, make investment in shares more attractive, stimulate saving and investment, and "make more of the investment flow 'stand the test of the market place.'" Yet he goes on to reject this argument[24]:

> The realities of the Colombian situation suggest, however, that company reinvestment is a major source of growth funds and would not adequately be replaced by shareholder savings out of, or in response to, increased dividend payments on stock.

Moreover, the economic efficiency argument assumes that a functioning capital market exists in the country. To the extent that there is no such market, the argument fails. Even with the best of capital markets, not all corporations have equal access to the market (as is the case in the United States). Corporations with less than full access to the capital market are forced to rely as far as possible on retained earnings. "Debt aversion" must also be taken into account. Those who have never owed large amounts of money overlook the fact that debt financing "has its own peculiar

23. The Musgrave Commission on Fiscal Reform for Colombia recommended against integration for a variety of reasons, one of which was that "integration would probably tend to encourage distribution (or to remove the possible retarding effect of the present system) and thereby reduce the rate of saving in the economy." Musgrave and Gillis, *Fiscal Reform for Colombia* 81. The marginal propensity to save from dividends and other private disposable income is "extremely low," Professor Bird reports, adding: "Increased retentions are probably desirable in Colombia today, given the low rate of personal saving of dividend recipients." Bird, *Taxation and Development: Lessons From Colombian Experience* 6, 142.

24. Slitor, "Reform of the Business Tax Structure: Analysis of Problems and Alternative Remedial Proposals," in Musgrave and Gillis, *Fiscal Reform for Colombia* 463, 497.

hazards."[25] Even a corporation with access to the capital market may invest retained earnings more readily than money that it has to borrow from third parties (and repay).

Given the importance of retained profits as an element in private saving and as a source of funds for economic growth, any penalty put on distributions by an unintegrated tax system may be desirable (especially in a developing country). Professor Bird reports of one such country[26]:

> A major agent of private industrial capital formation in Colombia today is the corporation, and a large part of corporate investment is at present financed out of retained earnings..... In the present Colombian situation, both revenue and equity considerations demand a relatively high absolute profits tax (with no offsetting concessions to shareholders on their personal taxes)....

Opposing distribution relief by way of integration for Great Britain, Professor Kaldor put the matter this way[27]:

> As far as publicly quoted companies are concerned (and these account for much the greater proportion of business investment) there is a close correlation (at least over a run of years) between the amount of retained profits and the level of investment. Publicly quoted companies (and particularly companies with widespread ownership) do not retain profits which are not required for business expansion. The profit which they retain is essential in order to ensure the growth of the business over longer periods; it is naive to suppose that a growing company can finance its long-term requirements by continued borrowing or continued share issues in *substitution* of retentions. A fast growing company will need both internal and external finance: the two are *complementary* to each other and not substitutes.

Many years ago, Professor Groves concluded that the unintegrated U.S. system of "unbalanced burdens upon distributed and undistributed income

25. Goode, *The Corporation Income Tax* 124.
26. Bird, *Taxation and Development: Lessons From Colombian Experience* 69, 80. See also Slitor, "Reform of the Business Tax Structure: Analysis of Problems and Alternative Remedial Proposals," in Musgrave and Gillis, *Fiscal Reform for Colombia* 463, 491 (recommending against integration in part because of the need of a developing country to retain earnings).
27. Kaldor, "The Economic Effects of Alternative Systems of Corporation Tax," in United Kingdom, Parliament, House of Commons, *Report From the Select Committee on Corporation Tax* 248, 249. Professor Kaldor added (at 251) that "the proposed reform of the corporation tax which redistributes the burden of taxation between companies in favour of the high distributors will thus necessarily cause the fastest-growing companies to be more severely handicapped by financial limitation; it will thereby reduce both the volume and the quality of business investment at any given level of business taxation."

was admirably adapted to an economy that needed to encourage business saving and discourage spending."[28] A summary of the recommendations made by tax missions to underdeveloped countries concluded that tax discrimination in favor of retained profits, which is the opposite of integration, "is a rough, but reasonable, incentive in the right direction."[29] One tax survey asserted that "business retention of profits" is "historically the primary source of capital accumulation in Western industrialized nations."[30] In this light, two-tier taxation of corporations and shareholders may be desirable to the extent that it encourages retention. In summary, integration is adopted (as in the German example cited earlier) "in order to encourage corporate distributions"; therefore, a country should adopt integration only if it has decided that corporate distributions are more in its national interest than retentions.

b. Discrimination Against New and Expanding Corporations

One economic efficiency argument in favor of integration is that it reduces tax discrimination against the corporate form of business organization. Within the corporate sector, however, it may be argued that integration discriminates against the new, small, or expanding corporation and in favor of the mature, wealthy, and well-established corporation. By definition, integration offers tax relief to the distributed, not the retained, component of corporate profits. Yet a new, small, or expanding corporation is more dependent on retained earnings as a source of capital than is a mature, well-established firm. Corporations are rarely able to pay dividends in the early years of their lives. Whatever the tax considerations, a new, small, or expanding corporation is often not in a position to take advantage of tax concessions favoring the distributed component of corporate profits. Distribution relief may mean that the mature, established corporation will be taxed at a lower rate than the small, new, or growing corporation. Although integration systems sometimes include relief provisions for small or new corporations, it may be that some alternative (a retention allowance, for example, or a rate reduction that extends to retained as well as distributed profits) would be more helpful to the small, new, or expanding corporation.

28. Groves, "Equity and Expediency in Business Taxation," in Tax Policy League, *How Shall Business Be Taxed?* 33, 42.

29. Schlesinger, "Tax Policy Recommendations of Technical Assistance Missions: Evolution, Pattern, and Interpretation," in Joint Tax Program of the Organization of American States, Inter-American Development Bank, and Economic Commission for Latin America, *Fiscal Policy for Economic Growth in Latin America* 425, 438.

30. Joint Tax Program of the Organization of American States and the Inter-American Development Bank, *Fiscal Survey of Colombia* 246.

3/E.3. Other Policy Arguments

a. Transitional Measures for Developing Countries

Some of those who accept the proposition that the absence of integration means a discriminatory burden on corporate-source income do not accept the conclusion that this discrimination is evil. It may not be inequitable, they argue, to levy extra tax burdens on income from capital. Such burdens are often imposed by net wealth taxes or earned income allowances, for example; to single out the profit distributions of corporations for two-tier taxation, it is asserted, is merely to put a special burden on dividends as a special variety of income from capital.[31] Since most dividends go to shareholders in the upper-income brackets, the extra burden falls primarily on those brackets and may therefore contribute to a more equal distribution of wealth and to a reduction in income disparities.

A special problem may exist in those countries which use an unintegrated system of taxing corporate-source income and which are considering a move toward integration. The price paid by shareholders for their shares presumably reflects the existing tax structure (the tax burden, in other words, is "capitalized" in the price). If that is the case, the adoption of some form of integration may give windfall benefits to those shareholders.[32]

b. Preferential Treatment of Capital Gains

Whether there is an "overtaxation" of corporate-source income and whether integration is therefore needed as a relief device may depend on the entire structure of corporation and shareholder taxation and not solely

31. For example, the Musgrave Commission on Fiscal Reform for Colombia recommended against integration for that country in part because "a strong tradition exists in Colombian tax thinking that it may well be desirable to tax capital income more heavily than wage or salary income." Musgrave and Gillis, *Fiscal Reform for Colombia* 81. See also Harberger, "Issues of Tax Reform in Latin America," in Joint Tax Program of the Organization of American States, Inter-American Development Bank, and Economic Commission for Latin America, *Fiscal Policy for Economic Growth in Latin America* 110, 113.

32. See Moore, "The Carter Report: Some Misgivings," 1 *Canadian Journal of Economics* 195, 198–202. (If integration were adopted, "windfall gains would accrue to those now owning Canadian shares. This must be counted on the negative side as a decrease in equity . . . ." Moore, at 199.) To reduce the scope of windfall benefits, some countries limit distribution relief to dividends paid on shares that were issued after the adoption of the integration scheme; no relief is given with respect to dividends paid on pre-existing shares. See the discussion of the dividend-deduction method in Chapter 5, which deals with integration at the corporate level.

on the two-tier taxation of distributed profits. In many countries, capital gains realized on the sale of shares by individual investors are free of tax or are taxed only at preferential rates. The yield from capital is made up of two separate elements: the appreciation in value of the capital and the periodic return on capital represented by dividends, rent, or similar payments. The favorable tax treatment of one element of the yield from share capital—appreciation—may compensate for any extra burden imposed, in the absence of integration, on the other element—dividends. The preferential taxation of capital gains, that is, may serve to raise the rate of return on capital invested in corporations by an amount sufficient to compensate for the reduction in the rate of return which results from the two-tier taxation of corporate-source income. As a practical matter, the absence of a tax on capital gains or the existence of a preferential rate for capital gains may be more important in inducing the retention of corporate profits than the two-tier taxation of distributed profits.[33]

In summary, the problem that proponents of integration hope to cure—the "overtaxation" of distributed corporate income—cannot be dealt with in isolation. The entire complex of corporation and shareholder taxation, and particularly the tax treatment of capital gains realized by shareholders, must be taken into account.

3/E.4. Revenue and Administrative Considerations

a. Revenue Considerations

Viewed as a separate economic entity, the corporation has a taxpaying capacity of its own. Moreover, in many countries, dividend income in the hands of shareholders, as well as profits in the hands of the corporation, can be taxed to produce significant amounts of revenue for the government. As will be noted below, integration amounts to selective rate relief, in that it involves a reduction in the rate of tax on corporate-source income at either the corporate or the shareholder level (in some countries, at both levels). In the short run, at least, the result is a decline in the amount of the government's tax receipts. The larger the degree of integration, the greater

33. "It has often been suggested that adoption of a partial integration plan should be contingent upon improved and increased taxation of capital gains." Goode, *The Corporation Income Tax* 200. See also Surrey, "Statement by Assistant Secretary of the Treasury Surrey, April 21, 1966, at the School of Law of the State University of New York [at Buffalo], on Federal Tax Policy in the 1960's," in United States, Treasury Department, *Annual Report of the Secretary of the Treasury on the State of Finances for the Fiscal Year Ended June 30, 1966*, 366, 377. This speech is reproduced in Hellmuth and Oldman (eds.), *Tax Policy and Tax Reform: 1961–1969—Selected Speeches and Testimony of Stanley S. Surrey* 115, 127.

may be the decline in tax revenue. In a world of rising revenue needs, this factor cannot be ignored. In its enumeration of "a number of reasons" why it recommended against the integration of corporation and individual income taxes, the Musgrave Commission on Fiscal Reform for Colombia made this blunt remark: "To begin with, the revenue loss involved would be substantial."[34]

Professor Surrey also emphasizes the loss of tax revenue which integration involves. After discussing the varying approaches to integration found in use in the Common Market, he points to the enormous tax revenues provided by the unintegrated corporate tax structure in the United States and adds[35] that the system

> is certainly efficient in this sense and is thus not easily displaced by any rival approach that disperses the tax collection and complicates the task of administration. Thus any approach which looks more to the shareholder for the tax on corporate profits must devise a more efficient system of collecting the tax on dividends than we possess today.

b. ADMINISTRATIVE DIFFICULTIES OF INTEGRATION AND ITS ALTERNATIVES

1. The alternative of rate reduction. Another argument against integration is grounded in the administrative difficulties that any method of integration involves. The difficulties vary from method to method, but even the simplest adds some element of complexity to the income tax structure. Particularly in less developed countries, the extra administrative difficulties of integration suggest the wisdom of considering alternatives.

One alternative is rate reduction. Integration itself amounts to a sophisticated form of rate reduction which operates at either the corporate or the shareholder level (sometimes at both levels) to reduce the effective rate of tax on distributed corporate earnings. Whenever any particular method of integration is under consideration, it may be appropriate to ask these questions: How much corporate-source tax revenue will be lost? How far

34. Musgrave and Gillis, *Fiscal Reform for Colombia* 81. To take another example, Germany not long ago proposed to give a far larger degree of integration relief to its shareholders. It was estimated that to make up for the lost revenue, Germany's value-added tax rate would have to be increased by one percentage point (an increase of approximately 10%). "Germany Changes to Tax Credits," *The Economist*, 13 November 1971, p. 79.

35. Surrey, "Statement by Assistant Secretary of the Treasury Surrey, April 21, 1966, at the School of Law of the State University of New York [at Buffalo], on Federal Tax Policy in the 1960's," in United States, Treasury Department, *Annual Report of the Secretary of the Treasury on the State of Finances for the Fiscal Year Ended June 30, 1966*, 366, 377.

would relinquishing the same amount of tax revenue in a less complicated way—for example, by a simple reduction in the rate of tax on corporate profits—accomplish comparable economic goals with fewer administrative difficulties?

To put the matter another way, the adoption of any kind of integration may mean a reduction in the tax revenue obtained from corporations and shareholders if compared with the revenue that would be obtained under an unintegrated tax system. The benefits of this tax reduction may be less than the benefits that might be obtained from some alternative form of tax reduction.

2. The alternative of special rules for closely held corporations. The view that a corporation is essentially like a partnership and that it is improper to tax both corporations and shareholders without offering integration relief may be obsolete with regard to the widely held corporation. This view retains some force, however, with regard to the typical closely held corporation; in this latter case, ownership and management are ordinarily in the same hands. It is no distortion of reality to assert that in most closely held corporations, the shareholders are essentially similar to partners. As a practical matter, much of the pressure for integration comes from those who are particularly concerned with the situation of the closely held corporation (which is generally, but not invariably, a small corporation). Much of the argument relating to closely held corporations may be irrelevant, however, if applied to widely held corporations.

A country may adopt a single solution for all corporations—integration for all, or integration for none. For example, France and Sweden offer the same degree of integration (the former at the shareholder level, the latter at the corporate level) to all corporations, whether widely held or closely held.

Yet there is an alternative—the provision of different tax systems for the two corporate categories. For the widely held corporation, it may be reasonable to use an unintegrated tax structure, in recognition of the separateness and the taxable capacity of the widely held corporation and in order to avoid the administrative problems and revenue losses of integration's being applied to that category of corporation. At the same time, it may be equally reasonable to provide some alternative method of taxation for the closely held corporation (for example, giving such a corporation the option of being taxed as a partnership if it and its shareholders so desire).[36]

This practice is followed in the United States, which since 1954 has given closely held corporations the option of being taxed under the partnership method if they and their shareholders so desire. Most of the corporations in the United States are closely held and are in a position to claim the benefits of partnership taxation (that is, to enjoy the complete integration of the corporation and individual income taxes with regard to retained as well as distributed profits). The number of corporations exercising this option has grown steadily. In 1970, income tax returns were filed by almost 1,665,000 active corporations; of these, more than 257,000 corporations (over 15% of the total) exercised their option for taxation under the partnership method[37]. (In 1960, the proportion was less than 8%.)

3. International complexities. In any given country, some degree of integration may appear desirable at any given time in the context of a closed national economy. Even in that case, however, a full consideration of the country's national interests requires that the international impact of the proposed integration scheme—both on domestic investors considering investment abroad and on foreign investors considering investment within the country—be carefully scrutinized. Any system of integration may distort the pattern of international investment. The problems involved, particularly the administrative and technical difficulties of adjusting the integration scheme to reduce the distortions in international investment patterns which it may cause, are explored in detail in Chapter 7.

36. Canada, Minister of Finance, *Proposals for Tax Reform* (the Canadian "White Paper," 1969), stressed the differences between widely and closely held corporations and added (para. 4.4): "It is little wonder that it has always been difficult to design a tax system that can be applied appropriately to all of these different types of corporations and corporate relationships." The Canadian proposal, therefore, was "to create one set of rules for the closely-held corporation—the incorporated proprietorship or partnership—and another set of rules for the widely held, public corporation. This distinction reflects the difference in the relationship between the two types of corporations and their respective shareholders" (para. 4.19). The proposal (to give closely held corporations an option to elect taxation as a partnership) was not adopted, however; instead, Canada provided other varieties of small business relief.
37. United States, Department of the Treasury, Internal Revenue Service, *Statistics of Income—1970 Corporation Income Tax Returns* 1, 3, 137. The great majority of the closely held corporations electing the partnership method of taxation were small corporations. Of the 257,000 corporations involved, more than 174,000 had assets totaling under $100,000, and only 3,100 had assets totaling over $1,000,000.

3/F. Conclusion: The Prevalence of Partial Integration

Whether some form of integration should be included in the tax structure of any given country is not a question that can be answered in the abstract. The answer must depend on political, economic, and revenue considerations and policies that appear from time to time in that country.

Some years ago, a British Royal Commission asserted that a country decides on its system of taxing corporations and shareholders or makes changes in a pre-existing system "by reference to the current policy of favouring company investment at the expense of personal income or personal income at the expense of company investment, as the case may be."[38] Because that policy varies from time to time, and because there is little agreement on how best to carry out a policy even after it has been established, the matter of integration is characterized by a large degree of fluctuation and instability. Nevertheless, a close scrutiny of the various tax structures would seem to permit the following assertions of fact.

1. In the usual case of an ordinary business corporation, every developed country treats the corporation for tax purposes as an entity separate from its shareholders and levies a corporation income tax on corporate profits, whether distributed or retained. Such countries also tax to the shareholders, under the individual income tax, that portion of corporate profits which is distributed to the shareholders as dividends.
2. No developed country uses the "partnership method" as its normal method of taxing the profits of ordinary business corporations. In addition, in the usual case of the ordinary business corporation, none of the developed countries provides for the full integration of the corporation and the individual income taxes. Full integration, as defined at the beginning of this chapter, is integration that is comprehensive enough to cover retained as well as distributed profits.
3. For the distributed component of corporate profits, however, a large proportion, but not all, of the developed countries provide integration by offering tax relief to such profits at either the corporate or the shareholder level (in some cases, at both levels) to take account of the tax paid at the other level. Usually, the relief is only partial, in that it does not provide complete relief even for distributed profits; that is, in addition to tax at the individual income tax rates, a portion of the corporate tax is still payable on distributed profits.
4. Some countries offer a degree of integration for closely held (ordinarily

38. United Kingdom, Royal Commission on the Taxation of Profits and Income, *Final Report*, para. 57.

small) corporations which is not available to widely held corporations; others provide other varieties of relief from the corporation income tax to closely held corporations.

The pattern summarized above amounts to a compromise among the various arguments discussed earlier. With regard to shifting and incidence, for example, partial integration amounts to a compromise between the unproven view that the corporation income tax is not shifted, but falls on the owners of the corporation, and the equally unproven view that the tax is shifted to workers, consumers, or both. Professor Prest argues that partial integration may be justified on the grounds that the corporation income tax is partially shifted in the short run.[39]

Partial integration may also be regarded as a compromise between the view of the corporation as a mere agglomeration of individuals associated for profit-making purposes and the view of the corporation as a separate decision-making entity with its own economic autonomy and taxable capacity. Similarly, the grant of special integration rules or other forms of tax relief to closely held corporations steers a middle course between conflicting views of the corporation.

And, finally, partial integration lightens the additional burden of the corporation income tax on distributed profits without substantially diminishing the government's tax receipts, whereas the complete elimination of that burden might result in a severe revenue loss.

39. Prest, "The Select Committee on Corporation Tax," 1972 *British Tax Review* 15, 18, 19.

4

Choice of the Level (Corporate or Shareholder) at Which Integration Is To Be Provided

4/A. In General

If the burden of the two-tier taxation of corporate-source income is to be eased by integration, the first question to be answered is this: at what level should integration be provided? Should an adjustment be made at the corporate level—that is, should the corporation income tax on the distributed component of the corporation's profits be reduced because that component will also be taxed in the shareholders' hands? Or should there be an adjustment at the shareholder level—that is, should the individual income tax on the shareholder's dividend be reduced to take account of the fact that the dividend is paid from profits that were previously taxed to the corporation?[1]

This chapter will discuss the arguments for and against the choice of one level or the other. This choice, however, is one of tax technique rather than of substantive effect. The choice of level does not control the amount of relief given. The integration of the corporation and the individual income taxes can achieve whatever amount of tax relief for distributed profits is desired, whether it is applied at the corporate level or the shareholder level (or at both levels). As far as the total amount of tax is concerned, the same reduction can be provided at one level just as well as at the other level.

Moreover, whatever level is chosen and whatever the formal differences between techniques of integration, integration reduces the effects of the two-tier taxation of corporate-source income by diminishing the impact on distributed profits of the *corporation* income tax, not that of the individual

1. Some countries (Japan and Germany, for example) use a combination of methods, which provides some reduction in the taxes on distributed earnings at both the corporate level and the shareholder level (see below).

income tax. It is the additional burden imposed by the corporation income tax (see Table 1 in Chapter 3) which is reduced or eliminated by integration.

Some methods of integration reduce the burden of the corporation income tax by operating at the corporate level; they impose a rate of tax on the distributed component of a corporation's profits which is lower than the rate imposed on the retained component. Yet even those methods of integration which operate at the shareholder level (reducing, in one way or another, the individual income tax on the shareholder's dividend receipt) do so by treating the corporation income tax merely as a collection device. The payment of income tax by the corporation on the distributed component of its profits is treated, in whole or in part, as an advance payment by the corporation on account of the income tax due from the shareholder. In other words, the corporation income tax on the distributed component of the corporation's profits is treated as a tax "withheld" for the shareholder's account from his share of that component. Only because a portion of the corporation income tax is deemed to have been paid or withheld for the account of the shareholder does the latter receive correlative relief from the individual income tax.

With the warning, then, that the discussion of the relative merits of integration at the corporate level as opposed to integration at the shareholder level involves matters of form rather than of substance, the remaining sections of this chapter will examine certain considerations that enter into the choice of the level (corporate or shareholder) at which integration is to operate in a technical sense.

4/B. Ease of Administration

Integration is generally easier to administer at the corporate level than at the shareholder level. Integration at the corporate level is not, however, entirely free of administrative difficulties; it does introduce some additional complexity into the corporate tax structure. This complexity is rarely beyond the capability of most tax administrations and corporations, however. Corporations are more skilled at bookkeeping than individual shareholders; and the computation of tax by the taxpayer, as well as audit and review by the tax administration, tends to be easier at the corporate level than at the shareholder level.

At the shareholder level, the fact that integration involves some complexity may be more serious than at the corporate level. Far more taxpayers are involved. Except in cases in which integration takes the form of an outright exemption of dividends from the individual income tax (which is true only in some relatively underdeveloped countries, as indicated in

Chapter 6), integration at the shareholder level requires some adjustment of each shareholder's tax base or tax liability. The degree of complexity involved in this adjustment varies from one method to another, as will be apparent from the discussion in Chapter 6 of particular methods. As a practical matter, some of the burden of complexity at the shareholder level may be shifted to the corporation. For example, the corporation may be required to advise the shareholder of the exact amount of the adjustment to which the latter is entitled.

Moreover, integration at the shareholder level is based on the assumption that the full tax has been paid at the corporate level on the profits from which the shareholder's dividend is paid. For a variety of reasons, however, corporations often pay tax at less than the full nominal rate. Particularly complex adjustments may be required to ensure that distribution relief is not given to shareholders with respect to taxes that have *not* been paid by the corporation.[2] At best, therefore, integration at the shareholder level tends to be more complicated for the taxpayer and more difficult for the tax administration than integration at the corporate level.[3]

4/C. Effects on Tax Revenue and Compliance

Although, as pointed out in the beginning of this chapter, tax revenues may be made equal under the two systems of integration, integration at the corporate level may in practice cost the government more in lost tax revenues than integration at the shareholder level. One argument for the use of a corporation income tax is its strength as a revenue producer. Because integration at the corporate level operates by reducing the corporation income tax on a portion of a corporation's profits (the distributed portion), however, integration at that level results in an immediate decline in the yield of the corporation income tax. Although this decline can be compensated for by an increase in the rate of tax on the retained com-

2. See, for example, the discussion of the French *précompte mobilière* in Chapter 6.

3. Professor Prest asserts that as far as comparisons of integration at the corporate and shareholder levels are concerned, "The arguments of principle ... seem to be very weak ones"; for that reason, he thought it appropriate to go along with the views of the tax administrators that, in the English case, integration at the corporate level would be preferable because easier to administer. Prest, "Minutes of Evidence Taken 6 July 1971," in United Kingdom, Parliament, House of Commons, *Report From the Select Committee on Corporation Tax* 110.

Unlike Professor Prest, who favors integration, Professor Kaldor opposes integration. If forced to choose between alternative systems of integration, though, Professor Kaldor would also prefer it at the corporate level. Kaldor, "The Economic Effects of Alternative Systems of Corporation Tax," in United Kingdom, Parliament, House of Commons, *Report From the Select Committee on Corporation Tax* 248, 255.

ponent, such an increase may reduce retained earnings below reasonable business needs.

Integration at the shareholder level has the advantage of leaving undiminished the yield of the corporation income tax. This advantage may be more apparent than real, however. At the beginning of this chapter, it was pointed out that integration at the shareholder level in effect treats a portion of the corporation income tax as a mere prepayment of the individual income tax. With integration at the shareholder level, some of the tax collected from corporations in the first instance therefore serves merely to reduce the tax collected from shareholders in the second instance. As a result, it is difficult to isolate the impact of integration on tax revenues and to attribute this impact specifically to one level of taxation rather than another.

Nevertheless, a country contemplating the adoption of distribution relief at the corporate level must consider that the tax revenue lost at that level may not be compensated for by higher tax revenues at the shareholder level. Even if dividend disbursements increase, the relatively large number of shareholders and the problems of enforcement and administration of the individual income tax (particularly to the extent that that tax bears on unearned income) mean that a considerable degree of erosion is likely. Pointing to the efficiency of the corporation income tax as a revenue producer, Professor Surrey warned that "any approach which looks more to the shareholder for the tax on corporate profits must devise a more efficient system of collecting the tax on dividends than we possess today."[4] If this is a consideration in a developed country, such as the United States, which has an experienced and presumably efficient income tax administration, it must be an even greater consideration in developing countries in which the income tax is relatively new.

Integration at the corporate level may be appropriate, therefore, only to the extent that tax compliance at the shareholder level is good. Moreover, integration at the shareholder level may actually improve taxpayer compliance. Except in those countries in which integration takes the form of an outright exemption of dividends, the tax benefits of integration at the shareholder level are available only to the individual who reports his dividend income on his tax return and then claims integration relief. The French, for example, in defending their post-1965 system of integration at the shareholder level (see Chapter 6), emphasized that its benefits "go only

4. Surrey, "Statement by Assistant Secretary of the Treasury Surrey, April 21, 1966, at the School of Law of the State University of New York [at Buffalo], on Federal Tax Policy in the 1960's," in United States, Treasury Department, *Annual Report of the Secretary of the Treasury on the State of Finances for the Fiscal Year Ended June 30, 1966*, 366, 377. This speech is reproduced in Hellmuth and Oldman (eds.), *Tax Policy and Tax Reform: 1961–1969—Selected Speeches and Testimony of Stanley S. Surrey* 115, 127.

to honest taxpayers." Those who fail to report their dividend income cannot use the system.

To eliminate or at least reduce the problems of shareholder compliance, a country adopting integration at the corporate level may find it expedient to adopt a withholding system that would collect from every dividend disbursement a preliminary tax for the shareholder's account. With such a withholding system in effect, compliance may be as good under integration at the corporate level as under integration at the shareholder level.[5] In the absence of actual withholding from dividends, however, integration at the corporate level may reduce tax revenues at that level by an amount greater than that of any increase in revenues at the shareholder level.

4/D. Effect on Business and Investment Behavior

Integration is generally adopted with the hope that it will influence taxpayer behavior—for example, that it will increase the portion of corporate profits paid out as dividends or encourage equity rather than debt financing. If it is assumed that corporate managers consider the total tax on corporate-source income (the corporation income tax and the individual income tax on dividends), then the two systems of integration do not differ in their effect on such behavior (see Chapter 3). But corporate managers may not give equal attention to the two taxes imposed at the two levels. They may respond more strongly to integration at the corporate level, which directly reduces the corporation income tax. At least in the case of widely held corporations, it is often argued that what matters to management is the tax payable by the corporation itself.[6] Integration at the corporate level should therefore have a greater impact on corporate dividend policy.

In contrast, integration at the shareholder level may be said to have less effect on business decisions than integration at the corporate level. If integration is provided at the shareholder level, the tax due from the corporation is the same whether earnings are retained or distributed. For

5. "Having a tax withheld by a payor, that is, deducted from the payment and paid instead to the government, is universally recognized as the most effective and inexpensive way of collecting income taxes. . . . . A withholding tax is not an income tax but a means of collecting that tax, inasmuch as whatever is collected is applied toward the payment of the total income tax liability." Yudkin, *A Legal Structure for Effective Income Tax Administration* 3/B1.

6. See Musgrave, "The Carter Commission Report," 1 *Canadian Journal of Economics* 159, 166 (1968). Professor Musgrave has also put it this way: "With widely-held corporations it may well be that management simply looks at what corporation tax must be paid at the corporate level, and not at the net payments by the shareholders." Musgrave, "Taxation of Corporations," in Canadian Tax Foundation, *Report of the Proceedings of the Twenty-Second Tax Conference* 124, 135–136.

the corporation, integration at the shareholder level means there is no discrimination against the retention of earnings. If the directors of a corporation conclude that the needs of the business require the retention rather than the distribution of earnings, no tax penalty on the corporation results. Quite apart from tax factors, retained earnings may be the cheapest and the most readily available source of corporate capital. If so, it might be appropriate to arrange the tax system so that it does not work at cross-purposes with nontax considerations.

If constructive dividends or noncash dividends (dividends in shares, for example) qualify for distribution relief, however, even integration at the corporate level may operate without unduly depleting corporate cash reserves or unduly influencing the directors' decisions about the amount of earnings to be retained. On the whole, though, integration at the shareholder level may more easily avoid tax discrimination against retained earnings at the corporate level. Belgium, for example, adopted distribution relief at the shareholder level as its primary method of integration because it feared that integration at the corporate level "would have the effect of discouraging self-financing. Self-financing is of considerable importance in Belgium . . . ."[7]

With the change from the two-tier system of taxation, integration at the shareholder level may even permit increased retentions by corporations without causing any reduction in shareholder income.[8] Because integration at the shareholder level reduces the shareholder's tax on dividend receipts, each unit of distributed profits becomes more valuable (after tax) to the shareholder. The corporation may therefore be able to meet shareholder net (or after-tax) dividend requirements despite a reduction in its gross (or before-tax) dividend outlays. In short, integration at the shareholder level may permit an increase in the shareholder's effective income without draining the corporation of the profits needed for investment in the business.

On the whole, however, integration at the shareholder level is generally assumed to leave the shareholders (generally well-to-do individuals) with more after-tax income than they would have without integration. Whether the result will be more investment by individuals and a greater flow of funds into capital markets or more consumption expenditures depends on

7. "European Communities: The Corporation Income Tax Split Rate Versus the Shareholders' Tax Credit As a Means of Easing the Double Taxation Burden on Corporate Distributions," 8 *European Taxation* 197, 201–202 (1968).

8. See the discussion in Chapter 6 of the French dividend practice since France's adoption of integration at the shareholder level. As noted there, the increase in retention is not the effect of the system itself but the effect of a change in the system. In other words, a reduction of the tax on corporate-source income resulted partly in increased corporate retentions and partly in increased net dividends for shareholders.

such local variables as the presence or absence of a functioning capital market, patterns of investment and spending, and so on.

All of these considerations are theoretical, however. As a practical matter, there is no conclusive evidence that integration is effective in raising dividend distributions, promoting investment in corporate shares, or accomplishing any similar results. There is still less evidence that integration at one level is more effective than integration at the other. Professors Bird and Oldman state that "no one has ever shown that what system is employed makes much difference in economic results on saving and investment."[9]

4/E. Shifting and Incidence

The proponents of integration at the corporate level perhaps depend less on unproven assumptions about the incidence of the corporation income tax than those who support integration at the shareholder level. At present, the incidence of the corporation income tax is shrouded in doubt; the burden of the tax may be on the shareholder, or on the consumer, or on the worker, or on some combination of the three. Yet integration at the shareholder level is generally defended on the grounds that the burden of the corporation income tax falls, at least in part, on the shareholder and that the shareholder is therefore entitled to an equivalent measure of tax relief when he receives a dividend. To the extent that this assumption about incidence is incorrect, such relief may be unwarranted.

Regardless of the assumptions about incidence, however, it may be easier to defend integration at the corporate level. Suppose, for example, that the burden of the corporation income tax falls not on the shareholder but on the consumer, to whom it may be passed on as a cost. Even in this case, integration at the corporate level may be defensible as a device to reduce (tax) costs. In other words, there may always be a case for integration at the corporate level. In contrast, integration at the shareholder level may be largely defensible only to the extent that the burden of the corporation income tax actually falls on the shareholder, who gets the relief.

Any argument based on the thorny problem of incidence is likely to be inconclusive, however, and will therefore throw little light on the choice of the level at which integration should be offered.

9. Bird and Oldman, "Tax Research and Tax Reform in Latin America," 3-3 *Latin American Research Review* 5, 13 (Summer 1968). To the same effect, see van den Tempel, *Corporation Tax and Individual Income Tax in the European Communities* 9.

4/F. Equity and Political Factors

Whether a particular method of integration is equitable is generally measured by this test: does it remove, at all income levels, the same proportion of the additional burden imposed on distributed profits by the corporation income tax?[10] All of the alternatives for integration at the *corporate* level which are discussed below meet this test, but some of the methods proposed for integration at the *shareholder* level do not (see Chapter 6). The more common methods of integration at the shareholder level do, however, operate equitably by the test. The argument of equity does not, therefore, point to the choice of one level or the other but, rather, depends on the particular technique by which integration is implemented.

Even if it is deemed equitable according to the test above, integration at the shareholder level may involve a special difficulty of "apparent" equity. Integration at this level generally means that if only the shareholder's tax burden (rather than the combined corporation-shareholder burden) is considered, dividend income appears to be taxed less heavily than other income—earned income from labor or a profession, for example. Especially since dividend income is received primarily by well-to-do individuals, this apparent preference for a particular form of unearned income may raise more political problems than a system of integration at the corporate level. France offers an example of the political problems that may follow from integration at the shareholder level: in 1972, the Prime Minister was forced out of office after it was revealed that he had paid no income tax for several years because of the tax savings he had enjoyed (as a shareholder) as a result of France's having adopted a system of integration at the shareholder level. (This episode is discussed in more detail in Chapter 6.)

4/G. International Aspects: Effect on Nonresidents

4/G.1. In General

The above arguments are inconclusive; none is strong enough to point compellingly to the choice of one level of integration over the other. In one respect, however, integration at the shareholder level is significantly different from integration at the corporate level. This difference may be important enough to determine a country's choice of the level, corporate or shareholder, at which integration is to be provided.

The difference concerns the effect of choice of level on nonresident shareholders. Integration at the corporate level reduces the tax burden on

10. Pechman, *Federal Tax Policy* (rev. ed.) 142.

all distributed profits, including those paid to nonresident shareholders. Integration at the shareholder level, in contrast, ordinarily benefits only resident shareholders; it offers no benefits to nonresident shareholders.[11] A study for the European Economic Community concluded that this differing impact on resident and nonresident shareholders constitutes the "*essential difference*" between integration at the shareholder level and integration at the corporate level.[12]

In a country in which foreign ownership is so extensive as to be a matter of concern, the preferential treatment of resident, as compared to nonresident, shareholders which follows from integration at the shareholder level may be the single most important factor inducing such a country to integrate at that level. Canada and France are conspicuous examples. In 1965, France adopted integration at the shareholder rather than the corporate level because integration at the shareholder level gives relief only to resident shareholders (see Chapter 7).[13] In Canada, the Carter Commission regarded integration at the corporate level (by way of a deduction to the corporation for dividends paid) as "a reasonable alternative." However, the Commission then added[14]:

> Its main drawback, however, would arise from the deduction of dividends paid to non-residents. The allowance of such deductions would result in unwarranted revenue costs and would serve to increase the amount collected by foreign treasuries.

The United Kingdom provides another example. It adopted a new integration scheme that became effective in April 1973. The British government's first preference was for integration at the corporate level; but in the end, the government chose integration at the shareholder level. The major consideration in this choice was that integration at the shareholder level would provide no relief to nonresident shareholders—particularly U.S.

11. The international aspects of integration are considered in detail in Chapter 7.

12. Communauté Économique Européene, Commission, *Le Développement d'un marché européen des capitaux* 225.

13. "In 1965, when the French first introduced this system, there was strong opposition from abroad because the benefit of the [system] was not extended to foreign investors. Of course, this was the intention of the French government. . . ." Rädler, "International Aspects—II," in Canadian Tax Foundation, *Report of the Proceedings of the Twenty-Second Tax Conference* 299, 301.

14. Canada, Royal Commission on Taxation, 4 *Report of the Royal Commission on Taxation* 44. Professor Musgrave similarly indicated Canada's preference for integration at the corporate level but recognized that it might "not be quite suitable to the Canadian setting"; given the importance of foreign shareholders in Canada, integration at the shareholder level might be preferable because it "readily permits limitation to resident shareholders." Musgrave, "Taxation of Corporations," in Canadian Tax Foundation, *Report of the Proceedings of the Twenty-Second Tax Conference* 124, 136.

parent corporations of British corporate subsidiaries. (See Chapter 7, which deals with the international aspects of integration.)

Integration at the shareholder level does more than deny relief to nonresident shareholders; it also denies relief to those resident shareholders who own shares in domestic corporations but who conceal those shares abroad. It is apparently not uncommon for residents of a country (particularly a developing country) to transfer wealth secretly to a safe haven in a foreign country (Switzerland, for example). The transfer may be made because of fear of political disturbances, fear of devaluation or exchange controls, or a desire to evade income, wealth, or death taxes. Often, some of the wealth transferred will include shares of corporations resident in the transferor's country. Even though the shares are beneficially owned by a resident of that country, they will be held by a nonresident nominee in the transferee country and, for purposes of distribution relief, will be treated as shares owned by a nonresident. Integration at the corporate level will extend distribution relief to dividends paid on these pseudo-foreign shares, but integration at the shareholder level will deny relief to dividends paid on such shares.

Much of the Italian capital transferred to Switzerland is said to consist of shares in Italian corporations. Similarly, it is believed that much of the French capital concealed in Switzerland consists of shares in French corporations. The French government's desire not to provide tax relief for dividends paid on those shares was a factor in France's choice of integration at the shareholder rather than the corporate level; in the French view, integration at the former level discourages the expatriation of capital.

Any country that has reason to fear the flight of capital or to believe that a significant portion of the shares nominally held by nonresidents is actually owned by residents must take account of this argument in choosing the level at which integration is to be offered.[15]

4/G.2. Possible Effect of New French Tax Treaty Pattern

A development in France since 1969 may, however, have reduced the force of the argument that integration at the shareholder level is in a country's national interest because it gives no relief to nonresidents. As noted earlier, France chose integration at the shareholder level in 1965, primarily to favor resident over nonresident shareholders. However, pressure from France's Common Market partners and from other capital-exporting nations (as well

15. Musgrave, "International Aspects—II," in Canadian Tax Foundation, *Report of the Proceedings of the Twenty-Second Tax Conference* 308, 325.

as certain changes in France's attitude toward foreign investors) led France to modify its position.

France announced that it was willing, by treaty or treaty amendment, to extend the same relief it offered to its own resident shareholders to shareholders in any country with which it had a tax treaty (see Chapter 3). Because France has treaties with virtually all developed and many undeveloped countries, there is little merit (as far as France is concerned) in the argument that a country may prefer integration at the shareholder level as a means of favoring residents over nonresidents. In fact, by the end of 1977, France has extended dividend relief to nonresident shareholders in 12 countries (Australia, Austria, Belgium, Brazil, Finland, Germany, Luxembourg, the Netherlands, Sweden, Switzerland, the United Kingdom, and the United States). Moreover, the United Kingdom, after adopting an integration scheme at the shareholder level, decided to follow the French pattern and actually extended dividend relief across its borders. By treaty arrangement, it has afforded the same treatment as France to foreign shareholders in seven European countries (Denmark, Finland, France, Ireland, Spain, Sweden, and Switzerland) and a number of less-industrialized countries.[16]

Underlying the tax treaty patterns of France and the United Kingdom is the requirement of the European Community (Common Market) treaty that capital be allowed to move freely within the Community so that the goal of a unified capital market throughout the whole Community can be attained. In other words, a resident of one member country must eventually be able to invest in the other member countries without impediments (tax or other); a corporation of one member country must, similarly, be able to raise capital in the other member countries without tax or other obstacles.[17] Countries outside the European Community have no such obligation, however. Japan, for example, does not extend to nonresident shareholders the same distribution relief that it gives residents at the shareholder level. Although Belgium is a member of the European Community, it had not, as of 1977, extended its shareholder distribution relief to nonresidents.

A developing country adopting integration at the shareholder level may therefore be able in its tax treaties to follow the Japanese and Belgian pattern (of not extending relief to nonresident shareholders) rather than the French pattern.

As a general rule, then, the fact that integration at the shareholder level favors resident over nonresident shareholders, whereas integration at the

16. The same treatment is provided to U.S. shareholders by the U.S.-U.K. income tax treaty which was ratified in 1980.

17. See Article 4(1) of the "Proposed Directive for the Harmonisation of Systems of Company Taxation and of Withholding Taxes on Dividends," 16 *European Taxation* 52, 59 (1976).

corporate level gives as much relief to nonresidents as to residents, remains the "essential difference" between these two levels of integration. In a number of cases, this difference appears to have been the decisive factor in the choice of the shareholder level.

4/H. Conclusion

Given the importance of local variables as well as the fact that few of the arguments considered above point strongly in one direction or the other, no definitive answer can be given to the question whether a system of integration, if it is to be adopted, should be implemented at the shareholder rather than the corporate level. Administrative capabilities, revenue needs, political factors, attitudes toward progressive taxation, national economic goals, investment and spending patterns, the presence or absence of a functioning capital market, the relative importance of nonresident shareholders, and the extent to which a country seeks to limit foreign ownership, to give a tax incentive to foreign shareholders, or merely to provide "neutrality" in the tax treatment of nonresidents—in every case, these and other local variables must be considered, and the alternatives must be weighed in the light thereof. Moreover, each of these factors will vary from time to time; for example, a system beyond the capabilities of a country's tax administration at one time may be feasible 10 or 20 years later.

In the absence of arguments that point conclusively to the choice of one level of integration over the other, it is perhaps not surprising that some countries have chosen to adopt measures of integration at both levels. Japan and Germany, for example, provide some relief for distributed profits at the corporate level and rather more relief at the shareholder level. Such a system capitalizes, at least to a limited extent, on the advantages of integration at each level. Yet by requiring tax adjustments for distributions at both the corporate level and the shareholder level, such a system of relief doubles the administrative problems of integration.

5

Integration at the Corporate Level

5/A. Introduction

Methods of integration at the corporate level fall into two major categories. One category involves the use of the corporate rate structure. Integration systems in this category employ a differential rate schedule under which a corporation pays a lower rate of tax on the distributed component of its profits than it does on the retained component. Systems of integration that fall in the other category do not operate through the corporate rate structure, but instead through the rules governing the determination of taxable income. For such systems, only one rate of tax, equally applicable to distributed and retained profits, is used; in determining the amount of corporate taxable income subject to that uniform rate, however, some or all of a corporation's dividend outlays are allowed as deductions.

Depending on the rates selected and the extent to which dividends are deductible, either category of corporate-level integration system may be used to provide a specific amount of relief to the distributed component of a corporation's profits. In the extreme case, for example, either type of system may be used to convert the corporation income tax into a tax on undistributed profits, under which only retained profits would be subject to tax at the corporate level. Nevertheless, the differences in technique and form between the two categories are substantial. For that reason, this chapter will treat separately the alternative methods of reducing the tax at the corporate level on the distributed component of corporate profits.

Except if otherwise indicated, this discussion of integration at the corporate level is based on the assumption that both the corporations and the shareholders involved are residents of the same country. The problems that arise if one party or the other is a nonresident are discussed in Chapter 7, which deals with the international aspects of integration.

5/B. Differential Rate Structures: The "Split-Rate" System

5/B.1. In General

In a system of integration at the corporate level which operates through the rate mechanism, the rate of the corporation income tax levied on the distributed component of corporate profits is lower than that levied on the retained component. Hence, this method of corporate-level integration is generally referred to as the "split-rate" system.[1] Germany, Japan, Israel, and Austria are among the countries using this method of partial integration. Under a split-rate system, a corporation's net profits are divided, for purposes of the corporation income tax, into two segments, retained and distributed. The retained segment is taxed at one rate, and the distributed segment is taxed at a different, lower rate. The rate reduction for the distributed segment takes into account the fact that this segment is subject to the individual income tax in the hands of the dividend recipients. To some extent, therefore, the rate differential reduces the overtaxation of corporate-source income which is said to result when the income tax imposed at one level—corporate or shareholder—takes no account of the tax imposed at the other level.

In the extreme case, the rate of the corporation income tax on distributed profits is zero, and the corporation income tax becomes merely a tax on undistributed profits (5/B.3b). Ordinarily, however, some tax is levied at the corporate level on distributed profits, though at a rate lower than that imposed on retained profits. Like other systems of partial integration, therefore, the split-rate system amounts to a compromise: it reduces, but does not wholly eliminate, the burden of the corporation income tax on distributed profits. To that extent, the system helps to maintain the yield of the corporation income tax.

5/B.2. Equity

Table 1, in Chapter 3, shows the additional burden of the corporation income tax (when imposed at the rate of 30% on corporate profits, both retained and distributed, without integration) on shareholders in the 0%, 10%, 20%, and 40% brackets of the individual income tax. In Chapter 4, it

1. In Professor van den Tempel's study of the corporation and the individual income taxes, an unintegrated system (such as that of the United States) is referred to as a "classic system" or "System A"; a split-rate system, such as that analyzed in this chapter, is referred to as "System B"; and a shareholder-credit system, such as that analyzed in Chapter 6, is referred to as "System C." See van den Tempel, *Corporation Tax and Individual Income Tax in the European Communities* 7.

was pointed out that corporate-level methods of integration reduce this additional burden by a uniform percentage for shareholders in all brackets. Table 2 below demonstrates this effect for a country that adopts a split-rate system of integration at the corporate level.

TABLE 2: *Portion of the Additional Burden of the Corporation Income Tax Removed by the Split-Rate Method of Integration at the Corporate Level**

Shareholder Marginal Individual Income Tax Rate (1)	Additional Burden of Corporation Income Tax (2)	Reduced Corporation Income Tax (Paid to Shareholder As Dividend) (3)	Tax on Additional Dividend (4)	Additional Income to Shareholder (5)	Percentage of Additional Burden Removed (6)
0%	30	20	0	20	66.66%
10%	27	20	2	18	66.66%
20%	24	20	4	16	66.66%
40%	18	20	8	12	66.66%

*This table has been adapted from Table 5-9 in Pechman, *Federal Tax Policy* (rev. ed.) 144.
Explanation: Column 2 = Column 7 of Table 1
Column 3 = 30 − 10% of 100
Column 4 = Column 3 × Column 1
Column 5 = Column 3 − Column 4
Column 6 = Column 5 / Column 2

Table 2 assumes that, instead of the 30% rate on total corporate profits used in Table 1, country *X* adopts a split rate of 30% for retained profits and 10% for distributed profits and that corporation *C* has pretax profits of 100 units and distributes the maximum amount available (90 units) after paying a corporation tax at the 10% rate. The shareholder rates in Table 2 are the same as those in Table 1. Because the split-rate method of integration reduces the additional burden of the corporation income tax by the same proportion for shareholders in all income tax brackets (Column 6), it is regarded as equitable in its operation. This is true whatever the differential between the rates on distributed and retained profits.

5/B.3. Differential Between the Rates of Tax on Retained and Distributed Profits

a. In General

There is no agreement among countries using split-rate systems of integration at the corporate level about the appropriate size of the gap between the rates on retained profits and distributed profits. Depending on the degree of integration desired, on revenue needs and the amount of corporation tax revenue which can be forgone, and on other factors, the differential between the rates imposed on distributed and retained profits may be large, small, or medium in amount. For some years, Germany used rates of 51% for retained profits and 15% for distributed profits.[2] (The German system described in the text throughout this chapter is that in effect prior to 1977. The present German system is described briefly in the Appendix.)

In Finland, by contrast, the gap between the two rates in a recent year was only two percentage points—49% for retained profits and 47% for distributed profits.[3] Japan uses a rate schedule with a differential that is midway between the wide gap of Germany and the narrow gap of Finland. In Japan, the present rates are 40% on retained profits and 30% on distributed profits.

Depending on a country's goals, either of the rates of a split-rate system may be made progressive or regressive. If the primary purpose is to encourage dividend distributions, the rate on the retained component may go up as the proportion of profits retained goes up. A rate of this kind, designed to increase dividend distributions, was used by the United States for a short period in the 1930s. In the years preceding the adoption of a progressive rate structure for retained profits, the tax rate for U.S. corporations had been lower than the individual rates applicable to most shareholders. This difference was thought to have resulted in an excessive retention of profits within the corporate structure. The progressive levy on retained profits was designed to discourage retentions, rather than to reduce the tax burden on distributed profits.

Even if the rates of the corporation tax levied on the retained and the distributed components of corporate profits are not formally progressive in a country using a split-rate system, however, the split-rate system becomes progressive in its operation. Assume, for example, that the effective rate of tax is 51% on retained profits and 23% on distributed profits. In such a case, the rate of tax paid by a corporation will range from 23% (if all of its profits are distributed) to 51% (if all of its profits are retained). Depending on the proportion of profits distributed, every corporation in the country (except those at the extremes because they distribute all or no profits) will be subject to a different rate of tax.

In unusual circumstances, a split-rate corporate tax structure may be used to encourage retention and discourage distribution. Shortly after

2. The German rate of 15% for distributed profits is only the nominal rate; because the 15% tax due on the distributed profits has itself to be paid from the retained profits, which are taxed at 51%, the effective rate on the distributed component is 23.4375%.

3. Finland gave up the split-rate system for the dividend-deduction system, which is discussed in section 5/C below.

World War II, for example, the United Kingdom levied its "profits tax" on corporations at the rate of 2.5% for retained profits and 27.5% for distributed profits. The aim of this system was to encourage capital formation by the corporate sector and to restrain consumption by holding down the dividend component of personal income.

Germany is by far the most important industrialized country using a split-rate system. The development of the German system from its beginning in 1953 will illustrate some of the reasons for choosing this method of integration, as well as some of the factors that enter into the choice of a particular differential between the rates on retained and distributed profits. Before 1953, Germany taxed corporate income by applying a flat rate of 60% uniformly to retained and distributed profits; dividends were taxed again in the hands of individual recipients. World War II had left Germany with a shortage of capital, and in order to help meet the corporate sector's needs for funds for rehabilitation and growth, the government "fostered the withholding of profits."[4] By 1953, a considerable portion of Germany's postwar needs had been met, and German policy changed. There was some demand for a reduction in the 60% rate, but the government decided that "in order to encourage corporate distributions as a means of reviving the then dormant market"[5] and to reduce self-financing through the retention of profits,[6] it would be preferable to reduce the rate only for distributed earnings. The rate for such earnings was cut to 30%; for retained earnings, it stayed at 60%. In 1955, the rate on retained earnings was reduced to 45%, and the rate on distributed profits remained at 30%.[7]

The 45%–30% differential was not great enough, however, to increase dividend outlays substantially, and the rate of retention by German industry remained high. In 1958, the differential was therefore broadened drastically: the rate on retained profits was increased to 51%[8] and the rate on distributed profits was cut by one half, to 15%.[9] Although the corporate

4. Häuser, "West Germany," in National Bureau of Economic Research, *Foreign Tax Policies and Economic Growth* 97, 136.

5. WTS: *Germany* (2d ed.), 11/5.8b3, n. 279.

6. Rädler and Edwards, "The Split Rate of Corporation Income Tax in Germany—A Tax Advantage for Foreign-Owned Subsidiaries," *CCH Common Market Reports* (Transfer Binder) ¶ 9051 (1963).

7. At the same time, the rule of the "taxable minimum" was repealed. Under this rule, taxable income could not be less than the amount of a corporation's distributions to shareholders. This rule was regarded as an obstacle to dividend payments.

8. Added to other tax burdens on corporations, the 51% rate was believed to approximate the highest rate of the individual income tax.

9. The German rate on retained profits (51%) is so much higher than the rate on distributed profits (15% nominal, 23.43% effective) that Professor Musgrave has called the German system not a method of integration but rather a method of discriminating against retentions. Musgrave, "Taxation of Corporations," in Canadian Tax Foundation, *Report of the Proceedings of the Twenty-Second Tax Conference* 124, 126.

rate preference for distributions is greater in Germany than in other industrialized countries, there is no conclusive evidence that the wide differential has significantly increased the ratio of distributions to retentions in Germany over that in other countries at comparable stages of industrialization.

b. The Undistributed Profits Tax

In discussions of split-rate systems, the emphasis is generally on the fact that the rate of the corporation income tax on the distributed component of corporate profits is *lower* than the rate on the retained component. Yet, in some countries using differential rates at the corporate level, the emphasis may be put on the fact that the rate of tax on the retained component is *higher* than the rate on the distributed component. Although the effect may be the same, the difference in emphasis may lead to a difference in nomenclature. If the fact that the rate on retained profits is higher than the rate on distributed profits is emphasized, the system may be referred to as one that involves an "undistributed profits tax." Such terminology is especially likely if the system involves a "normal" tax levied at a single rate on all profits, both distributed and undistributed, and a "surcharge" on retained profits (which is generally limited to profits retained beyond a certain level). Under Panama's company tax, for example, one rate schedule applies to all profits, whether retained or distributed, and then a surcharge of 10% (formerly 8%) to the difference between the amount of distributed profits and a figure equal to 40% of the profits remaining after payment of the company tax.

In some cases, the rate of tax at the corporate level on distributed profits is reduced to zero, and the corporation tax in effect becomes a tax solely on undistributed profits in that it bears only on retained profits. In such a case, only the individual income tax applies to distributed profits; integration is therefore complete with regard to the distributed component of corporate profits.

No industrialized country using a split-rate system goes to the extreme of levying a tax on distributed profits at a zero rate. The reason may be that an undistributed profits tax is often regarded as a form of "compulsory distribution." In essence, an undistributed profits tax is a method of creating pressure—pressure on the corporation to distribute its profits so that they will be subject to the individual income tax. (Objections to compulsory distribution are discussed in Chapter 2.)

An abortive attempt to adopt an undistributed profits tax was made in the United States in 1936, when President Roosevelt suggested that the corporation income tax be replaced by a progressive tax applicable only to distributed profits.[10] The proposal called for a zero rate, at the corporate level, on distributed profits; retained profits were to be subject to progressive rates that would increase as the proportion of retained profits went up. The rate was to be zero if no profits were retained and was to increase to a maximum of 42.5% of retained profits if 57.5% or more of total profits were retained.

American industry objected sharply to the proposed undistributed profits tax. Business needs ordinarily taken into account in determining dividend outlays would be overridden by tax considerations. It was argued that the anticipated increase in dividend payments would increase personal consumption at the expense of capital formation. Opponents of this argument claimed that the failure to subject retained profits to the full weight of the progressive individual income tax amounted to a tax subsidy to corporate profits.

The result was a compromise: a corporation income tax, applicable to both retained and distributed profits, was kept, but it was supplemented by a surtax applicable only to retained corporate profits. The rates of this surtax were graduated from 7% (if less than 10% of net income was retained) to a maximum of 27% (if 60% or more was retained). Opposition continued, however, and the surtax was abolished within three years. In the meantime, the disparity between the rate of the corporation income tax and the rates for the top brackets of the individual income tax had been reduced by increasing the corporation tax rate. A revival of the undistributed profits tax has not been seriously considered in the United States at any time since.

In 1965, the Chancellor of the Exchequer explicitly rejected such a tax for Great Britain[11]:

> ... a tax confined to undistributed profits penalises investment and growth; it severely handicaps the young and dynamic companies which must rely on ploughed-back profits for expansion. A tax on the whole profit has the opposite effect. It makes it possible to shift the burden of taxation in such a way as to relieve the faster-growing companies, which are generally low distributors, and thus enable them to expand even faster. It will place more of the burden on those companies which are high distributors. It gives a strong incentive to all companies to plough back more of their profits for themselves.

10. In the years preceding this proposal, the rate of the corporation income tax had been substantially lower than the rates of the individual income tax payable by the majority of shareholders in the United States. It was charged that, as a result, corporations had accumulated profits beyond their reasonable business needs in order to shelter those profits from the individual income tax. "Tax avoidance by the rich" was said to have resulted from the disparity between the rates of the corporation and individual income taxes.

11. Great Britain, Chancellor of the Exchequer, "Budget Statement," *Hansard*, 6 April 1965, col. 265.

In the most comprehensive tax study of recent years, Canada's Royal Commission on Taxation recommended against an undistributed profits tax on the ground that "it would run the grave risk of creating tax pressure for the increased distribution of cash of the detriment of capital investment."[12]

The difference between a split-rate system, with a rate for distributed profits which is more than zero but less than the rate for retained profits, and an undistributed profits tax proper, with a zero rate for distributed profits, is only a matter of degree. The split-rate system merely uses less pressure to encourage distributions than a tax confined to undistributed profits.

When it is not carried to the extreme of a zero rate on distributed profits, the split-rate system (like other forms of partial integration) amounts to a compromise. On the one hand, it reduces the burden of the corporation income tax on distributed profits. On the other hand, by collecting some tax at the corporate level even on distributed profits, the system gives fiscal recognition to the advantage of the corporate form of business organization and helps maintain the yield of the corporation income tax.

c. Portion of Profits Used To Pay Tax

Except in the rare case in which the rate of the corporation income tax on distributed profits is reduced to zero, some portion of a corporation's earnings must be used to pay the tax due on the distributed component of those earnings. Generally speaking, the tax payable on the distributed component does not itself qualify as a distribution and is not entitled to the benefit of the reduced rate for distributed earnings. In Germany, for example, the split-rate system provides a rate of 51% for undistributed earnings and a rate of 15% for distributed earnings. A corporation wishing to distribute all of its current after-tax earnings and to pay the amount of tax due out of its current earnings pays an effective rate on its distributed earnings of 23.4375%, not 15%.[13]

12. Canada, Royal Commission on Taxation, 4 *Report of the Royal Commission on Taxation* 46.

13. WTS: *Germany* (2d ed.), 12/2.1a. The rate of 23.4375% is determined by the following formula:

y = taxable income
x = profits needed for payment of tax
.51 = rate of income tax on retained profits
.15 = rate of income tax on distributed profits
$x = .51x + .15(y - x)$

If taxable income is 100, for example, then

$x = .51x + .15(100 - x)$
$x = .51x + 15 - .15x$
$x = .36x + 15$
$.64x = 15$
$x = 15/.64 = 23.4375$

d. CONSENT DIVIDENDS

In principle, at least, the preferential rate for distributions which is provided by the split-rate system may cause such a great increase in dividend outlays that the corporation may find itself short of cash for investment and other purposes. To mitigate this effect, especially for closely held corporations, the definition of distributions qualifying for the preferential rate may be expanded to include "consent dividends"—noncash distributions that the shareholders agree will be taxed to them individually on the same basis as cash distributions. Consent dividends add administrative complexity to the system, however; special accounts on the corporation's books, tracing rules, and the like may be required.

e. CEILING ON THE PROPORTION OF EARNINGS ENTITLED TO THE PREFERENTIAL RATE

Distribution relief at the corporate level is sometimes limited to "normal" or "basic" dividends; dividends in excess of the "normal" or "basic" amounts may be denied relief. The reasons for this kind of limitation, ordinarily found in countries using the dividend-deduction method, are discussed below in connection with that method. Even under a split-rate system, however, a country may choose to limit distribution relief to "normal" dividends by putting a ceiling on the proportion of total profits which qualifies for the lower rate applicable to distributed profits.[14]

A ceiling of this kind, which bars relief to "excess" dividends, takes account of the fact that some retention of earnings is normal and for many corporations even essential. Distribution relief may be limited, for example, to one half or two thirds of total profits; if a higher proportion is distributed in any year, the excess is subject to the rate usually applied to retained profits. The proportion chosen by a country will depend on patterns of retention and distribution in that country, the balance between the need for retained capital and the desire to encourage distributions, and other factors. Systems with such ceilings put a limit on the incentive to distribute which may result from the lower rate for distributed profits. If a corporation chooses to pay to its shareholders dividends in excess of the normal return on share capital, the excess amounts will receive no integration relief.

14. Similarly, if the split-rate system takes the form of a surcharge on retained profits, the surcharge may apply only to retained profits in excess of a presumably "normal" level. In the example cited above, Panama levies its surcharge only on retained profits in excess of 40% of the profits available for distribution. That is, the retention of 40% of profits is considered "normal."

In some countries, provisions other than tax provisions may place a legal limit on the proportion of profits available for distribution. For example, the laws of some countries require the retention of a specified portion of profits in a legal reserve. Bond indentures, bank loan agreements, and similar private financing arrangements may also limit the proportion of its earnings which a corporation may legally distribute. Equity and fairness may suggest that such restrictions be taken into account; otherwise, new or expanding corporations (presumably borrowing to the limit of their capacity and presumably subject to restrictions imposed by cautious lenders) may be in a less favorable position than old or stagnant corporations. The need to take account of dividend restrictions, particularly those imposed by private contract rather than public law, may, however, impose major administrative burdens on the tax authorities of a country.

f. Current Versus Past Earnings

The problem of defining which distributions should qualify for the reduced rate of tax concerns the issue of current versus past earnings. If the profits earned in one year are retained and taxed at the higher rate applicable to retained earnings, what rate is to be applied if those earnings are distributed in the following year?

In Germany, for example, only distributions from the current year's earnings qualify for the reduced rate applicable to distributed profits. If a corporation has earnings of 100 units in a year and pays out 10 units in dividends, the 90 units retained are subject to the 51% rate for retained earnings. If in the following year, the corporation chooses to pay a dividend out of those retained 90 units (for example, because it has no current earnings in that second year), Germany's system provides no way by which the corporation can reclaim any part of the tax previously paid at the higher rate on the sum now distributed to shareholders. As it applies in Germany, therefore, the split-rate system operates as an incentive only to the *current* payment of dividends.

In contrast, Israel's system does not require that earnings be immediately distributed in order to qualify for the reduced rate of tax. Israel provides rates at the corporate level of 46% for retained profits and 28% for distributed profits.[15] For purposes of computing income that is subject to

15. Israel taxes corporations by means of two separate taxes, a "company tax" and an "income tax." The company tax is levied at a uniform rate of 28% on all corporate profits, retained and distributed. The "income tax" is then levied, at a rate of 25%, on the 72% of corporate profits which remains after payment of the company tax. For purposes of the income tax, dividends are deductible in determining taxable income. The effective rate of the income tax on retained profits, therefore, is 18% (25% of 72%); the total tax at the corporate

the Israeli income tax, a dividend is deductible from income in the year of distribution; if dividends in any year exceed taxable income, the excess may be carried back to the first previous year in which taxable income was not fully paid out.

In contrast with the German system, then, Israel's system may permit a corporation to maintain dividend payouts at a consistent level without incurring any tax penalty. A corporation may maintain its dividend rate in a year of reduced profits, for example, by paying the current year's dividend out of past retentions and may still enjoy the reduced tax rate applicable to distributed profits. The system may also be of some help to new, expanding corporations that seek to retain as large a proportion of their profits as possible in years during which their capital requirements are high. Such corporations can postpone dividend distributions until later years and still claim the reduced rate for the distributed component in those years—retroactively, in effect. The German system of extending the preferential rate for distributions only to the current year's earnings has, however, the advantage of simplicity.

5/B.4. Qualifying Shareholders

a. In General

Apart from the question of which distributions qualify for the reduced rate in a country using a split-rate system, there is also the question of which shareholders qualify. For example, will payments to individual and corporate shareholders, to taxable and tax-exempt shareholders, and to resident and nonresident shareholders all qualify? Or must the corporation, in calculating its taxes, distinguish among the various kinds of shareholders it may have?

Limiting distribution relief at the corporate level to distributions made to particular categories of shareholders is cumbersome, but not impossible. Shareholders may, for example, be required to file statements certifying that they are not tax-exempt charities or that they are subject to tax as residents. Generally speaking, however, countries using split-rate systems give corporations the right to claim the reduced rate for distributed profits in the case of all distributions that otherwise qualify, without reference to

level on retained profits is therefore 46% (company tax of 28% plus income tax of 18%). Since distributed profits are not subject to income taxation at the corporate level (because they are deductible in determining the amount of income subject to that tax), the total tax at the corporate level on distributed profits is only 28% (that is, the company tax only).

Recent increases in these rates and the Israeli tax concession for retained and reinvested earnings are ignored for purposes of this discussion.

the tax status or other characteristics of the recipients. Assigning to the corporation the task of determining the status of each of its shareholders—whether taxable or tax-exempt, whether an individual or a corporation, whether a resident or a nonresident—may be thought to impose too heavy an administrative burden on the corporation. If, for any reason, distributions to a particular category of shareholders (other corporations, for example) are to be regarded as not entitled to distribution relief, a simpler means of imposing this restriction is to apply it to those shareholders directly, rather than to the distributing corporation.

b. Intercorporate Dividends

A typical example of the application of this rule may be seen in the German treatment of intercorporate dividends. Most countries provide some form of tax relief for intercorporate dividends. In Germany, this relief takes the form of the "affiliation privilege": dividends received by a corporation are not included in its taxable income if that corporation owns at least 25% of the capital of the distributing corporation. Germany makes its lower rate for distributed profits available even for dividends paid on shares owned by an affiliated corporation that is not subject to tax on the dividend receipt. In short, the paying corporation is not required to distinguish between dividends paid to taxable shareholders and dividends paid to exempt shareholders. It is at the shareholder level that Germany takes steps to prevent any abuse arising out of the combination of (1) a reduced rate of tax on the distributing corporation and (2) a zero rate of tax (due to the intercorporate dividend exemption) on the receiving corporation.

If a corporation that receives a dividend is not subject to tax thereon because of the "affiliation privilege," Germany requires the receiving corporation to pay a supplementary tax on the exempt dividend to the extent that this corporation fails to redistribute its dividend receipts to its own shareholders. The amount of the supplementary tax due from the receiving corporation is equal to the tax saving enjoyed by the distributing corporation—that is, to the difference between the reduced rate on distributions (15%) and the rate on retentions (51%), or 36%.

If, however, an additional tax is levied on a corporation that receives tax-preferred dividends from other corporations but fails to distribute an equivalent amount to its own shareholders, it becomes necessary to set up rules to trace the source of the dividend payments made by the receiving corporation. Should a parent company's dividend be deemed to come first from its operating profits, for example, or from its dividend receipts? In Germany, the operating profits are deemed to be distributed first, and it is only after those profits have been distributed that a corporation can claim to be distributing its dividend income. Japan follows the German practice of levying an additional tax on corporations that receive dividends but fail to distribute a commensurate amount to their own shareholders. In contrast to Germany, however, Japan presumes that the dividend receipts are distributed first (before operating profits), but in turn limits the benefit of the lower rate to the dividend distributions that are presumed to be made out of operating profits. That is, dividend receipts, which have already enjoyed the distribution relief provided for the paying corporation, are denied the same relief when they are redistributed by the receiving corporation. The results of these differing presumptions are that the supplementary tax yields considerable amounts of tax revenue in Germany, but very little in Japan, and that, for the same reason, the revenue losses arising from distribution relief are quite substantial in Germany, but relatively less in Japan.

c. Nonresident Shareholders

The essential difference between integration at the corporate level and integration at the shareholder level is that corporate-level integration gives distribution relief even to dividends going to nonresident shareholders (see Chapter 4). This is true of the split-rate system at the corporate level and gives rise to one of the major problems involved in the use of that system. This matter is discussed in detail in Chapter 7, which deals with international aspects of integration.

5/B.5. Treatment of Small Corporations

Small corporations, it is generally argued, have a greater need to retain earnings than larger corporations, which may have easier access to outside sources of capital. One problem in the use of the split-rate system is whether to take this factor into account by providing a rate schedule for small corporations which is different from that applied to large corporations, at least with respect to the retained component of corporate profits. Many countries using split-rate systems do provide preferential rate schedules for small corporations. Such a solution requires both a definition of "small corporation" and a determination of the appropriate rates to be used. Germany, for example, offers an optional rate schedule for corporations that meet certain requirements—notably, that their net worth does not exceed DM 5,000,000.[16] Japan, which uses a split-rate system resembling that of Germany, also makes special provision for small cor-

16. WTS: *Germany* (2d ed.), 12/2.1b.

porations.[17] Under the Japanese system, the first Y 7 million of the profits of a small corporation, even if those profits are retained, are taxed at the rate of 28%, rather than at the 40% rate ordinarily applicable to retentions.

5/C. Deduction of Dividend Disbursement by Corporations

5/C.1. In General

As noted at the beginning of this chapter, corporate-level integration can occur in either of two ways. Integration may be achieved through a rate mechanism, such as that used in the split-rate system described in section 5/B above; in that case, the corporation income tax is levied on distributed profits at a rate lower than that levied on retained profits. Instead, however, corporate-level integration may also be achieved through the rules for the determination of taxable income; in that case, only one rate of tax is levied on the taxable income of the corporation, but some portion of the corporation's dividend payments is deductible in determining the amount of income subject to that rate. This dividend-deduction method, described in this section, has authoritatively been called "the simplest and most effective method of dealing" with the problem of integration.[18] The method is used in Scandinavian countries and from time to time in some of the Common Market countries as well.

The dividend-deduction method squarely meets one of the arguments against the corporation income tax—namely, its alleged bias in favor of debt financing and against equity financing. Interest on loan capital is generally deductible in determining the amount of corporate income subject to taxation. In countries in which dividends on equity capital are not also deductible (or in which some other form of integration is not provided), discrimination against equity capital and in favor of loan capital is said to result. Such discrimination becomes more important as the rate of the corporation income tax rises.

The practical consequences of this discrimination for the determination of patterns of financing are not clear. Here, too, the situation of the publicly held corporation must be distinguished from that of the closely held corporation. In the case of a closely held corporation, the persons

17. In Japan, a small corporation is defined as a corporation whose capital is not more than ¥ 100 million.

18. Pechman, "Taxation: Personal Income Tax," 15 *International Encyclopedia of the Social Sciences* 529, 535 (1968). To the same effect, see Slitor, "Reform of the Business Tax Structure: Analysis of Problems and Alternative Remedial Proposals," in Musgrave and Gillis, *Fiscal Reform for Colombia* 463, 497 (stating that the dividend-deduction method is "perhaps the simplest and most effective approach to company-individual tax integration").

interested in the enterprise have some choice among methods of financing; often, borrowed funds come from the shareholders, who lend money to the corporation in proportions similar to their relative equity interests. As a practical matter, the line between "equity" capital and "loan" capital provided by the owners of the equity is hazy for a closely held corporation—a matter of nomenclature rather than of substance. In the case of bankruptcy, for example, the "loans" made by the owners to the corporation may rank equally with the claims of outside creditors, whereas contributions in the form of equity capital rank after those claims.[19]

For the publicly held corporation, however, there is little evidence to support the charge that the corporation income tax leads corporations to finance their operations by debt rather than equity capital. In the United States, which is the major industrialized country with no system of integration, a comprehensive study has found that the "deductibility [of interest] has not been responsible for a major increase in the use of debt."[20]

In any event, some countries provide partial integration of the corporation and individual income taxes by granting a deduction from corporate income for some portion of dividend payments. Total deductibility is rare because it converts the corporation income tax into an undistributed profits tax.

Supporters of the dividend-deduction method of integration argue that, in order to function, corporations need equity capital just as they need labor, machinery, and—as a general rule—loan capital. The cost of labor (wages) is deductible; the cost of machinery (depreciation) is deductible; and the cost of loan capital (interest) is deductible. It therefore follows, according to this argument, that the cost of equity capital (dividends) should also be deductible. In determining taxable income for purposes of the corporation income tax, all costs are deductible except the cost of equity capital (dividends). If the corporation income tax seeks to tax net income, no sufficient reason exists to discriminate against this particular cost. Because of the discrimination, moreover, the amount of a corporation's income tax will vary not merely with the amount of its earnings, but also with the extent to which it uses equity rather than loan capital.

Another method of equalizing loan and equity capital is to deny a deduction for interest outlays. Yet because interest payments are so widely

19. In the case of a closely held corporation, however, a bank or other outside lender will ordinarily consider loans from shareholders to be equivalent to equity capital as a practical matter and will therefore require shareholder loans to be subordinate to its own loans before it will advance any funds to the corporation.

20. Miller, "The Corporation Income Tax and Corporate Financial Policies," in Commission on Money and Credit, *Stabilization Policies* 381, 441, n. 12. Outside the United States, too, "debt aversion" is recognized as a factor in corporate behavior. Lindbeck, "Theories and Problems in Swedish Economic Policy in the Post-War Period," 58 *American Economic Review, Supplement* 1, 37 (1968).

regarded as a business expense, the denial of an interest deduction is rarely considered except to meet abuses.[21]

At least with regard to publicly held corporations, theoretical support for dividend deductibility has increased as the number of shareholders has proliferated and the gulf between ownership and control has widened. Berle and Means have asserted that in widely held corporations, the public shareholder has lost his right to participate in management; he is "simply a supplier of capital on terms less definite than those customarily given or demanded by bondholders." Despite the legal distinctions still drawn between the "bondholder as a lender of capital and the stockholder as a quasi-partner in the enterprise, economically the positions of the two have drawn together."[22] Schumpeter takes the view that in the modern corporation, the "only realistic definition of stockholders is that they are creditors (capitalists) who forego part of the legal protection usually extended to creditors, in exchange for the right to participate in profits."[23]

Opposed to this view, however, is the argument that whatever the economic realities, dividends as a matter of law stand on a different footing from interest. Hence, the deductibility of interest does not support the deductibility of dividends, it is argued.[24]

21. Such abuses may include, for example, the payment of interest on loans used to earn tax-exempt income; the payment of excessive interest that may amount to a concealed or constructive dividend; and the organization of a corporation with a disproportionately low amount of share capital and a disproportionately high amount of loan capital ("thin capitalization").

22. Berle and Means, *The Modern Corporation and Private Property* 279. Father Harbrecht asserts that in the modern, publicly held corporation, ownership has been separated from control, but the nomenclature appropriate to the old system is still used; "thus, a share of stock is still called an equity, which indicates ownership, though it is in reality only a claim upon income." "The Modern Corporation Revisited," 64 *Columbia Law Review* 1410, 1413 (1964).

23. Schumpeter, 1 *Business Cycles* 104. See also Goode, *The Corporation Income Tax* 178, on the case of large, publicly held corporations: "The difference in tax treatment of corporate earnings used to pay interest and those available for dividends is often illogical." Kaldor, *Indian Tax Reform* 98, states that from the point of view of equity, "the ideal system is one which treats dividend distributions in the same manner as interest charges and other expenses for the purpose of assessing profits to company tax."

24. Under U.S. tax law, interest is deductible, whereas dividends are not (with a minor exception for certain dividends on preferred stock). A U.S. court distinguished interest from dividends in these terms:

> . . . where a corporation pays [interest] for the use of money which it will return, it is in effect allowed a deduction for a business expense, just as it is allowed a deduction for the expense of renting a building. Where, however, a corporation pays dividends, it is not incurring a business expense; it is distributing profits. While interest and profits are not always distinguishable, they are distinct concepts, and the distinction, however imperfect it may be in a particular case, lies in the degree of risk involved.

Gilbert v. *Commissioner*, 248 F.2d 399, 406–407 (2d Cir. 1957).

Some countries nevertheless achieve partial integration of the corporation and individual income taxes by permitting the partial deduction of dividend payments. The deduction of dividends has the great advantage of simplicity. For both the corporations and the tax administration involved, it is no more complicated than the familiar deduction of interest. It is a far simpler method of integration than, for example, the shareholder dividends-received credit (with gross-up), which is discussed in Chapter 6. For developing countries, this relative ease of administration may be an important argument in support of a corporate dividend-deduction scheme as opposed to alternative methods of integration.[25]

The deduction of dividends, moreover, is not a new method of integration; it is an old and well-established device. It was a feature of the old Prussian income tax. It is used currently in Sweden, Norway, and Finland. For some years, France permitted deductibility essentially as an incentive measure for certain government-approved share issues. In order to encourage equity financing, Japan also used a similar system, permitting the deduction of dividends on newly issued shares, for a number of years after World War II. In the special case of preferred shares of public utilities issued before 1 October 1942, the United States also permits the deduction of dividends.[26] The Shoup Mission to Venezuela recommended that "to mitigate the problem of overtaxation of corporate income, . . . corporations should be allowed to deduct a fractional part of dividends paid to shareholders, in computing the corporate net income subject to tax, or, alternatively, shareholders should be given some credit for income tax paid by the corporation."[27]

In Canada, the Royal Commission on Taxation approved the dividend-deduction method of integration; indeed, had it not been for the importance of nonresident shareholders in the Canadian economy and the fact that distribution relief under the dividend-deduction system spills over to the benefit of nonresidents, it appears that the Commission would have preferred the dividend-deduction method to the method recommended (namely, integration at the shareholder level, limited to resident shareholders).[28]

25. The simplicity of the dividend-deduction method, compared with alternative integration devices, is emphasized in Slitor, "Reform of the Business Tax Structure: Analysis of Problems and Alternative Remedial Proposals," in Musgrave and Gillis, *Fiscal Reform for Colombia* 463, 497.

26. U.S. Internal Revenue Code §247(b)(2)(B). Dividends may also be deducted on public utility preferred shares issued on or after 1 October 1942 to "refund or replace bonds or debentures issued before 1 October 1942."

27. Shoup *et al.*, *The Fiscal System of Venezuela* 15.

28. Various international aspects of integration are discussed in Chapter 7.

5/C.2. Equity

Integration by way of a dividend deduction has the same effect as the split-rate system of integration at the corporate level which was considered in the previous section. It removes the same proportion of the additional burden of the corporation income tax for resident shareholders in all income brackets (see Table 2 above). The system thus operates equitably for all resident shareholders. The impact on nonresidents is considered in Chapter 7.

5/C.3. Amount of Deduction

a. Normal Versus Excess Dividends

If dividends are deductible in full, the corporation income tax becomes simply an undistributed profits tax (5/C.3b4). The deduction of all dividends is distinctly *not* the usual pattern, however. In virtually all of those countries which use a dividend deduction as a method of integration, there is a limit on the extent of the deduction. Generally speaking, the deduction is limited by one device or another to a "primary," "normal," or "basic" dividend; dividend distributions beyond that level are regarded as "excess" profits, paid to the shareholder as compensation for his entrepreneurial risk, and are not entitled to distribution relief. In Professor Schumpeter's terms, the return paid to the shareholder as a creditor is deductible, just like the return to a bondholder as a creditor. But the return to the shareholder which is derived from his right to participate in profits is not deductible and remains subject to taxation at both the corporate and the shareholder level.

The remainder of this section considers the reasons for limiting the dividend deduction to a "normal" or "basic" dividend (that is, to the shareholder's return as a creditor) and alternative methods of arriving at an appropriate limit. If distribution relief at the corporate level is to be limited to "normal" dividends, it appears that the dividend-deduction method is administratively more convenient than the split-rate method described in section 5/B above.

b. Determining the Amount of a "Normal" Dividend

1. Limitation to a rate related to the interest rate. One argument in support of providing integration at the corporate level by the dividend-deduction method is that dividends represent (at least in part) a "cost" of equity capital and that this cost portion should be deductible in determining taxable income. In effect, dividends (viewed as the cost of equity capital) are treated in the same way as interest (the cost of loan capital). The question that arises at once, however, is whether the entire amount of a dividend is to be treated as a cost or whether there ought to be some limitation.

As already noted, most countries using the dividend-deduction method of integration at the corporate level place a limit on the amount of dividends which may be deducted. In effect, dividend disbursements are divided into two portions, one representing the "cost" of capital (which is deductible) and the other representing "excess" distributions, or distributions of profits over and above the cost of capital; the excess is not deductible. The question, then, is how to determine what is "cost" and what is "excess."

A common method is to relate the amount of deductible dividends to the rate of interest. The amount deductible as a dividend is often limited to some figure approaching (but not equaling) the price of money in the country in question—for example, 5% of the amount paid in to the company on the original issue of the shares.

The rate of the deductible "basic" or "primary" dividend is generally lower, however, than the market rate of interest on loan capital. A shareholder enjoys the possibility of a gain in the capital value of his shares, to say nothing of higher dividend payments in future years; to compensate for these potential gains, the shareholder is often willing, as a practical matter, to accept a lower current yield than a bondholder would be.[29] In the market, that is, there is often a "yield gap": bonds frequently give higher current yields than common shares.

The dividend-deduction method often takes account of this "yield gap." When Sweden, for example, first adopted a partial dividend deduction as an integration device, one of its primary aims was to eliminate the "double taxation" of the "normal interest cost of money." The deduction was limited to 4% of the amount paid in to the corporation for the shares; later, after the general level of interest rates had risen, the deduction was increased to 5%. France, too, originally limited its dividend deduction to 5%, and then raised it to 7.5%. In all of these cases, the amount of the dividend deduction probably fell short of the going interest rate at the time.

In support of limiting the dividend deduction to a figure related to the cost of money, it is argued that a dividend may be seen as consisting of two separate components: (1) a component equivalent to interest which com-

29. For the same reasons, the current rate of interest on bonds or other debt securities convertible into equity is usually lower than the rate offered on debt securities of comparable quality but without the conversion feature.

pensates the shareholder for the current use of his money and (2) a profit-sharing component that is equivalent to the shareholder's aliquot share of the corporation's earnings in excess of all costs (including, for this purpose, the cost of its equity capital). The second, or profit-sharing, component may be regarded as the shareholder's reward for the entrepreneurial risk of equity investment. It is argued that the first component is analogous to interest and thus should be deductible; however, no comparable analogy supports the deduction of the shareholder's participation in profits in excess of all costs. The denial of distribution relief to dividends beyond a "primary" or "basic" figure may be regarded, indeed, as equivalent to an excess profits tax, limited to "excess" income on equity capital. "Normal" profit distributions are exempt from and relieved of two-tier taxation, but no relief is given to distributions in excess of the "normal."

Put another way, the limitation of distribution relief to a "normal" dividend amounts to recognition of the fact that some retention of earnings is the common pattern and, for many corporations, is essential. The limitation ensures that distribution relief will not encourage distributions to a point that will jeopardize the retention of earnings needed in the business.

A limitation of the dividend deduction to a figure related to the cost of money (5%, for example) sharply reduces the revenue loss that may follow from integration. Yet it raises the problem of the base on which the deductible percentage is to be calculated. Generally, the base is taken as the value of the cash or property originally paid in to the corporation for the shares. Only that amount is available to the corporation for its use. For this reason, the base is not the sum paid by the shareholder (to a third party, for example) for the particular shares he happens to own from time to time.

In some countries, "property" paid in to the corporation for its shares is defined, for purposes of this rule, to exclude shares in other corporations. This rule is designed to deny the benefits of the dividend-deduction method to holding companies and other nonoperating companies.

2. Limitation to a proportion of dividends paid. To limit the rate of dividends deductible to a percentage of the capital sum paid in to the corporation on the original issue of the share in question is workable if the deduction is limited to newly issued shares (that is, shares issued after a specified date). If the right to a deduction based on the original issue price is extended to dividends paid on all shares, then problems arise. If the original issue occurred some years in the past and if the corporation has prospered, a large number of the current shareholders may have acquired their shares on the market at prices much higher than the original issue price; hence, a deduction based on the original issue price may no longer have any practical significance.

For this reason, countries that do not confine the deduction to dividends paid on newly issued shares often express the limitation on the deduction as a percentage of the total dividend paid, rather than as a percentage of the original issue price. For example, Finland's integration scheme permits 40% of all dividends paid to be deducted even if the dividend equals 100% or 200% of the issue price of the shares.[30]

The Shoup Mission to Venezuela suggested that if the dividend-deduction method of integration is chosen, the deduction should be set at an amount that is one third or one half of the dividend payment. Sweden, France, Japan, and Belgium, which permit a dividend deduction calculated as a percentage of the capital paid in for the share, make the deduction available only for dividends on newly issued shares, whose issue price is known and presumably bears some relation to current market value.

Calculating the dividend deduction as a percentage of total dividends paid has one advantage over calculating it as a percentage of the capital sum originally received by the corporation for the shares. If applied to all shares, any specific rate chosen under the latter system may tend to become the norm for dividend outlays and thus to exert some restraint on the discretion of the corporate directors. For example, if a dividend of 5% is deductible, the directors may seek to pay a dividend of that amount—no less and no more—even though the corporation's needs and financial condition may be thought to warrant a higher or a lower dividend. A deduction expressed as a percentage of the dividend (one half, for example), whatever the amount of the dividend, avoids the rigidity of a deduction expressed as a percentage of the capital value of the shares; yet it makes the relationship of the deduction to the interest rate somewhat tenuous.

3. Deduction of the imputed cost of equity capital. The dividend-deduction system is available only to corporations whose profit level is high enough, and whose working capital and financial position are good enough, to permit the payment of dividends. Under the dividend-deduction system, a corporation making a profit but unable to pay out dividends finds itself at a tax disadvantage in comparison to a corporation paying out dividends. In some cases, the disadvantaged corporation will be a new and growing enterprise—the very kind of enterprise which the government may wish to encourage. In an effort to put all profit-making corporations on an equal plane whether or not they actually pay dividends, at least one country

30. Finland adopted the dividend-deduction method of integration in 1969 to replace its previous split-rate system.

allows a deduction for "imputed dividends," or the imputed cost of equity capital. Before 1974, Denmark allowed corporations to deduct a sum equal to 2.5% of paid-in capital (but not more than 50% of net income).

In effect, this system permits a minimum return on equity capital to be tax-free at the corporate level. It bears a superficial resemblance to those individual income tax systems which (by way of a personal exemption or otherwise) exempt an amount of individual income necessary for a "minimum level of subsistence." Presumably, many of the corporations receiving the deduction actually pay dividends equal to or greater than the deduction. For the others, however, the system may be said to relieve two-tier taxation even in cases where there is no tax at the shareholder level (because there is no current dividend). Since the deduction is available whether or not dividends are paid, it reduces the impact of tax considerations on dividend policy. To some extent, moreover, the deduction for imputed dividends reduces the advantages of "thin capitalization"—the organization of corporations with a small proportion of equity capital and an excessive proportion of loan capital (the interest on which is deductible).

The allowance of a deduction for imputed dividends has the advantage of simplicity and serves to equalize the tax position of all profit-making corporations, whether or not they actually pay out dividends. In effect, the deduction of imputed dividends amounts to a reduction in the rate of the corporation income tax, the amount of the reduction varying in proportion to the amount of equity capital used in the business.[31]

4. No limitation: The undistributed profits tax. Countries seeking to tax corporations only on retained profits may do so by means of a split-rate system that taxes distributed profits at a zero rate at the corporate level (5/B.3b). These countries may accomplish the same result by making all dividend disbursements fully deductible at the corporate level (which is the procedure followed by Greece, for example). In either case, the corporation income tax becomes an undistributed profits tax.

Norway formerly limited the amount of its dividend deduction. Since 1970, however, it has permitted the deduction, without limitation, of all dividends paid provided that they come from profits of the current year. Dividends paid from past profits are not deductible. Norwegian corporation law, however, in effect limits the deduction: each corporation must maintain a "legal reserve fund" to which it must credit an amount equal to the

31. Because interest on borrowed capital is also deductible, it could equally be said that the deductibility of interest amounts to a selective rate reduction, with the amount of the reduction varying in proportion to the amount of loan capital used in the business. The deduction of imputed dividends thus tends to equalize the tax position of dividends and interest.

dividends paid each year (to the extent that those dividends exceed 5% of the share capital plus the amount of the reserve fund itself).

5. *Deduction of sums set aside for future dividends.* In many countries, the steady and continued payment of dividends without reduction is a mark of sound management. Corporations are reluctant to increase their dividend outlays unless it seems likely that the new level of payment can be maintained. To take account of these circumstances, Norway, as of 1972, not only permitted the deduction of all dividends paid (subject to the limitations just mentioned), but also allowed corporations to deduct amounts not actually paid out but allocated to a "dividend equalization fund" for disbursement in future years. Amounts in the fund not paid out as dividends within five years were treated as taxable income at the end of that time, however.[32]

6. *Use of a dividends-paid credit in lieu of a dividend deduction.* Although the dividend deduction is the more common method of taking account of the argument that dividend outlays may represent, at least in part, the "cost" of share capital, it is also possible to integrate the corporation and individual income taxes by providing a credit against the corporation tax which is linked to the amount of dividends paid. In the United States, for example, the Revenue Act of 1938 fixed the rate of the corporation income tax at 19%, subject to a credit of 2.5% of dividends paid. In no event, however, could the credit reduce the corporate rate to a level below 16.5%. This dividends-paid credit was short-lived; it was abolished the year after its adoption.

In 1971, prior to the final decision on corporate tax reform in the United Kingdom, the Chancellor of the Exchequer recommended to Parliament the adoption of integration at the corporate level by way of a tax credit for dividends paid. Under his proposal, corporations would have been taxed at a flat rate of 50%, subject to a credit against tax equal to 30% of dividend outlays.[33] The proposal was not adopted, however.

Depending on the rate structure of the corporation income tax, it may be possible to provide a dividends-paid credit that will give the same distribution relief as a dividends-paid deduction. On the whole, however, a credit against tax is generally designed to take account of a tax already paid by a taxpayer or deemed to have been paid for his account, whereas a deduction generally represents an item in the nature of an expense. A deduction for dividends may thus be more appropriate than a credit. The

32. The Norwegian Ministry of Finance proposed that the deduction for allocations to the fund for future dividends be limited to 1% of the total of paid-in share capital plus the amount of the legal reserve fund.

33. United Kingdom, Chancellor of the Exchequer, *Reform of Corporation Tax* 5.

credit may, however, be viewed as a rough method of taking account of the fact that the dividend will presumably be subject to tax in the hands of the shareholder.

There may be some difficulty in relating the amount of the credit to the "cost" of equity capital. Generally speaking, credits against tax are more difficult to administer than deductions from taxable income; as a result, dividends-paid deductions are common, but dividends-paid credits are found only rarely.

5/C.4. Temporary Use of the Dividend Deduction As a Tax Incentive

a. In General; New Shares

The dividend-deduction method is far more likely to be adopted as a temporary tax incentive than other methods of integration. A country whose basic tax structure is not integrated (such as Sweden) or whose tax system already includes some other integration device may permit some dividends to be deducted for a period of years in order to encourage the greater use of equity rather than loan capital. To accomplish this purpose, the deduction is limited to dividends paid on new shares (that is, shares issued for cash or property within a given period). In countries in which a deduction is made available for dividends paid on all shares, a greater deduction may be allowed for dividends paid on new shares than for dividends paid on old (that is, pre-existing) shares.

For purposes of this tax incentive, "new" shares are defined as shares issued by corporations that are newly organized after a certain date, or additional shares sold by existing corporations after that date to raise additional equity capital. To extend the deduction to dividends paid on all shares, whatever their date of issue (new shares and old alike), would also serve as an incentive to the greater use of equity capital for the future. The extension of the deduction to dividends paid on shares already outstanding would cost the government a larger amount in lost tax revenue, however, and might push dividend disbursements to unreasonable levels[34] and give windfall gains to existing corporations with respect to their existing shares. Yet, to offer the deduction only for new equity capital provides an

34. When Sweden adopted the dividend deduction, it restricted it to dividends (limited in amount) on new shares. It did not adopt a general dividend deduction or a split-rate system based on the German model, because it feared that either of the latter devices might stimulate dividend disbursements to a level undesirable in the context of Sweden's economy. Indeed, Sweden makes extensive use of a tax device to encourage the retention of earnings (namely, a deduction for profits allocated to a reserve for future investment). See Norr, *Reserves for Future Investment: A Swedish Tax Incentive.*

incentive to new corporations to increase their proportion of equity capital and to existing firms to raise new capital by equity rather than loans.[35] For such reaons, Sweden, France, Belgium, and Norway, for example, all limited the dividend deduction, when it was adopted as a method of partial integration, to dividends paid on new shares; at least in the beginning, no deduction was allowed for dividends paid on pre-existing shares. By stimulating the issuance of new shares, such restrictions may broaden local equity capital markets.

Limiting the deduction to dividends paid on new shares concentrates the effect of the revenue losses involved on the new shares in question and thus may have a more stimulating effect on new issues than extending distribution relief to all shares. Moreover, the price of the latter shares presumably reflects or "capitalizes" the pre-existing tax structure, and the extension of distribution relief to these shares will give windfall benefits to those who hold outstanding shares.

Even if a country permits the deduction (within limits) of dividends paid on all shares (old and new), it may encourage the issuance of new shares by allowing a greater deduction for dividends on new shares. Finland, for example, gave up a split-rate system based on the German model and adopted a dividend-deduction system (in which 40% of dividends paid are deductible). As an incentive, however, 100% of dividends paid are deductible on shares issued between 1 January 1969 and 31 December 1978.

Apart from its general encouragement of the greater use of equity, the restriction of the deduction to dividends on new shares may offer another advantage. It may permit some transfer of the corporate tax burden from new or expanding corporations (which need additional capital and hence are likely to issue new shares qualifying for the deduction) to old or stagnant corporations (which need no additional capital and hence are not likely to issue new shares in any event). This aspect of the matter was stressed by the Swedish Ministry of Finance when the new-share dividend deduction was adopted in Sweden in 1960. Moreover, a dividend deduction that is not limited to new shares may have exactly the opposite effect; it may favor old, stagnant corporations at the expense of new and expanding firms. The new or expanding corporation may have so great a need to retain earnings that it is unable to pay dividends and claim the deduction; the mature corporation, having no need for additional capital, may be able

35. The Segré report on the development of a European capital market approves of temporary dividend deductions on new shares for this reason. Communauté Économique Européene, Commission, *Le Développement d'un marché européen des capitaux* 232. At another point (225), however, the report points out that the various measures adopted in the Common Market to provide tax reductions for distributed profits do not seem to have had the hoped-for results.

to claim the full deduction. Unless the deduction is limited to new shares, a mature corporation may pay tax at a lower rate than a new corporation.

The effect on two corporations of the enactment of a dividend deduction for new shares, including the shares of newly organized corporations, is summarized below.

	Corporation *A*	Corporation *B*
Earnings before tax	$300,000	$300,000
Dividend paid	50,000	50,000
Dividend deduction	50,000	—
Taxable income	250,000	300,000
Corporation income tax at 30%	75,000	90,000

Corporation *A* was organized with paid-in capital of $1,000,000 after the enactment of the dividend deduction. Its earnings, before tax and before dividends are paid, amount to $300,000 after several years of operation. Dividends are deductible up to an amount equal to 5% of paid-in capital, or $50,000. Corporation *A* pays a dividend of $50,000, and the dividend is deductible because *A*'s shares qualify as "new shares." Corporation *B*, which was organized before the deduction became effective, also has paid-in capital of $1,000,000 and pretax earnings of $300,000. It, too, pays a dividend of $50,000; this dividend is not deductible because corporation *B*'s shares do not qualify as new shares. With a corporation income tax rate of 30%, *A*'s tax is $15,000 less than *B*'s tax because of the difference in the amounts of their taxable income. As a result, *A* has retained earnings totaling $175,000 and *B* has only $160,000, even though they have the same pretax income, make the same dividend outlays, and pay tax at the same rate.

Although the limitation of the deduction to dividends paid on new shares (whether they are shares issued by new corporations or additional shares issued by existing corporations) may serve as a tax preference for certain corporations, it raises certain administrative problems. Rules will be needed to prevent "wash transactions"—that is, the dissolution of existing corporations followed by the organization of new ones or the sale of new shares (qualifying for the deduction) preceded or followed by the redemption of existing shares (not so qualifying). Precautions must be taken to ensure that only genuine increases in the use of equity capital benefit from the limited dividend deduction.

b. LIMITATION OF DEDUCTIBILITY TO A PERIOD OF YEARS

Related to the limitation of the dividend deduction to dividends paid on new shares is another common restriction. The deduction often applies only to dividends on shares issued within a comparatively short period of time from the date of the enactment of the governing statute—three, five, or seven years, for example. Moreover, even for shares issued within this qualifying period, the deduction does not cover all dividends paid indefinitely into the future, but only those which are paid within a specified period of time—five, six, or ten years, for example. Such limitations serve both to reduce the revenue loss that might result from the adoption of the deduction and to encourage the immediate issuance of shares. In addition, such limitations give a country time to test the usefulness of the device before adopting it as a permanent part of its tax structure. Sweden, Norway, France, and Japan began by adopting the dividend deduction provisionally. Later, Sweden and Norway accepted the device as a permanent part of their tax structures; France, in contrast, replaced it with a different integration system, the dividends-received credit at the shareholder level (see Chapter 6).

If a dividend deduction is to be available only for a limited period of years, what number of years should be chosen? A new corporation is not very likely to be profitable at the outset, and even an existing corporation may need several years to show a return on new share capital invested in a new plant or a new product. When France first adopted the dividend deduction, which was limited to seven years, it sought to solve this problem by providing that the first year of deduction for companies should be the fourth year of the corporation's existence, not the year of incorporation. Under this rule, which was designed to permit a new corporation to recover its initial losses and "launching costs," the deduction was available from the fourth to the tenth year of the corporation's existence.[36] Sweden offers the taxpayer more flexibility in that it permitted the deduction (available for ten years in total) to be claimed in any ten of the fifteen years following the issuance of the shares on which the dividend is paid.

The argument in support of limiting the amount of the dividend deduction—namely, that it is appropriate to limit the deduction to an amount in the neighborhood of the "interest cost" of money—does not support a limitation in time, however. If reasonable in amount, interest is deductible for the life of a loan, not for a mere five or seven years. If the dividend equivalent of the interest cost of equity capital should not be subject to

36. France later returned to a second, temporary dividends-received deduction for shares issued between 1976 and 1981, with a different set of limitations.

taxation at both the corporate level and the shareholder level, it should presumably be immune from such taxation indefinitely, not just for a few years. The limitation in time appears to be related principally to revenue considerations and to the use of the deduction as a short-term tax incentive. In short, the deduction may reflect economic and financial circumstances at the time of its adoption rather than abstract notions of "equity" or "double taxation."

c. Miscellaneous Policy Goals

Apart from its use as an incentive to the greater use of equity capital, the dividend deduction can be fashioned much more explicitly to take account of specific policy goals of the government. As noted earlier, France adopted a limited dividend deduction some years ago, partly in order to stimulate French capital markets. To carry out that aim, it made the deduction available only to those corporations which, within a given period, arranged for the listing of all their shares (not just those new shares eligible for the deduction) on a public exchange.

If the administrative competence of a country permits, even more specific limitations on the right to the deduction can be imposed as tax incentives. France limited the deduction to dividends paid on new shares whose investment purpose had first been specifically approved by the government. Each corporation seeking the right to deduct dividends on proposed share issues had to file an application for approval with the National Planning Commission, which would be considered by a special committee of government officials. The committee scrutinized each application for conformity with national policy objectives.[37] To support a policy of industrial decentralization, for example, the right to deduct dividends was granted to a corporation issuing shares designed to raise funds for a plant in an underdeveloped area that was suffering from local unemployment. At the same time, the right to deduct dividends was denied to a corporation seeking funds for expansion in Paris.

A recent survey considers the limited dividend deduction analyzed here to be relatively simple and relatively effective in influencing the capital market. It concluded: "There is thus no reason why its temporary use, confined to new issues, should not be stimulating."[38] As is the case with other methods of integration, however, there is little quantitative evidence that the dividend-deduction method actually stimulates a wider resort to

37. See WTS: *France* 7/2.6.

38. Cardyn, "General Report: The Multiple Burden on Dividends and Shares by Taxation on Income and Capital of Both Corporations and Shareholders," 55a *Cahiers de droit fiscal international*, I/39, I/66 (1970).

equity than to loan capital. A survey carried out after Sweden's adoption of the limited dividend deduction found, for example, that out of 27 public share issues in the following year, only two had been influenced by the availability of the deduction.

5/C.5. Qualifying Distributions

As under the split-rate system, constructive dividends generally do not qualify for distribution relief under the dividend-deduction system. Because the amount of the deduction is generally limited, moreover, there may be little need to make provision for consent dividends under this system. For the same reason, rules defining whether qualifying dividends must come from current or past profits may not be required.[39] In short, the partial dividend deduction operates with relative administrative simplicity.

5/C.6. Qualifying Shareholders

a. In General

Integration at the corporate level generally makes distribution relief available for dividend payments to all resident shareholders, without regard to their tax status. In some cases, the result may be tax relief at the corporate level for dividends not subject to tax in the hands of shareholders. Yet, because the dividend deduction is almost invariably limited in amount and because the number of tax-exempt resident shareholders is not likely to be large, administrative considerations suggest that, at least for resident shareholders, the deductibility of a dividend should not depend on the tax status of the shareholder. This rule is generally followed by those countries which permit the deduction of dividends.

There may be two exceptions to this rule, however. One relates to intercorporate dividends, which are discussed just below; the other relates to dividends paid to nonresident shareholders, which are discussed in Chapter 7.

39. If, however, there is no ceiling on the proportion of dividends that may be deducted, it may be appropriate to limit the deduction to dividends paid out of current profits, as Norway did (see above).

b. INTERCORPORATE DIVIDENDS

To avoid "chain taxation," most countries exempt corporations from all, or nearly all, taxes on dividends received from other domestic corporations. A country that provides such an exemption may deem it appropriate to make rules to prevent double tax relief (that is, relief to the paying corporation through a dividend deduction and relief to the receiving corporation through an intercorporate dividend exemption). In Sweden, for example, intercorporate dividends are generally exempt from taxation; as a result, Sweden allows no dividend deduction to a corporation more than half of whose shares are owned by another Swedish corporation. Norway at first followed the same rule; it exempted intercorporate dividends but denied the dividend deduction to any corporation that qualified as the subsidiary of another. Such a rule may, however, bar distribution relief to the paying corporation for dividends paid to outside shareholders who do not enjoy the intercorporate dividend exemption.

The opposite rule—allowing the dividend deduction to the paying corporation for all otherwise qualifying dividends and denying the intercorporate exemption to the receiving corporation for dividends that entitle the payor to a deduction—may be deemed preferable in some circumstances. Norway, for example, changed its practice in 1970; it allows the dividend deduction for all dividends that are otherwise qualified and at the same time abolished the intercorporate dividend exemption.

Finland, too, provides an intercorporate dividend exemption; to prevent double tax relief, only dividends paid in excess of dividends received qualify for the 40% dividend deduction. Swedish tax policy generally aims to favor operating companies over holding companies; as a result, the right to deduct dividends on new shares is available only to operating companies.

5/C.7. Treatment of Small Corporations

Provisions for small business relief are found in many corporation income tax structures. In some cases, such relief serves as an alternative to a general integration scheme. In other cases, however, some degree of integration and some measure of small business relief are both provided.

At least in principle, a dividend deduction may therefore be combined with small corporation relief. Consent dividends may be made deductible only by small or closely held corporations and not by publicly held corporations. (In any event, consent dividends are not likely to be practicable for the latter.) The rate on the nondeductible earnings of small or closely held corporations may be fixed below the rate on the nondeductible earnings of other corporations. The alternative device of providing a greater deduction for dividend outlays by small corporations than for dividend outlays by large corporations ignores, however, the greater need of small corporations for retained earnings; as far as it is known, no country uses that method of small business relief.

As a practical matter, the dividends-paid deduction method of integration does not seem to lend itself particularly well to small business relief. Special provisions for the latter are not common in countries that use this method of partial integration.

6
Integration at the Shareholder Level

6/A. Introduction

Systems of integration at the shareholder level may be divided into two major categories. Under the relatively crude systems in use in certain countries, the shareholder simply excludes from his taxable income all or part of his dividend income. The principle underlying these systems is that the profits from which the dividend was paid have previously been taxed to the corporation and that it is improper to tax to a shareholder a dividend from such previously taxed profits. Systems of this kind, and objections to them, are discussed in section 6/B below.

The use of more sophisticated systems of integration at the shareholder level is increasing. In these systems, profits are first taxed to the corporation as earned. When and if dividends are paid from those profits, the shareholder includes the full amount of the dividends in his income subject to tax. After calculating the individual income tax due on that income, the shareholder is allowed a credit against the total tax found to be due. For convenience, the shareholder's tax credit is generally calculated as a percentage of his dividend income rather than as a portion of the tax paid by the corporation on the profits from which the dividend was paid. Nevertheless, the principle underlying these systems is that a portion of the corporation income tax paid on those profits was paid for the account of the shareholder receiving the dividend and that the shareholder is entitled to a credit for that portion. Put another way, the creditable portion of the corporation income tax is treated as though it were an "advance" payment of the shareholder's tax on his dividend receipt, or as though that portion had been "withheld" for the shareholder's account.

A shareholder dividend credit of this kind was adopted by France in 1965; such a credit was introduced in Belgium earlier. In 1973, the United

Kingdom abandoned its unintegrated system, which had been in effect since 1965, and adopted in its place a system of shareholder-level integration based on a similar credit.[1] In 1976, the German government agreed in principle to reform its system so that shareholders would be allowed to credit the tax on distributed profits (to be raised to 36%) against their personal tax liabilities.[2]

The three largest countries in the European Economic Community (EEC)—Germany, France, and Great Britain—have thus integrated their corporation-individual income tax structures by offering a shareholder dividends-received credit. Moreover, the EEC, in the process of harmonizing the tax structures of its member countries has proposed that a shareholder credit for dividends received be adopted as its common method of integrating the corporation and individual income taxes.[3] If adopted, this mode of integration will therefore be the method applied to a very large proportion of the world's corporations and shareholders. Countries with different corporation-shareholder tax structures (for example, those with no integration, such as the United States, and those with integration at the corporate level, such as the Scandinavian countries) will then be required to re-examine their tax structures to see whether they should follow the Common Market example.

Various methods of integration at the shareholder level are discussed in the following sections. Some countries (Japan, for example) have "mixed" systems, using one of these methods of shareholder-level integration in addition to some degree of integration at the corporate level. Such countries must first decide how much integration or distribution relief is to be provided in total and then what proportion of that total is to be provided at each level, corporate and shareholder. Generally speaking, it appears that these mixed systems emphasize integration at the shareholder level as their primary method of providing distribution relief and offer a minor degree of relief at the corporate level merely as a supplement. Mixed systems are discussed in section 6/D below.

1. The United Kingdom adopted a value-added tax at the same time that it adopted a new integration system; the revenue produced by the former was expected to make up for revenue lost by the latter.

2. The proposed dividend credit for shareholders was linked to other tax changes and was adopted in 1977.

3. See Article 4(1) of "The Proposed Directive for the Harmonisation of Systems of Company Taxation and of Withholding Taxes on Dividends," 16 *European Taxation* 52, 59 (1976).

6/B. Exemption or Exclusion of Dividends From the Individual Income Tax Base

6/B.1. Total Exemption or Exclusion

The simplest method of integration at the shareholder level is the exemption of all dividend income from tax in the shareholder's hands. Under such a scheme, corporate profits (whether distributed or retained) are taxed to the corporation in the first instance, and dividends are then exempted from tax in the hands of shareholders. Argentina offers an example: Argentine corporations pay tax on all of their profits, retained and distributed, at a flat rate of 33%[4]; dividends are exempt from tax in the hands of resident shareholders. An exemption of this kind is a crude form of integration; it is based on the argument that a dividend represents income that has already been taxed, rather than on an argument that a dividend is not income to the recipient. Indeed, as a British Royal Commission said of dividends many years ago, it is hard to imagine a receipt that is more obviously income.[5]

Full exclusion—the total exemption of dividends from the individual income tax—is relatively rare, however, among countries that levy a corporation income tax at a flat rate. The total exemption of dividends in the shareholder's hands is found primarily in those less-developed countries which tax corporations at progressive rates that are the same as, or similar to, the progressive rates applied to the incomes of individuals. It is argued that if corporate profits are taxed at highly progressive rates at the corporate level, the distributed component of these profits should not again be subjected to progressive rates at the shareholder level. The objection is thus not merely to "double taxation," but to "double progression." In Guatemala, for example, corporations are subject to the same progressive rates as individuals (from 5% in the lowest bracket to 48% in the highest); dividends are then tax-free in the hands of individual shareholders.

But dividend income is rarely exempt from tax (or excluded from taxable income) in countries in which the corporation tax is levied at a flat (or essentially flat) rate and in which progression is limited to the individual income tax. The exemption of dividend income in such circumstances is undesirable because it substitutes a flat-rate tax (the corporation tax) for a progressive tax (the individual income tax) on an element of individual income (namely, dividends). Such a substitution is considered to operate inequitably because the proportion of the additional burden of the cor-

4. From 1965 to 1968, Argentine corporations paid an additional tax of 8% on the portion of their profits distributed as dividends. Brazil, too, levied an additional tax (5%) at the corporate level on any profits distributed as dividends.

5. United Kingdom, Income Tax Codification Committee, 1 *Report* 63.

poration income tax relieved by the dividend exclusion is different for shareholders in different brackets and, indeed, increases as the shareholder's tax bracket increases.[6]

As is often the case, the matter of rate structures and progression becomes crucial. The argument that the dividend-exclusion method of relieving the two-tier taxation of corporate-source income is inequitable does not apply if the individual income tax is levied at a flat rate rather than progressive rates. In Norway, for example, the local income tax is levied at a flat rate; as a simple method of accomplishing partial integration, dividends are exempt from this flat-rate tax (though they are subject to the progressive national income tax).

A somewhat similar pattern may be found in some of the countries that subject individuals to both a basic, flat-rate income tax (primarily schedular in nature) and a supplemental, or complementary, global progressive tax (sometimes called a surtax and ordinarily applicable only to upper-income individuals). Some of these countries exclude dividends from the basic flat-rate tax but include them in taxable income for purposes of the progressive tax, or surtax. In the past, the United States followed this practice; Italy did also prior to its tax reforms of 1974 and 1977.[7] As a practical matter, a device of this kind may give full relief to small taxpayers (who are not subject to the surtax) while leaving dividends subject to progressive taxation in the hands of the upper-bracket individuals who, although fewer in number, receive the bulk of all dividend payments.

6/B.2. Methods of Correcting Inequity

As noted above, the total exemption of dividends from a progressive individual income tax operates inequitably because the proportion of the additional burden of the corporation income tax which is thereby relieved is different for shareholders in different income brackets. At the cost of a certain amount of complexity, various devices may be used to remove or diminish the inequity of a total dividend exclusion or exemption.

One such device is termed "exemption with progression." First, integration is accomplished through the total exclusion of dividend income from taxation in the shareholder's hands. Then, in order to reduce the inequity of the exclusion, and in recognition of the fact that, whether or not previously taxed to the paying corporation, dividends contribute to the

6. See Tables 3 and 4 in section 6/C.2b4 below.

7. Starting in 1978, Italy offered a shareholder dividend credit with gross-up, similar to that adopted by France in 1965 (discussed below). See Fantozzi, "Italy: The New Method of Taxation of Dividends: The Imputation System," 18 *European Taxation* 260 (1978).

shareholder's standard of living and taxable capacity, the dividends are taken into account in determining the progressive rate applicable to the shareholder's nonexempt income. At one time, New Zealand and Colombia followed this practice.

The "shrinking exemption" is another device that may be used. The dividend exemption or exclusion may be complete in the lower income brackets and may then decrease in amount as the shareholder's rate bracket increases. South Africa, for example, offers a 100% dividend exclusion to any taxpayer whose taxable income (including dividends) does not exceed SAR 2,600. The percentage excludable drops rapidly so that a taxpayer whose taxable income (including dividends) exceeds SAR 4,600 may exclude only 33-1/3% of his dividends from income subject to tax.

In the extreme case, the "shrinking exemption" may be converted to a "vanishing exemption," with no dividend exclusion or exemption at all for shareholders above a certain rate or income bracket. The Musgrave Commission recommended a vanishing provision for Colombia, for example. Colombian law provided an exemption or exclusion for the first P 12,000 of dividend income received by taxpayers whose net wealth did not exceed P 600,000; interest income enjoyed the same treatment, even though deductible by the payor. Although it recommended generally against the integration of the corporation and individual income taxes in Colombia, the Musgrave Commission did advise that (1) the traditional dividend exclusion be continued and indeed increased to P 20,000, but that (2) the dividend exclusion be made subject to a "vanishing provision" under which the exclusion would begin to decrease when net income exceeded P 40,000 and would disappear entirely when net income reached P 140,000.[8]

6/B.3. Partial Exemption or Exclusion

Some countries exempt small amounts of dividend income from taxation, and dividend income above the low exemption threshold is then taxed in

8. Musgrave and Gillis, *Fiscal Reform for Colombia* 41, 45. With the addition of the "vanishing provision," the limitation of the dividend exclusion to taxpayers with net wealth below P 600,000 could be eliminated.

The increase in the dividend exclusion to P 20,000 and related measures "are recommended not because they would serve business and personal income tax integration, but because they would encourage saving and investment by the small investor." Musgrave and Gillis, *Fiscal Reform for Colombia* 81–82. In Colombia, however, "most shares are owned by a relatively few large holders," and Professor Bird argues that, although the exclusion "costs relatively little," "it seems unlikely that much incentive is provided to shareholding by this exemption . . . ." It may result in a "small increase in saving," but only "by making the income distribution even more unequal than before." Bird, *Taxation and Development: Lessons From Colombian Experience* 82, 141.

full at the ordinary rates. In practice, this device is used less as an integration scheme than as a concession to small taxpayers and as a method of easing the administrative burden of dealing with small amounts of income from capital. In the United States, for example, single individuals may exclude the first $100 of dividend income from their taxable income (for married couples filing joint returns, the figure is $200). This exclusion is available to all individual taxpayers, whatever the total amount of their taxable income or dividend income.[9]

In other countries, a similar result is achieved by providing a small "standard expense deduction" even for those shareholders who incur no actual expenses in connection with their dividend income. In Sweden, for example, an individual who receives income from capital (dividends and interest, for the most part) may deduct his actual costs of collection and the like; even in the absence of actual expenses, he is entitled to a

9. In the United States, the limited dividend exclusion and a dividends-received credit for shareholders (equal to 4% of dividend income) were introduced by a Republican Administration in 1954. In his first tax message, in 1961, President Kennedy asked for the repeal of both measures. (At the time, Professor Stanley S. Surrey was Assistant Secretary of the Treasury for Tax Policy.) The message said in part:

> Proponents argued that [these measures] would encourage capital formation through equity investment, and that they would provide a partial offset to the so-called double taxation of dividend income. It is now clear that they serve neither purpose well; . . . .
>
> The dividend credit and exclusion are not an efficient stimulus to capital expansion in the form of plant and equipment. The revenue losses resulting from these provisions are spread over a large volume of outstanding shares rather than being concentrated on new shares; and the stimulating effects of the provisions are thus greatly diluted, resulting in relatively little increases in the supply of equity funds and a relatively slight reduction in the cost of equity financing. In fact, such reduction as does occur is more likely to benefit large corporations with easy access to the capital market, while being of little use to the small firms . . . .
>
> The dividend credit and exclusion are equally inadequate as a solution to the so-called problem of double taxation. Whatever may be the merits of the arguments respecting the existence of double taxation, the provisions of the 1954 act clearly do not offer an appropriate remedy. They greatly overcompensate the dividend recipient in the high income bracket, while giving either insufficient or no relief to shareholders with smaller income.
>
> . . . . The tax saving from the exclusion is substantially greater for a dividend recipient with a high income than for a recipient with low income. Moreover, on equity grounds, there is no reason for giving tax reduction to that small fraction of low-income taxpayers who receive dividends in contrast to those who must live on wages, interest, rents or other forms of income.

United States, Congress, House of Representatives, Committee on Ways and Means, *President's 1961 Tax Recommendations—Hearings* 11–12.

As a result of the President's message, the shareholder dividend credit was repealed. Congress refused to repeal the exclusion, however, and it remains in U.S. tax law.

"standard deduction" from such income of SKr 400; for married couples, who are required to aggregate their unearned income, the figure is SKr 800. Because few small shareholders incur any actual expenses of collection or administration, the SKr 800 standard expense deduction is equivalent to the exemption of the first SKr 800 of their dividend (and interest) income.[10]

The U.S. and Swedish exemption devices give full tax relief to persons with small amounts of dividend income. Like any deduction from income taxed at progressive rates, however, these exemptions become more valuable as the individual's tax rate increases. In principle, the exemption device is regressive and inequitable. Yet, the bulk of all dividend payments goes to individuals with high incomes and high dividend receipts; for them, the amount of relief given by a dividend exclusion of $100 or $200 is negligible, in practice. Negligible or not, however, the exclusion or the "standard deduction" continues to be available no matter how high the individual's income. In Colombia, by contrast, the dividend exclusion is now available only to shareholders whose wealth is below P 3,400,000.

A partial dividend exclusion such as that offered in the United States generally does not permit a small taxpayer to ignore his dividend income entirely, even if it is below the exclusion level and hence fully exempt. Ordinarily, the taxpayer must report his dividend income and then deduct the amount deductible (or deduct the amount of the "standard expense deduction," in Swedish practice). The result is therefore to render the individual income tax return more complicated, rather than less.

6/B.4. Integration Through the Individual Rate Mechanism

The methods of shareholder-level integration discussed above operate through the rules for determining taxable income; all or part of an individual's income from dividends is simply excluded from the tax base. It is also possible for a country to integrate at the shareholder level by means of the individual income tax rate schedule. Whether the rates of the individual income tax are flat or progressive, the rates applicable to dividend income may be made different from, and lower than, the rates applicable to other varieties of income.

The application of such a dual rate structure to all income brackets is relatively uncommon. More often a ceiling provision is used to limit the top

10. In some countries, information returns are required from dividend-paying corporations only if the dividend exceeds some minimum figure—$10 or F 300 or a similar amount. As a practical matter, taxpayers in those countries tend to regard these rules as the equivalent of a right to exclude from their income all payments below the figure that the payor must report. For a discussion of information returns, see Yudkin, *A Legal Structure for Effective Income Tax Administration* 14.

rate applicable to dividend income in the shareholder's hands. Such a provision recognizes that a corporation (at least in the ordinary case) has paid a corporation income tax on the profits from which the dividend was paid. In 1972, New Zealand taxed corporate profits in excess of NZ$ 7,200 at a rate of 42.5%. Individuals were taxed at progressive rates ranging from 15% to 60%. Dividends were subject to the individual income tax on the same basis as other income except that the maximum rate of tax on dividend income could not exceed 35% (for this purpose, dividends were treated as the last part of taxable income).

Still another system, one which is generally adopted as a device for combating tax evasion rather than as a method of distribution relief, also puts a rate ceiling on dividend income in the hands of shareholders. A country, particularly one in which bearer shares are common, may offer shareholders an option (1) to declare their dividend income and pay tax thereon at the ordinary rates or (2) to pay tax at the source at a relatively high rate in full discharge of their obligation to report and pay tax on dividend income. In 1974, for example, Italian corporations normally withheld a preliminary tax of 10% at the source from dividends paid to resident owners of registered shares. If the shareholder reported his dividend as income, as he was required by law to do, he paid tax on the dividend at ordinary rates and received a credit for the tax of 10% withheld at the source. The shareholder could, however, elect to have tax withheld at the source at the rate of 30%; in that case, the shareholder was not required to report his dividend income, and the 30% withheld at the source became the definitive tax on the dividend. Only those shareholders whose marginal rate exceeded the optional 30% rate were likely to elect this method of taxation.[11] Such a system may increase the possibility that some tax will be paid on dividend income, which is relatively easy to conceal in a country in which bearer shares are in common use (such as Italy). The system is regressive and inequitable, though, in that it benefits only upper-bracket individuals.

Japan uses a system that differs from the Italian one in only one essential respect. The benefits of the Japanese system are available primarily to small shareholders. As its major integration device, Japan uses a dividends-received credit at the shareholder level, supplemented by a split-rate system at the corporate level. In addition, a temporary savings incentive allows individuals to elect "separate taxation" of their dividends (and interest). In the case of dividends, for example, a preliminary tax of 20% is

11. The 30% rate was the same as the withholding rate applied (in the absence of a treaty) to dividends payable to nonresidents. The Italian system is said to have been adopted as a tax concession to upper-bracket taxpayers in order to reduce the tax advantages of expatriating capital to Switzerland, where their shares could be held for them in bearer form or in the name of a nonresident nominee.

withheld at the source; for dividends received between 1 January 1971 and 31 December 1972, an individual may elect "separate taxation," in which case the preliminary tax withheld at the source becomes the definitive tax. For dividends received in 1977, the rate of the optional tax had risen to 35%. If a shareholder elects separate taxation, the ordinary dividends-received credit is lost. Moreover, the benefits of separate taxation are not available for a dividend from a single corporation which exceeds ¥ 500,000 per year or for a dividend from a corporation in which the shareholder owns 5% or more of the equity capital. For "small dividends" (less than ¥ 100,000 per year from a single corporation), a lower preferential rate is available; for these dividends, the shareholder may elect definitive taxation through withholding at the source at the rate of only 15%.

As a result, Japan's taxation of corporate-source income is extremely complicated. Distribution relief takes three different forms: (1) a dividends-received credit at the shareholder level, (2) a split rate at the corporate level, and (3) definitive taxation of dividends, at two different rates, for dividends below certain amounts.[12] Before a country adopts such a complex scheme, it might consider whether the simple alternative of rate reduction might not be equally beneficial to the economy and involve much less administrative difficulty.

6/C. The Dividends-Received Credit to the Shareholder

6/C.1. In General

By far the most important method of integration at the shareholder level is the shareholder dividends-received credit. In summary, this method involves the following steps: (1) at the corporate level, a tax is imposed on corporate profits, whether distributed or retained[13]; (2) at the shareholder level, the shareholder includes his dividend receipts in his taxable income; and (3) against the tax due on his taxable income, the shareholder takes a credit for some portion of the dividend receipts included in that income. For purposes of the shareholder's dividends-received credit, the dividend consists of two separate and distinct parts—the shareholder's cash payment from the corporation and the credit against his individual income tax

12. In 1980, the Japanese government was actively considering the abolition of the optional tax. Abolition was recommended in the 1979 report of the Tax Commission, an advisory body to the Minister of Finance.

13. In this system, the rate of the corporation income tax is not necessarily the same for retained profits and for distributed profits; in some countries using the shareholder dividend credit, the rate on distributed profits at the corporate level is somewhat lower than the rate on retained profits.

to which that cash receipt entitles him.

In the interests of simplicity, the amount of the credit is usually fixed as a percentage of the shareholder's dividend receipt. It is not set as a percentage of the tax paid by the corporation on the profits from which the dividend was paid. Nonetheless, the premise underlying the system is that a portion of the tax paid at the corporate level on those profits should be treated as though it had been paid by the corporation not for its own account but for the account of the shareholder. In effect, the creditable portion of the corporation income tax is treated as if it had been "withheld" from the dividend payment for the account of the shareholder. For this reason, this method of integration is sometimes referred to as "deemed withholding." The remaining portion of the corporation income tax—the portion not creditable by the shareholder—is regarded as a "real" tax, imposed on the corporation as such and not withheld for the account of the shareholder.

"Deemed withholding" as a method of integration must be distinguished from actual withholding as a method of collection, either preliminary or final. Some countries, for example, require the withholding of a preliminary tax from dividends as a collection device, just as some countries require the withholding of a preliminary tax from wage of interest payments.[14] When the income recipient files his tax return and reports the income in question, he is given a credit against his final tax for the preliminary tax withheld from his income receipts.

The terminology used to describe the shareholder's dividends-received credit parallels the terminology used in connection with the U.S. foreign tax credit.[15] The shareholder's credit for tax actually withheld at the source from his dividend is sometimes called a "direct credit," and the shareholder's credit for the portion of the corporation income tax deemed to have been paid for the shareholder's account on the profits from which his dividend was paid is called an "indirect credit." In all cases, the shareholder's direct credit (for a preliminary tax actually withheld at the source from his dividend income) must be distinguished from his indirect credit (for a portion of the corporation income tax paid by the corporation on the profits from which the dividend came).

A country may use both a direct credit and an indirect credit. Japan, for example, uses both. France, however, abandoned the use of actual withholding and a direct credit when it adopted an indirect credit in 1965. The indirect credit was thought to be a sufficient guarantee of tax compliance to make actual withholding and the direct credit no longer necessary.

14. For a discussion of withholding as a collection device, see Yudkin, *A Legal Structure for Effective Income Tax Administration* 32.
15. See WTS: *United States*, 11/3.2. See also Owens and Ball, 1 *The Indirect Credit*, 1/2.

6/C.2. The Credit and "Gross-Up"

a. "Gross-Up" Defined

At least in the past, the question of "gross-up" was a major problem in the use of the shareholder indirect dividend credit. The question may be put this way: for purposes of determining the shareholder's income subject to tax, should the amount of his actual dividend receipt be increased ("grossed up") by the amount of the indirect tax credit to which the dividend entitles him?[16]

Suppose, for instance, that a country using a 30% corporation income tax rate enacts a dividends-received credit equal to 20% of dividend receipts. If a corporation earns pretax profits of 100 units, for example, and disburses all of its after-tax profits as a dividend to its sole shareholder, it will pay a dividend of 70 units; a 20% dividends-received credit will then give the shareholder a credit of 14 units. The question is whether the shareholder should be required to add the 14 units of tax credit to the 70 units of actual dividend receipts and report 84 units on his tax return as his income from the corporation, or whether he should be required to report only the 70 units of dividend income actually received. In either case, he will receive a credit of 14 units against the tax found to be due.

The practice of increasing the actual dividend receipt, for purposes of computing the shareholder's income, by the amount of the credit to which the dividend entitles him is ordinarily referred to as "grossing up." Among the countries now or formerly using a dividends-received credit, there has been no uniformity on the matter of gross-up. Japan, for example, uses a credit without gross-up.[17] For years, Canada provided a shareholder dividend credit without gross-up, and countries following the Canadian model also did not use gross-up (the United States, for example, used a 4% dividend credit without gross-up from 1954 until the repeal of the credit in 1965).[18] Canada switched to gross-up in 1972, however. The French credit introduced in 1965 involves gross-up, and the current German and British shareholder dividend credits also include gross-up, as does the proposed harmonized Common Market system. For the future, it seems likely that at least those developed countries which adopt a shareholder dividend credit

16. No question about "gross-up" appears to arise in the case of the direct credit for a preliminary tax withheld at the source from a dividend paid by a resident corporation. In this case, the dividend is always grossed up; the taxpayer is required to report as taxable income the gross amount of the dividend (without any reduction for the tax actually withheld at the source) and then to claim his credit for that preliminary tax against the final tax due from him.

17. Japan uses another device, however, to reduce the discrimination against low-bracket shareholders which is inherent in the use of a credit without gross-up. See section 6/C.2b4 below.

18. Reasons for the U.S. repeal of its 4% dividend credit are explained in note 9 above.

will include gross-up as an essential part of their systems. The reasons are considered in the next section.

b. ARGUMENTS FOR AND AGAINST GROSS-UP

1. In general: Administrative complexity and taxpayer confusion. The element of complexity in the grossing-up process is the major argument against it. The shareholder in the illustration above who receives a dividend of 70 units may find it difficult to understand why he must report 84 units as income and how the figure of 84 is reached when the sum actually received was 70 units. Moreover, the illustration tends to simplify the facts of corporate life. In the United States, for example, many dividends are paid in round amounts—$0.10 quarterly, for example. Odd amounts are not uncommon, however ($0.0325 quarterly, for example, or $0.052). Extra and special dividends may add to the problem. Whether the dividend credit is 4%, 10%, or 50% of the dividend, the shareholder and the tax administrator may have difficulty in carrying out the grossing-up process and in determining the exact amount of income to report. In Belgium, where the basic corporation tax rate was 30% and the shareholder's indirect credit was one half of that rate, or 15%, up to 1973, the shareholder was required to gross up each dividend by 15/70 of the net amount received.

Because of the complexity involved, the Shoup Mission recommended, after World War II, that Japan adopt a dividends-received credit without gross-up. It also recommended that after the Japanese tax system (particularly its administration) had developed further, a gross-up provision could be added to the system.[19]

Perhaps the administrative burden of gross-up has been exaggerated, however. It is relatively easy to shift most of the burden to the corporation and to require any corporation to advise the shareholder of the following when it makes a dividend payment: (1) the actual or net amount of the dividend; (2) the amount of the credit to which the dividend entitles him; and (3) the grossed-up figure that he must report as income. Information returns of this kind were required in the United Kingdom when it was using a dividends-received credit with gross-up.

The information that the corporation must provide to the shareholder under such a system is no different, in fact, from the information that an employer must provide to each employee in a country that requires employers to withhold a preliminary tax from wage payments (the United

19. In accordance with the Shoup Mission's recommendation, Japan adopted a dividends-received credit without gross-up. As of 1 January 1981, gross-up had not yet been enacted; whether or not to provide for it is a matter of continuing discussion in Japanese tax circles. See note 12 above.

States and Sweden, for example): (1) the amount of tax withheld from wages for the employee's account (that is, the amount of tax credit to which the employee is entitled) and (2) the gross amount of wages (that is before the deduction for withholding tax) which the employee must report as taxable income.

With the aid of such an information return from each corporation from which he receives dividends, the shareholder should have no more difficulty in determining his gross income from dividends than an employee has in determining his gross income from employment (in a country in which a preliminary tax is withheld from wages). Moreover, the shareholder's difficulty in understanding the grossing-up process will probably be limited to the first year or two of its operation. Those countries which in the past required dividends to be grossed up by the amount of the accompanying tax credit seem to have had no particular difficulty, and those which have adopted gross-up more recently (France, for example) appear to have overcome the transitional difficulties in short order. As with other tax matters, the administrative problems of gross-up may be more terrifying in prospect than in reality.

Complexity and taxpayer confusion stand on a different footing, however. Shareholders are among the wealthiest and the most sophisticated of taxpayers and have access to professional help. Nevertheless, in France, for example, the shareholder credit with gross-up remains a source of complexity and confusion for shareholders. Reporting in 1972 on a study of the French tax structure, the French Tax Council (*Conseil des Impôts*), an official body charged with the duty of reviewing various aspects of the structure, found that the shareholder credit had the "serious inconvenience of being relatively complicated." When introduced, the credit was not clearly understood by taxpayers, and seven years after its introduction, the credit remained "poorly understood."[20]

2. Impact on tax revenues and on size of dividend distribution. Gross-up makes the individual income tax base more comprehensive by extending the tax base to include the portion of the corporation income tax for which the shareholder receives credit. A dividend credit of any given amount will result in a smaller revenue loss with gross-up than the same credit without gross-up.

Moreover, depending on its magnitude, a dividends-received credit with gross-up may have another advantage over a credit without gross-up. One argument against distribution relief (at either the corporate or the shareholder level) is that it may lead to excessive distributions, which deplete

20. Conseil des Impôts, "Rapport au Président de la République, juillet 1972," *Journal Officiel*, 3 août 1972, pp. 629, 696.

the corporation's retained earnings below the level required to meet reasonable business and development needs (see Chapter 2). Yet a dividends-received credit with gross-up may permit corporations to increase their cash retentions and still satisfy shareholders' dividend needs.

Until France adopted integration in 1965, for example, it used an unintegrated system: if a corporation paid a dividend of F 100, the shareholder reported taxable income of F 100 and received no tax credit or other relief.[21] When France adopted a dividends-received credit of 50% of net dividend income with gross-up, the situation changed. If a corporation pays a dividend of F 100, the shareholder reports a gross dividend of F 150 and is entitled to a tax credit (or refund) of F 50. French corporations are careful to emphasize to shareholders the value of the tax credit attached to each dividend. A typical dividend announcement in France is phrased in much these terms: "dividend of F 10, carrying a tax credit of F 5, for a total of F 15."

The result is that a French corporation is in a position to reduce its dividends below the 1965 level, to increase the proportion of profits retained in the business, and at the same time to increase the net yield to the shareholder. In the case of the corporation mentioned above, which paid a dividend of F 100 before 1965, the shareholder's taxable income from that dividend was only F 100. Suppose that the corporation reduces its dividend from F 100 to F 80, or by 20%. The shareholder's taxable income becomes F 80 plus his tax credit of 50% of that amount, or F 40, for a total taxable income of F 120. In other words, despite the reduction in the corporation's cash dividend, the shareholder's gross taxable dividend is 20% higher than it had been before the adoption of the shareholder tax credit scheme. The result is that a corporation can retain a larger proportion of its earnings than before, reduce its cash dividends to shareholders, and give the shareholders a higher after-tax return than before.[22]

As indicated at the beginning of this section, in a country that uses a shareholder dividend credit as a method of integration, a dividend will consist of two separate elements: (1) the cash payment by the corporation and (2) the claim against the government to which the cash dividend entitles the shareholder. The existence of the second element may permit a reduction in the amount of the first element and at the same time provide the shareholder with an increase in his after-tax income. The saving to

21. Until the 1965 reform, a preliminary tax of 24% was withheld from dividends as a collection device; the shareholder reported F 100 as income and claimed a direct credit for F 24. This withholding scheme is disregarded in the discussion above.

22. The argument is not just a theoretical one; the Segré report asserts that there have been a number of dividend reductions since France adopted the dividend credit. Communauté Économique Europêene, Commission, *Le Développement d'un marché européen des capitaux* 225.

corporations and shareholders is paid for by the government, whose tax revenues (by comparison with those available in the absence of integration) are reduced by the amount of the tax credit involved.

3. *Refunds.* Closely linked to the problem of gross-up is the problem of refunds. A country that does not require gross-up generally does not provide for a refund to any individual whose dividends-received credit exceeds the amount of his tax. By the same token, countries that do require shareholders to gross up their dividend income by the amount of the dividends-received credit generally give a refund to any taxpayer whose credit exceeds his tax liability. The rationale for the dividend credit lies in the view that a part of the tax paid by the corporation was "withheld" for the shareholder's account; if so, any taxpayer who cannot use the credit fully as an offset against his tax liability should have the difference refunded to him. If there is no provision for refunds, the credit system will operate unfairly and inequitably for low-income taxpayers who cannot make use of the credit.

Operating a system of refunds is a complicated matter for a tax administration (though most countries that withhold a preliminary tax from wages generally provide refunds of any sums withheld in excess of the tax liability finally determined).[23] The need to audit claims and to control disbursements to what may be a relatively large number of taxpayers may put some strain on the administration. As distinguished from grossing-up, much of the administrative burden of which may be shifted to the corporation, the burden of issuing refunds cannot be shifted; it must be borne by the tax administration itself.

Against the argument that a refund of tax should be made to any shareholder whose income is so low that the credit exceeds his tax liability, it is argued that the dividends-received credit is designed to relieve the shareholder of a portion of the tax allocable to his dividend income. If the shareholder owes no individual income tax, then he has been taxed at only one level (the corporate); hence, it is argued, the shareholder is not entitled to a refund. Yet the argument overlooks the fact that integration seeks to reduce the burden of the *corporation income tax*; for that reason, even a shareholder who owes no individual income tax and hence cannot make use of his dividend tax credit should, in principle, receive a refund representing his aliquot portion of the corporation income tax paid on the profits from which his dividend was paid.

23. In some cases, however, the tax withheld from wages at the source is definitive, not preliminary, and there are no refunds of any tax "overwithheld." This was true, for example, of the tax on seamen's wages in Sweden; WTS: *Sweden*, 8/1.6. The idea of definitive wage taxation at the source has attracted increasing attention.

4. Equity. The need for a workable and relatively simple tax structure may argue against the use of gross-up and refunds. Yet the absence of any provision for gross-up and refunds makes the dividends-received credit inequitable in its operation. (Equity is defined, for this purpose, as the use of a method of integration which removes an equal share of the additional burden of the corporation income tax for shareholders in all income brackets (6/B.2).)

In recommending that Canada amend its dividends-received credit, which applied for years without gross-up or refunds, and that it require both gross-up and refunds, Canada's Finance Minister summarized the matter in these terms: "The dividend tax credit [without gross-up or refund] is of significantly greater value to high-income taxpayers than it is to low-income taxpayers."[24]

Without gross-up and refunds, that is, the dividends-received credit is inequitable because the credit removes an increasing proportion of the additional burden of the corporation income tax as the shareholder's income increases (see Column 6 of Table 3 below). Supporters of the credit deny the charge of inequity, however; they claim that the credit is equitable because (1) it offers all shareholders the same unit amount of relief and (2) an equal unit amount of relief means greater proportionate relief to lower-bracket shareholders (except those who owe no tax at all, even without the benefit of the credit).

Table 1, in Chapter 3, illustrates the additional burden of the corporation income tax if corporate profits are subject to a 30% corporation income tax and all after-tax profits are distributed to shareholders in the 0%, 10%, 20%, and 40% rate brackets of the individual income tax. Table 3 shows how much of that additional burden is removed for shareholders in the various brackets by a dividends-received credit equal to 20% of dividend receipts, without gross-up.[25] Column 4 of Table 3 shows that a dividend received credit of 20% of dividend income (without gross-up or refunds) offers all shareholders the same absolute amount of relief (14 units of tax in each case). But Column 7 of the same table shows that the percentage of the additional burden of the corporation income tax relieved by the credit goes up as the shareholder's individual income tax rate rises. That is, the wealthier the shareholder, the greater the relief (in terms of the percentage of the burden relieved).

The facts underlying Table 4 are the same as those for Table 3 except that

24. Canada, Minister of Finance, *Proposals for Tax Reform* 48.

25. In any particular case, the ratio between (1) the amount by which the credit without gross-up reduces the amount of the additional burden of the corporation income tax and (2) the amount of that burden may be determined by the following formula, in which K is the amount of the credit, C is the corporation income tax rate, and M is the individual shareholder's marginal income tax rate: $(K - CK)/(C - CM)$. See Shoup, *Public Finance* 316.

TABLE 3: *Effect of 20% Dividends-Received Credit Without Gross-Up or Refunds: Absolute Amount of Individual Income Tax Relieved and Percentage of Additional Burden of Corporation Income Tax Relieved*

Shareholder Marginal Income Tax Rate (1)	Additional Burden of Corporation Tax (2)	Shareholder Tax Before Credit (3)	Unit Amount of Credit (4)	Unit Amount of Shareholder Tax Relieved by Credit (5)	Percentage of Shareholder Tax Relieved by Credit (6)	Percentage of Additional Burden of Corporation Tax Relieved by Credit (7)
0%	30	0	14	0	0	0
10%	27	7	14	7	100%	25.92%
20%	24	14	14	14	100%	58.33%
40%	18	28	14	14	50%	77.77%

Explanation: Column 2 = Column 7 of Table 1
Column 3 = Column 5 of Table 1
Column 4 = Column 4 of Table 1 × 20%
Column 6 = Column 5/Column 3
Column 7 = Column 5/Column 2

TABLE 4: *Effect of 20% Dividends-Received Credit With Gross-Up and Refund**

Shareholder Marginal Income Tax Rate (1)	Additional Burden of Corporation Tax (2)	Dividend Received (3)	Credit (4)	Tax on Credit (5)	Net Credit (6)	Percentage of Additional Burden of Corporation Tax Relieved by Credit (7)
0%	30	70	14	0	14.0	46.6%
10%	27	70	14	1.4	12.6	46.6%
20%	24	70	14	2.8	11.2	46.6%
40%	18	70	14	5.6	8.4	46.6%

*This table has been adapted from Table 5-8 in Pechman, *Federal Tax Policy* (rev. ed.) 145.
Explanation: Column 2 = Column 7 of Table 1
Column 3 = 100 − 30
Column 4 = Column 3 × 20%
Column 5 = Column 4 × Column 1
Column 6 = Column 4 − Column 5
Column 7 = Column 6 / Column 2

gross-up and refunds are provided. That is, the corporation income tax rate is 30%; all after-tax profits are distributed to shareholders; the dividends-received credit is 20% of dividend income; and the shareholders' individual tax brackets are 0%, 10%, 20%, and 40%. Table 4 shows that the combination of gross-up and refunds with a dividends-received credit system removes the same proportion of the additional burden of the corporation income tax for shareholders in all brackets.[26]

Indeed, the failure to provide for gross-up and refunds may be seen as a violation of a basic principle of income taxation. If a debt or an item of expense attributable to one person, *A*, is paid for that person's account by a second person, *B*, it is generally the rule that *A* has enjoyed taxable income. The failure to provide gross-up violates that rule because the credit is based on the proposition that some portion of the corporation income tax paid by the corporation on the profits distributed as a dividend was paid (or "deemed" to have been withheld) for the account of the shareholder. To the extent that the shareholder's tax was paid for his account by another (the corporation), the shareholder has received income and should be taxed thereon, however.

The problem may be stated another way: a dividends-received credit

26. According to Professor Goode, the result of a shareholder dividend credit without gross-up and refunds is "exactly comparable to that of a method of withholding on salaries and wages that denied refunds for overwithholding and failed to include the amount withheld in the taxable income of the employee." Goode, *The Corporation Income Tax* 194.

without gross-up and refunds treats the corporation income tax (generally levied at a flat or nearly flat rate) as a partial substitute for the individual income tax (generally levied at progressive rates). With a flat-rate corporation income tax and a progressive individual income tax, indeed, the credit without gross-up and refunds introduces what amounts to a special, graduated rate schedule for distributed profits which is different from the rate schedule applied to other income.

As far as lost revenue is concerned, gross-up and refunds may have an advantage. Depending on the rate schedules and the pattern of share ownership in a country, a dividends-received credit with gross-up and refunds may cost the government less in tax revenue than a credit without gross-up and refunds. Although it is true that low-income shareholders will have to be paid refunds, upper-income shareholders—those who receive by far the larger portion of all dividends—must pay tax on their credit (see Column 5 of Table 4). Gross-up makes the individual's income tax base more comprehensive because it extends the base to include that portion of the corporation income tax for which he received credit. The progressive individual income tax then applies at the shareholder's marginal rate both to his net dividend and to his tax credit. The relationship between the rate of the shareholder's credit and the presence or absence of gross-up is examined in section 6/C.3 below, which deals with rates of credit.

To correct the inequity that may be thought to arise from the use of a dividends-received credit without gross-up and refunds, various modifications of the credit may be adopted. A "shrinking" credit may be used, for example; that is, the percentage of dividend income available as a credit would decrease as the taxpayer's income increased. In Japan, the shareholder's dividend credit is ordinarily 10% of dividends received. If the individual's taxable income from all sources, including dividends, exceeds ¥ 10,000,000, however, the 10% credit is available only up to the level at which his income (including dividends) equals the ¥ 10,000,000 ceiling; for any remaining dividend income, the credit is reduced to one half of its normal rate, or to 5% of dividend income.[27] This device provides no refund, however, for the low-bracket shareholder and may involve as much complication as gross-up itself.

In sum, a dividends-received credit without gross-up or refunds may have advantages in terms of simplicity, but disadvantages in terms of equity, in comparison with a credit with gross-up and refunds. The choice between the two will depend in each case on the administrative capabilities of the country in question and on the extent to which equity is preferred to simplicity.

27. The rate of the Japanese credit has been lowered from time to time. Before 1971, it was 15% for lower-bracket shareholders and 7.5% for upper-bracket shareholders. For 1971 and 1972, it was 12.5% and 6.25%; since 1973, the rates described in the text apply.

6/C.3. Rate and Base of the Credit

a. Rate

From time to time, a country has proposed that shareholders be given a full credit for the total amount of the corporation income tax attributable to the profits from which their dividends come. The Carter Commission made such a proposal for Canada, and a similar proposal was later made for Germany. The Canadian proposal for a 100% credit was rejected, however, and a credit was adopted for only part of the corporation income tax.[28]

Generally, the shareholder credits now in use give shareholders credit for only part of the corporation income tax. Under this system of semi-integration or partial integration, a part of the corporation income tax (the noncreditable part) is treated as a "real" tax on the corporation, and the government is thereby able to share in the fruits of corporate enterprise (see Chapter 2). The remaining part (the creditable part) is treated as a preliminary payment of tax on behalf of the shareholder.

The common use of a partial rather than a complete credit for the corporation income tax may reflect uncertainty about the shifting and incidence of the corporation income tax (see Chapters 1 and 3). Suppose, for example, that 50% of the corporation income tax is shifted to workers or consumers, and that only the remaining 50% is therefore borne by the shareholders. In that case, a shareholder credit for 50% of the corporation income tax amounts to a credit for 100% of the portion of the tax which falls on the shareholders.

As noted above, however, a shareholder dividends-received credit is almost invariably expressed as a percentage of the shareholder's dividend receipt, rather than as a percentage of the tax paid by the corporation on the profits from which the dividend was paid. The reason is administrative convenience. A shareholder is able to claim a uniform credit for all qualified dividends regardless of the rate of tax paid by the corporation. Temporary or permanent changes can therefore be made in the rate of the corporation income tax without affecting the manner in which shareholders compute their individual income taxes. Yet, however expressed, the credit is grounded in the premise that the corporation income tax has been paid on those profits and that some portion of that tax is to be treated as having been paid (or "deemed" to have been withheld) for the shareholder's account. A credit expressed as a proportion of the dividend paid can be recalculated as a proportion of the corporation income tax paid.

Suppose, for example, that the corporation income tax rate is 30% and that a dividend credit of 20% of dividend income is offered. If a cor-

28. See the Appendix for a brief description of the present German system, which grants a full credit.

poration earns 100 units of profits before tax, it will pay a tax of 30 units. If the corporation distributes the remaining 70 units as a dividend, the shareholder will receive a credit of 14 units against his tax. The credit thus equals 14/30 of the tax paid by the corporation. In other words, if the corporate tax rate is 30%, a 20% dividends-received credit is equivalent to a credit of 46.6% of the corporation income tax paid; a 10% credit is equivalent to 23.3% of the corporation tax paid; and so on. The relationship of the credit to the rate of the corporation income tax is therefore a crucial factor in any consideration of the amount of the dividends-received credit to be offered.

It is not the only factor, however. Just as important as the corporation tax rate may be the extent of the relief which the country in question wishes to offer, the amount of individual income tax revenue it can afford to forgo, and how much it believes that investment in corporate shares is a desirable activity which would be encouraged by distribution relief. As a result, although there is considerable uniformity among corporation income tax rates, the range of dividends-received credits is wide. In Japan, the credit was formerly 15% (7.5% for larger incomes), and then after transitional rates of 12.5% and 6.25% in 1971 and 1972, the credit became 10% and 5% in 1973 (without gross-up). In Japan, however, the tax rates (including that of the corporation income tax) are generally lower than those in other developed countries, and some degree of integration also exists at the corporate level. The effective rate of the Japanese shareholder credit (as a percentage of the corporation income tax paid) is therefore higher than the nominal rate would make it appear.

In Canada, the shareholder's credit was 20% without gross-up for many years; in 1972, the credit became 20% of the grossed-up dividend received. In 1973, when Britain's shareholder credit became effective, the rate of the British corporation income tax was 52% and the dividend credit was 3/7 of the dividend received. In April 1974, the credit became 34/66 of the dividend received.

How much integration any particular credit will provide depends, in short, on its relationship to the corporation income tax rate. In France, for example, the corporation income tax rate is 50%, and the shareholder is entitled to a credit equal to one half of his net dividend income (that is, of his dividend receipt before gross-up, which is also required). With the corporation income tax rate at 50%, the shareholder credit (one half of dividend receipts) is equivalent to a credit for one half of the income tax paid at the corporate level:

Corporate profits before tax	100,000
Corporation income tax of 50%	50,000
Distribution of after-tax profits	50,000
Shareholder credit of 50% of net dividend	25,000

In this illustration, the corporation has profits before tax of 100,000 units, pays the 50% corporation income tax of 50,000 units, and distributes its after-tax profits of 50,000 units. With respect to his net dividend receipt of 50,000 units, the shareholder is entitled to a credit equal to one half of that dividend receipt, or 25,000 units. That credit is equivalent to a credit for one half of the corporation income tax paid (50% of 50,000, or 25,000).

Whether or not a country requires gross-up and refunds in connection with its dividends-received credit is another factor affecting the amount of credit. Generally speaking, countries that require gross-up of the shareholder's net dividend by the amount of the credit are in a position, with little or no additional revenue loss, to offer a substantially larger credit than countries that do not require gross-up. The reason is that gross-up increases the shareholder's taxable income by the amount of the credit. The two illustrations below compare the revenue effects of credits with and without gross-up.

Assume, first, that shareholder *X* lives in a country that offers a shareholder dividends-received credit of 10% of dividend income and does not require gross-up. Shareholder *X* receives dividend income of 1,000 units and falls in the 40% income tax bracket.

Dividend income before tax	1,000
Shareholder tax before credit (40%)	400
Shareholder credit for 10% of dividend income	100
Net shareholder tax	300

Assume, second, that shareholder *Y* lives in a country that offers a credit twice as great—20% of dividend income—but requires gross-up. Shareholder *Y* also has dividend income of 1,000 units and falls in the 40% income tax bracket.

Dividend income before tax	1,000
Gross-up by amount of credit (20% of dividend income)	200
Income subject to tax	1,200
Shareholder tax before credit (40%)	480
Shareholder credit for 20% of dividend income	200
Net shareholder tax	280

These two illustrations show that a 100% increase in the shareholder's dividends-received credit (from 10% to 20%) results in only a 6.6% loss in shareholder tax revenues (from the 300 units paid by shareholder *X* to 280 units paid by shareholder *Y*) if gross-up is used.[29] Because gross-up is

29. The French Tax Council found that individual shareholders in France claimed a total tax credit of F 1,170,000,000 in 1970. But because of gross-up, the credit was subject to income tax, which was estimated by the tax administration to amount to F 503,000,000. Thus, the net loss in tax revenue resulting from the credit was F 667,000,000. For corporate shareholders,

generally combined with refunds to shareholders who are not able to take full advantage of the credit, a small loss of revenue from the individual income tax will also occur at the bottom end of the income scale.

b. BASE

Still another factor that may affect the size of the credit is the base on which it is calculated. Is the base to be the amount received by the shareholder, before any dividend-related deductions to which he may be entitled (interest and carrying charges on loans to buy shares, the cost of investment counsel, and the like) are taken into account? Or is the base to be the net amount reported as taxable income by the shareholder after he has subtracted from his dividend receipts the amount of any related deductions?

The 1972 change in Canadian law demonstrates the problem. Up to 1972, the Canadian credit was limited to 20% of the shareholder's *taxable* dividend income—that is, the amount remaining after interest and other charges had been deducted. The new law, which requires gross-up, takes the opposite position: the credit is based on the shareholder's dividend receipts before his deductions for expenses incurred in obtaining or protecting his dividend income are taken into account. This failure to decrease dividend receipts by dividend-related expenses before calculating the shareholder's credit may confer large benefits on any upper-bracket investor who is in a position to claim both (1) the 20% credit on dividend income before deductions and (2) deductions for interest, investment advice, bank vault and custodial expenses, and other expenses attributable to his dividend income. In the interests of administrative simplicity, however, many countries follow the Canadian practice and permit the shareholder's credit to be calculated on the basis of dividend income before the deduction of dividend-related expenses.

6/C.4. Qualifying Distributions

a. IN GENERAL

A country that adopts a dividends-received credit must determine which corporate distributions are to be treated as entitling the shareholder to the credit. As is true in other integration systems, "constructive" or "con-

the credit claimed amounted to F 472,000,000; after gross-up was taken into account, the net loss in tax revenue was estimated to be about F 221,000,000. Conseil des Impôts, "Rapport au Président de la République, juillet 1972," *Journal Officiel*, 3 août 1972, pp. 629, 695.

cealed" dividends (excessive salary or interest paid to shareholders, for example) are rarely permitted to qualify for integration relief in a dividends-received credit system. Rather, only dividends that are formally voted as such qualify. Other questions do arise, however, and they become especially important if the credit is large.

Generally speaking, dividends from foreign corporations do not qualify as distributions entitling the shareholder to a dividends-received credit. This matter is discussed in Chapter 7, which deals with international aspects of integration.

b. Previously Taxed Profits and Rate of Tax Paid

Underlying the use of the dividends-received credit as a method of integration are the assumptions, previously noted, (1) that the corporation has paid a corporation income tax on the profits it distributes and (2) that some portion of that tax may be deemed to have been paid or withheld by the corporation for the account of the dividend recipient. If the dividends-received credit is small (such as the 4% credit once used in the United States, for example), then the costs of (1) inquiring whether the corporation did, in fact, pay tax and at what rate and (2) making appropriate adjustments in the credit if no tax was paid or if tax was paid at a rate below the normal rate may exceed any potential benefits.

If the credit is substantial, however, then whether the corporation has paid tax on the profits used as the source of a dividend and the rate at which tax was paid become important. There is no reason to give shareholders substantial distribution relief with respect to distributions that have borne little or no tax at the corporate level. If some adjustment in the credit is thought necessary because tax has not been paid at the full rate at the corporate level, what form should that adjustment take? Should there be a reduction in the shareholder's credit or an increase in the amount of corporation tax on the dividend entitling the shareholder to the credit?

For the taxpayer's convenience and for ease of administration, it is preferable that all dividends be entitled to a uniform rate of credit. As a result, an adjustment in the credit at the *shareholder* level to take account of varying effective tax rates paid by corporations is almost never required, particularly if gross-up is also involved. An adjustment at the shareholder level is not impossible, however. The shareholder could be required, for example, to reduce his credit by so many points for each percentage point by which the tax paid by the corporation falls below some prescribed rate of tax (the current rate, for example). As a result, though, the taxpayer might be entitled to a different credit for each corporation in which he owned dividend-paying shares.

To enable the shareholder to claim a uniform credit for each dividend, any necessary adjustments should generally be required to be made at the *corporate* level. Complexity cannot be avoided, however. Tracing rules must be devised in order to determine the source of each dividend distribution, and the rate of tax paid by the distributing corporation must be ascertained. But, does "rate of tax paid" mean the effective rate of tax paid by the corporation in the year of distribution on the particular profits from which the dividend is deemed to have come? Or does it mean the average rate of tax paid by the corporation in that year—or over a span of years?

Solutions to some of these problems are suggested by the French experience. In 1965, when the rate of the French corporation income tax was 50%, France abandoned its unintegrated income tax structure and adopted a dividends-received credit system. The credit was fixed at a uniform 50% of net dividend receipts and was therefore equivalent to one half of the nominal corporate tax rate of 50%. Gross-up was required, and refunds were available. Yet France also provided that if any corporation paid a dividend from funds that had borne tax at a rate lower than 50%, that corporation would be required to pay an additional tax—the *précompte mobilière*—in an amount equal to the credit arising out of the dividend. If a corporation pays a dividend of F 100, for example, the shareholder is entitled to a credit of F 50, whatever the source of the profits from which the dividend came and whatever the rate of tax (if any) paid by the corporation on those profits. If, however, those profits have been taxed at any rate less than 50%, the corporation must pay the additional tax in an amount equal to the shareholder's credit (in this case, up to an additional F 50).

To implement such an adjustment, it is necessary to develop "tracing rules" for determining in a uniform manner the source of particular dividends. The French tax code establishes an irrebuttable presumption that dividends are paid first from the profits that most recently bore tax at the rate of 50%. Only when these profits have been exhausted is a dividend traced to other accounts in the order fixed in the statute. Although the nominal rate of the corporation income tax in France is 50%, the French tax structure is such that a considerable amount of corporate income is taxed at a lower rate and some is taxed at a zero rate. For example, income from foreign branches is exempt; most intercorporate dividends are fully exempt; and capital gains realized by corporations often qualify for a preferential rate. As a result, a considerable portion of French corporate profits is taxed at less than the nominal statutory rate of 50%. Virtually every large French corporation is said to pay some portion of its dividends out of income that has been taxed at less than 50% and is thus liable for some additional tax or *précompte*. To avoid double taxation in situations in which the payment of dividends from certain accounts gives rise to special tax payments by corporations, the amount of the additional tax may be credited against those special tax obligations. Although the complexities involved in implementing such an adjustment are fewer than those involved in performing an adjustment at the shareholder level, they are still formidable. "A new fiscal monster" is the label given the additional tax by a French business journal.[30]

In Canada, the Carter Commission and the Finance Ministry's White Paper agreed on a dividends-received credit as the preferable form of integration. They also agreed on the need for adjustments if corporations paid dividends out of profits taxed at less than the recommended corporate rate of 50%, but they disagreed about the level at which the adjustments should be made. The Carter Commission concluded that all distributions should "carry a uniform rate of tax credit" and that this rate should be based on the current rate of the corporation income tax. If the corporation had paid tax at less than that current rate, the burden of adjustment would rest with the corporation. Tracing rules would be enacted for determining the order in which dividends were to be attributed to particular sources, and if the tax on the profits deemed to be the source of a particular dividend was less than the current statutory rate, the corporation would be required to pay additional tax. The Commission recognized that even this solution "presents some problems,"[31] but considered it simpler than other alternatives. In contrast, the White Paper proposed to "restrict the credit to shareholders of Canadian corporations by reference to the Canadian corporate tax actually paid . . . ."[32] How this restriction was to be implemented was not indicated.

The Canadian tax reform law enacted by Parliament took still a different position. The dividend credit is available to resident shareholders, whatever the rate of tax (if any) paid by the corporation. This rule is said to have been designed to prevent any bias against investment by Canadians in Canadian corporations with large foreign investments. Such corporations may pay little or no tax to Canada because of Canada's foreign tax credit and other special provisions for the taxation of income from foreign sources. Similarly, the rule will prevent bias against investment by Canadian residents in Canadian corporations owing no Canadian corporation income tax because of large depreciation deductions, for example, or because of Canada's tax incentives for Canadian oil and mining opera-

30. The additional tax is so complicated that commercial French tax services publish special guides to the tax.
31. See Appendix H, "Accounting and Reporting Procedures for the Integration of Corporation and Personal Income Taxes," in Canada, Royal Commission on Taxation, 4 *Report of the Royal Commission on Taxation* 661, 677.
32. Canada, Minister of Finance, *Proposals for Tax Reform* 54.

tions. In effect, these tax incentives would have been greatly reduced if a corporation entitled to the incentives were required to pay an additional tax when distributing profits to shareholders. The Canadian dividend credit is available to resident shareholders on all dividends from resident Canadian corporations "regardless of corporation taxes paid."[33]

In any event, whether the shareholder's credit should be related in one way or another to the corporation's tax payments (if any) is a major problem in the use of the shareholder credit. If some connection between the shareholder's credit and the corporation income tax is to exist, the technique to be used poses another problem.

A special difficulty with the dividends-received credit relates to periodic changes in the statutory rate of the corporation income tax. Suppose a corporation earns profits in a year in which the corporation income tax rate is 25%, but makes no distribution of those profits until three years later, by which time the tax rate is 50% and the country has enacted a dividends-received credit based (directly or indirectly) on the 50% rate. Is the shareholder's credit in the year of distribution to be reduced because the rate of tax paid in the year in which the profits were earned was lower than 50%?

One common device reduces the scope of this problem and also puts a premium on the reasonably prompt distribution of earnings; that device is to limit the credit to distributions from relatively recent earnings. In France, for example, any dividend paid out of "stale earnings"—profits earned more than five years prior to distribution—makes the corporation liable for payment of the additional tax. This is true whatever the rate of tax paid on those profits. In Canada, the White Paper proposed that a credit be provided only for dividends paid to shareholders within two and one half years of the corporation's taxation year.[34] This provision was necessary, according to the White Paper, in order to limit the total amount of claims outstanding against the government; otherwise, corporations might be able to accumulate "creditable tax" for ten or fifteen years and then pay large dividends entitling shareholders to large credits.

c. DISTRIBUTIONS OTHER THAN CASH

One objection to integration is that the existence of distribution relief may induce corporations to distribute a larger proportion of their earnings and

33. Canada, Department of Finance, *Summary of 1971 Tax Reform Legislation* 36. Belgium, like Canada, follows a practice opposite to the French. Belgium imposes no additional tax on the corporation to compensate for the shareholder credit if the dividends are paid from profits that have not borne tax. The shareholder is entitled to a uniform dividend credit in all cases.
34. Canada, Minister of Finance, *Proposals for Tax Reform* 49, 51.

therefore to retain a smaller proportion than purely business needs might suggest. The larger the amount of relief provided, the more serious this problem may become.

Countries using a dividends-received credit often seek to permit creditable (and taxable) distributions to be made in forms other than cash. The aim is to allow shareholders to enjoy distribution relief and at the same time to enable corporations to retain cash for business needs.

One type of noncash distribution entitling a shareholder to a tax credit may be a "stock dividend"—a dividend paid in shares of the issuing corporation. The tax law of the country involved must be such, however, that a stock dividend is treated as taxable income (in many countries, it is not so treated). Moreover, as a matter of corporation law, the issuance of a taxable stock dividend ordinarily requires the capitalization of surplus, which is sometimes a cumbersome process.

In 1966, the Carter Commission proposed that Canadian corporation and individual income taxes be integrated through the use of a 100% dividends-received credit. The Commission recognized that distribution relief of this magnitude (which exceeded that offered in any other developed country) might lead to excessive distributions of cash. Because of Canada's shortage of capital and because retained earnings are a major source of capital for growth and development, it was feared that the resulting depletion of retained earnings might impair Canadian development and make Canada even more dependent than it had been on foreign (primarily American) capital. To permit Canadian corporations and shareholders to enjoy the benefits of distribution relief without undue depletion of retained earnings—particularly if the capitalization of earnings to permit stock dividends might be difficult or impossible as a matter of corporation law—the Commission suggested an intermediate form of qualifying distribution. The Commission proposed the use of "allocation certificates" that would have significance only for tax purposes. Their purpose would be "to permit the shareholders to obtain the benefit of a distribution for tax purposes without a distribution actually being made."[35]

Under this proposal, a corporation that showed a profit but needed to retain its after-tax earnings for business operations would have been able to allocate all or any part of those earnings to shareholders by issuing "allocation certificates"—in effect, paper dividends. The certificates, like cash dividends, would have been treated as taxable dividend income to shareholders, entitling them to a tax credit and (under the Carter proposal) requiring gross-up (or refund) by a commensurate amount. The portion of earnings allocated to each shareholder would have been added to his cost basis (for purposes of determining gain or loss in the event of a subsequent

35. Canada, Royal Commission on Taxation, 4 *Report of the Royal Commission on Taxation* 55.

disposition). The corporation would have been required to set up a separate account on its books showing the amount of income "allocated" to shareholders. If allocated income was later distributed in cash from this account to shareholders, no additional tax was to be due from the shareholder, but the cost basis of his shares would have been reduced accordingly (again, for purposes of determining gain or loss). The proposal for "paper dividends" involved many complications, however (such as the treatment of nonresident shareholders, the treatment of shares held in the names of brokers, banks, or other nominees, and problems of allocation to a shareholder followed by the sale of his shares and a later distribution of the allocated income in cash to the new shareholder).

The Canadian Finance Minister later recommended a dividends-received credit at only one half of the rate proposed by the Carter Commission, namely, 50% instead of 100%. In view of this proposed reduction in the scope of distribution relief, the Minister rejected the recommendation that paper dividends or "allocation certificates" be recognized for tax purposes. He did, however, recommend that dividends paid in shares entitle shareholders to the same tax benefits as dividends paid in cash. The inclusion of stock dividends was designed to ensure that the integration "process should not by itself force corporations to pay out in cash a higher proportion of their profits than they would under the present system."[36] Canadian law now defines taxable dividends as including stock dividends; the taxable value is the increase in the paying corporation's paid-up capital resulting from payment of the dividend. The shareholder credit, in turn, is available with respect to any dividend from a Canadian corporation which is "required to be included" in the shareholder's taxable income. The result of these provisions is that a profit-making Canadian corporation can, in appropriate circumstances, retain cash for business needs and pay a dividend in shares which will entitle the shareholder to the same tax credit as a dividend in cash.

How important it may be to recognize noncash distributions for purposes of distribution relief will depend on such factors as the size of the credit, the presence or absence of gross-up, and the extent of the need for corporate cash retentions. In each case, moreover, the administrative complexities of extending distribution relief to noncash distributions must be weighed against the benefits.

d. Dividends From Foreign Corporations

Countries that give distribution relief to shareholders by way of a dividends-received credit generally apply the credit only to dividends from

36. Canada, Minister of Finance, *Proposals for Tax Reform* 51.

domestic corporations. They do not extend the credit to dividends from foreign corporations. This matter is discussed in Chapter 7, which deals with international aspects of integration.

Distribution relief as an integration device must be distinguished from a credit for foreign taxes as a method of alleviating international double taxation. The foreign tax credit is generally limited to foreign withholding taxes imposed at the source on dividend payments to nonresidents, though the United States and Japan give parent corporations (but not individual portfolio investors) an "indirect credit" for the underlying corporation income tax paid by foreign subsidiaries (see Chapter 7).

6/C.5. Qualifying Shareholders

a. Resident and Nonresident Shareholders

One reason, and usually the controlling reason, for providing distribution relief at the shareholder level rather than at the corporate level is to give resident shareholders preference over nonresident shareholders. Countries providing integration by way of a shareholder dividends-received credit generally limit the credit to resident shareholders; it is ordinarily not extended to nonresident shareholders, at least in the absence of a tax treaty. The circumstances in which complaints by tax treaty partners have led a country to provide equivalent credit benefits to certain nonresidents are discussed in Chapter 7.

b. Corporate Shareholders

Most countries exempt intercorporate dividends, either in full or in large part, from income taxation. If distribution relief is available at the shareholder level, it becomes necessary to correlate that relief with the intercorporate dividend exemption in order to prevent double relief.

6/C.6. Special Treatment for Small Corporations

Many countries provide special, preferential rules for the taxation of small, closely held, or private corporations. These rules may be regarded as an alternative to integration. One argument for integration is that the corporation is merely a formal device, substantially equivalent to a partnership, by which a group of persons combine their resources in order to carry on a business activity jointly. With regard to publicly held corporations, this proposition may be, as Professor van den Tempel observed, "obsolete." It retains some validity, however, in the case of the closely held corporation, which has only a few participants (sometimes only one) and whose ownership and management are essentially the same. Because of this difference, even countries that as a general rule provide no integration relief may offer special tax treatment to small, closely held corporations. The United States is an example. Its tax structure makes no general provision for integration,[37] but certain closely held corporations may opt to be taxed as partnerships. The United States also provides a preferential rate for corporate income under $25,000 (or $50,000).

Such tax preferences for small corporations reduce the weight of the argument that integration is necessary for the benefit of small corporations and their shareholders. For example, the United States, after dealing with the problem of small corporations in the manner just outlined, provides no other integration system for shareholders and corporations (large or small) in other circumstances.

Certain other countries provide both integration at the shareholder level (available to shareholders in both large and small corporations) and special relief (reduced rates, for example) to small corporations. Canada serves as an example. Under the tax structure effective in 1976, Canada provides both a shareholder dividend credit and small business relief for Canadian-controlled, closely held corporations which takes the form of a retention allowance for profits reinvested in the business.[38] This allowance operates to reduce the corporation income tax by one half—from the normal 50% rate to a preferential rate of 25%—on the first $150,000 per year of income from active business operations (until $750,000 of such income has been accumulated).

The correlation of this small business relief with distribution relief presents complexities under the Canadian scheme.[39] The net result of the Canadian arrangement, however, is to provide full integration of the corporation and individual income taxes in the case of dividends from small or private corporations but only partial integration in the case of dividends from large, widely held corporations.

Under the Canadian scheme, the degree of integration provided depends on the nature and the size of the corporation paying the dividend. Japan takes another approach; the degree of distribution relief it provides through its dividends-received credit depends on the size of the income of the

37. The minor dividend exclusion available in the United States ($100 for each taxpayer) may be ignored for this purpose.

38. If the private corporation makes an "ineligible investment" (in portfolio securities, for example), the tax saving is recaptured.

39. Mitchell, "Corporate-Source Income Under the Tax Reform Bill," 19 *Canadian Tax Journal* 379 (1971).

shareholder receiving the dividend, rather than on the size or the nature of the corporation paying the dividend. The dividends-received credit in Japan (which does not require gross-up) is lower for upper-income shareholders than it is for low-income shareholders (6/C.2).[40]

6/C.7. Effect on Compliance

Because a dividends-received credit is available only to those shareholders who report their dividends as income and then claim the credit, the use of a dividends-received credit is generally thought to improve shareholder compliance. Yet the credit does not guarantee that upper-bracket shareholders, who receive the bulk of all dividend payments, will report their dividend income; in fact, by reducing the tax due from the honest shareholder, the credit may merely reduce the scope of the tax saving available to the defrauding shareholder.[41] In many cases, the reporting of dividend income will result in a higher tax, despite the credit, than will the fraudulent omission of dividends from income, coupled with loss of the credit. Even with a credit system in effect, the actual withholding of preliminary tax from dividend payments may be appropriate as a means of fighting dividend tax fraud.

As was mentioned above in connection with France, integration at the shareholder level (by way of a dividend credit, for example) does not extend to nonresident shareholders. Moreover, integration at the shareholder level does not give distribution relief to those resident shareholders who own shares in domestic corporations but deposit them in tax havens abroad in order to evade tax. It is said that most of the shares in French corporations held by Swiss nominees are owned by French residents. The desire to avoid giving distribution relief to residents who conceal their shares abroad was an element in France's choice of integration at the shareholder rather than the corporate level. Because wealthy residents of less-developed countries are said to keep much of their wealth in Swiss,

40. At the same time, however, Japan provides lower tax rates for small corporations than for larger ones.

41. The United States does not withhold preliminary tax from dividends paid to resident shareholders. After emphasizing the amount of revenue raised by the corporation income tax, Professor Surrey asserts that that tax "is thus not easily displaced by any rival approach that disperses the tax collection and complicates the task of administration. Thus any approach which looks more to the shareholder for the tax on corporate profits must devise a more efficient system of collecting the tax on dividends than we possess today." Surrey, "Statement by Assistant Secretary of the Treasury Surrey, April 21, 1966, at the School of Law of the State University of New York [at Buffalo], on Federal Tax Policy in the 1960's," in United States, Treasury Department, *Annual Report of the Secretary of the Treasury on the State of Finances for the Fiscal Year Ended June 30, 1966*, 366, 377.

Caribbean, and other tax havens, this factor may make integration at the shareholder level more appropriate for developing countries than integration at the corporate level.

6/C.8. The Political Impact of Integration at the Shareholder Level

Chapter 3 discusses factors that may enter into a country's choice between integration at the corporate level and integration at the shareholder level. The political factor was mentioned among the various factors influencing the choice of the corporate rather than the shareholder level. Because shareholders are generally in the upper-income brackets, integration at either level will give them tax relief, but integration at the shareholder level makes it clear to the population at large that it is these upper-bracket individuals who are enjoying tax benefits. Political dissatisfaction may result.

It must be recognized, however, that because shareholders are more numerous than corporations, providing distribution relief to shareholders may attract more votes than providing distribution relief to corporations. Moreover, the largest proportion of shares is held by upper-income taxpayers, who, though few in number, may be politically powerful.

France offers a graphic example of the proposition that integration at the shareholder level may have serious political repercussions. As noted above, France adopted a shareholder dividend credit (*avoir fiscal*) equal to 50% of dividend income in 1965. The credit is available against tax on income from all sources, not merely against tax on dividend income; in appropriate circumstances, a shareholder who cannot take full advantage of the credit receives a refund.

Early in 1972, a French journal revealed that, despite his high income, the Prime Minister of France (M. Chaban-Delmas) had paid no income tax for several years. The Prime Minister's income included dividends in substantial amounts, and his dividends-received tax credit had been large enough to wipe out the income tax due on both his dividend and his nondividend income. The revelation that because of this tax concession, the Prime Minister had not had to pay any income tax—despite his comparatively high income—resulted in sharp criticism from political opponents.

The Prime Minister and the Minister of Finance used television, radio, and the press to defend the shareholder dividend credit and to protest that the Prime Minister, in claiming the credit, had acted fully in accordance with the law and that no fraud was involved. All was in vain; the French public was outraged. As *The Economist* reported[42]:

42. "France: Yes, But Should It Be Like That?" *The Economist*, 19 February 1972, p. 37.

> The avoir fiscal system which enabled M. Chaban-Delmas not actually to write a cheque to his tax collector can perfectly well be defended.... But it has become the symbol of a tax structure, and therefore of a society, which favours the influential and the rich.

The New York Times summarized the story in the following terms, under the headline "Premier's Tax Avoidance Stirs French"[43]:

> The system, "l'avoir fiscal," or "tax credit," instituted originally to encourage investment and discourage expatriation of funds, has become a symbol of an inequity that allows a man with a high income to evade what wage earners are forced to pay.

The Times added that "the windfall to the shareholder can hardly be exaggerated."[44] *The Economist* of London put it this way[45]:

> ...the income tax affair has done M. Chaban-Delmas peculiar harm. Willy nilly, he has become the symbol of a tax system which enables wealthy shareholders who get tax credits on their dividends thereby apparently to pay no taxes at all. The expert may claim that tax has already been paid on the taxpayer's behalf by the company concerned. For the public at large M. Chaban paid no taxes and that's that.

The following week, *The Economist* added that "it is now abundantly obvious that the imputation system is wide open to misrepresentation and political attack."[46]

Labor unions and opposition political parties announced a street demonstration to demand "fiscal justice."[47] Popular resentment of the Prime Minister's tax credits soon had two major results: in France, the Prime Minister was forced to resign, and in Germany, consideration of a tax reform bill that would have enacted a shareholder credit on the French model and would have taken effect in 1974 was postponed. Despite the

43. *The New York Times*, 7 February 1972, p. 7. See also "French Premier Denies Tax Fraud; Chaban, on T.V., Sees Charge As 'Political Maneuver,'" *The New York Times*, 16 February 1972, p. 1.
44. "France: A Premier Explains, or at Any Rate, Tries," *The New York Times*, 20 February 1972, sec. 4, p. 2.
45. "Giscard Lets the Hounds Slip," *The Economist*, 5 February 1972, p. 34.
46. "Chaban-Fiscal," *The Economist*, 12 February 1972, p. 74. *The Economist* added that the tax credit system "is criticised for the outrageous favors it appears to confer on those with dividend incomes, who have, however, already indirectly suffered the full whack of company tax. In Germany, the government's plan to go over to it has run into bitter opposition for the same reason."
47. "Chaban-Delmas's TV Speech Fails To Still Critics," *The New York Times*, 17 February 1972, p. 4.

political storm, the French government announced that it had no intention of ending the shareholder dividend credit.

The French Tax Council nevertheless cited the episode to show that the complex shareholder credit was misunderstood by the population despite seven years of experience with it.[48] The French problem and its impact in Germany suggest that a country considering the enactment of a shareholder dividend credit must take into account the confusion and the political repercussions that may follow from a device that can be called the "symbol of inequity," or "the symbol of a tax structure . . . which favours the influential and the rich."

6/D. Mixed or Dual-Level Integration Systems

Certain countries—Japan, in particular—provide some degree of integration at the corporate level and additional integration at the shareholder level. In these countries, there is a split-rate system at the corporate level (with a preferential rate for distributed profits) plus relief at the shareholder level by way of an indirect credit for part of the tax paid by the corporation on distributed profits (even though that tax is paid at a reduced rate). Until 1973, such a mixed system was used by Belgium, but the 1973 tax reform replaced it with an indirect shareholder credit based on the French model.

The reasons for such dual relief seem to be largely historical and political. Japan, for example, following the recommendation of the Shoup Mission, first adopted integration at the shareholder level.[49] Afterwards, it also introduced integration at the corporate level, with a view toward encouraging corporate equity financing rather than debt financing. Sometimes, it seems difficult for political reasons to withdraw completely a preferential tax treatment once it has been offered, even if a new and similar treatment is provided. As a result, a complicated system is likely to emerge.

48. See "Au Sénat: M. Jean Taittinger: La Suppression de l'avoir fiscal ne peut être envisagée," *Le Monde*, 27 April 1972, p. 10.

49. See also the Appendix, which describes the German system that went into effect in 1977.

7

International Aspects

7/A. Introduction

7/A.1. In General

In other chapters of this book, the corporation income tax and its integration with the individual income tax are dealt with in the context of a closed national economy. Those chapters assume that only one country is involved and that the corporation and its shareholders are residents of that country and therefore subject to its tax jurisdiction and no other. This chapter, in contrast, will consider the special problems that arise when more than one country is involved—for example, when the corporation is a resident of one country and the shareholder is a resident of another.

Generally speaking, an individual is regarded as a resident of a country for tax purposes if he is physically present in the country other than as a mere transient or sojourner or if he makes his home—his principal place of abode—in that country.[1] A corporation is regarded as a resident of a country if its head office or seat of management and control is located in that country or if it is incorporated under the laws of that country.[2] For purposes of this chapter, a person (physical or juridical) will be referred to as a "resident" of a country if he meets these qualifications.

A "resident" of a country may also be described as one of the great mass of taxpayers in a country to whom its general rules of taxation apply. Yet in addition to the many persons throughout the world who have no contact whatsoever with the country and who therefore may be disregarded for tax purposes, there are some persons who do have some contact with the

1. WTS: *United States*, 11/4.2a2; WTS: *Sweden*, 11/3.1; WTS: *France*, 11/2.1a.
2. WTS: *United States*, 11/1.2; WTS: *France*, 11/2.2a.

country which is not such as to bring them within the definition of "resident" given above. Although the contact exists, it is not enough to amount to residence or to qualify the person for taxation under the general rules applied to residents. Such persons will generally be referred to here as "nonresidents." If a country taxes nonresidents, it will tax them according to special rules, which are different from the rules generally applied to the great mass of residents. For the most part, these special rules for nonresidents will involve assertions of *in rem* jurisdiction. Although the contacts of nonresidents with a country may be insufficient to warrant asserting jurisdiction over them as residents, the income generated by their contacts will be regarded as a *res*, a thing, over which the country has enough physical jurisdiction to levy and collect a tax.

Suppose, for example, that *A*, a resident of country *X*, buys shares of a corporation resident in country *Y* and that the corporation then declares a dividend on those shares. *A*'s ownership of those shares may be *A*'s sole contact with country *Y*. As a general rule, *Y* will not regard *A* as a resident and will not subject *A* to the income tax generally levied on *Y*'s residents. Yet, again as a general rule, *Y* will assert its jurisdiction over the dividend income of nonresident *A* by imposing a withholding tax.

Earlier chapters in this book indicated that any system of integration adds complexity to a country's national tax structure. The complexities of integration multiply, however, if international factors are introduced. Suppose that country *Y* adopts integration at the corporate level and allows resident corporations to deduct from their taxable income all "normal" dividends paid on their shares (see Chapter 5). Should the deduction include otherwise qualifying distributions paid to *A*, who is a nonresident and not subject to *Y*'s individual income tax? Or, suppose that *Y* adopts integration at the shareholder level and gives shareholders a dividends-received credit that is designed to refund a portion of the corporation income tax levied on the corporations paying the dividends (see Chapter 6). Should that credit, or any comparable relief, be extended to *A*, the nonresident shareholder? And are the answers to such questions different if the nonresident shareholder is not an individual, but rather a parent corporation that is a resident of country *X* and owns all of the shares of a subsidiary in country *Y*?

As a practical matter, the answers to international questions of this sort tend to vary with the nature of the country's integration system, with the amount of distribution relief involved, and particularly with the level (corporate or shareholder) at which integration is offered. Indeed, the essential difference between integration at the corporate level and integration at the shareholder level, according to the Common Market report cited in Chapter 4, lies in the international area.[3] Systems of integration at the corporate level generally offer distribution relief to any otherwise qualifying distribution, whether it goes to a resident or to a nonresident shareholder. By contrast, systems of integration at the shareholder level generally limit relief to resident shareholders and exclude nonresidents from their benefits.

Moreover, integration at the corporate level provides no benefits to resident shareholders who invest abroad; integration at the shareholder level provides no benefits to either nonresident shareholders or to resident shareholders who invest abroad. In either case, integration introduces elements of discrimination and nonneutrality into the tax structure. The meaning of these terms in this context is clear from Professor Surrey's comments after France adopted integration at the shareholder level in 1965. Speaking of the French and similar systems, Mr. Surrey said[4]:

> Some of these systems involve integration of the corporate tax with the individual shareholders' taxes on distributed dividends, through credits to these shareholders for the corporate tax. Their structure, by limiting those credits to domestic shareholders in domestic corporations, discriminates against both their domestic shareholders who invest abroad and the shareholders from abroad who invest in their domestic corporations.

Mr. Surrey added[5] that international tax relations should be grounded in

> two basic concepts: first, the concept of long-range neutrality in a country's tax system between those of its investors who invest at home and those who invest abroad; and second, the concept of non-discrimination in a country's tax system between its investors at home and investors from abroad.

Although Mr. Surrey left the U.S. Treasury Department, the Treasury continued to object vigorously to the international consequences of the adoption by other countries—especially the Common Market countries—of integration at the shareholder level based on the French model, which is described in Chapter 6. The French system, like other systems of integration at the shareholder level, gives relief only to French shareholders in French corporations; in the absence of a treaty, it gives no relief to U.S. shareholders in French corporations or to French shareholders in U.S. corporations. In 1972, the Treasury's Director for International Affairs

3. Communauté Économique Européene, Commission, *Le Développement d'un marché européen des capitaux* 225.
4. Surrey, "The United States Tax System and International Relationships—Current Developments, 1965–6," 20 *Bulletin for International Fiscal Documentation* 45, 46 (1966).
5. Surrey, "The United States Tax System and International Relationships—Current Developments, 1965–6," 20 *Bulletin for International Fiscal Documentation* 45, 46 (1966).

therefore asserted that "the long-range tendency of the French system is clearly in the direction of restricting capital flows."[6]

The remedy for the international discrimination and nonneutrality thus introduced by integration lies, Mr. Surrey suggested, in tax treaties. The negotiation of tax treaties is a slow and cumbersome process, however. Although developing countries are entering into tax treaties more and more often, their treaty network is not yet as comprehensive as that of the developed countries. For that reason, it may not be enough for a developing country that is considering the adoption of an integration scheme to expect tax treaties to solve any international problems that may result. In its own national interest, a developing country must consider how and to what extent the international problems of integration can be taken into account within its own statutory scheme.

Another factor that a country must consider in deciding whether to adopt an integration scheme is the element of international tax competition. When France adopted integration in 1965, the Minister of Finance emphasized that Germany and Belgium already provided integration to their residents. The result was that the French taxation of corporate-source income was "considerably more burdensome" than that of its Common Market competitors. The Finance Minister added[7]:

> If this difference of regime is not reduced, French capital will be induced to invest outside our frontiers, while an artificial depreciation of French security prices will facilitate the takeover . . . of our industry by foreign investors.
>
> It is appropriate, therefore, to reduce the tax on distributed income to a level comparable to that which has been adopted by Germany.

This kind of international competition in tax reduction may be particularly acute in such economic communities as the Common Market, but it is not necessarily limited to such communities. It may extend to developing countries as well. Suppose that a corporate investor from a developed country has the choice of establishing a subsidiary to build a plant in either of two developing countries, both located in the same part of the world. Will the nonresident corporation be influenced in its choice by either country's method of taxing corporations and shareholders?[8]

6. Gordon, "International Fiscal Arrangements Distorted by Foreign Tax Policies; New Rules Needed," 37 *Journal of Taxation* 113 (1972).

7. See Norr, "The French Reform of Dividend Taxation and Common Market Tax Harmonization," 44 *Taxes* 320, 322 (1966).

8. The answer to this question may be affected by the widespread use of tax incentives in the developing countries. If a country offers a tax holiday at the corporate level, or exempts dividends on approved foreign investments at the shareholder level, for example, the country's general method of taxing corporations and shareholders may be of little significance to the potential foreign investor.

Although it is necessary to recognize the possibility of such influence, it is equally necessary to avoid exaggerating the role of taxation in investment decisions. Years ago, Professor Butters' research indicated that "nontax considerations frequently are of much greater significance than tax considerations in determining the basic decisions" of business management.[9] Speaking particularly of the impact of integration on international investment, Professor Wheatcroft made the same point: "Don't overestimate the tax factor in investment. . . . . We all take tax into account when we do international business, but it isn't the decisive factor."[10]

Even if not decisive, international considerations must at least be taken into account by a country that is considering whether integration, or any particular method of integration, is in its national interest. The potential impact both on nonresident investors and on residents who may be considering either investment abroad or capital flight must be kept in mind.

The discussion in this chapter places a certain amount of emphasis on developments within the European Common Market. The reason is that the Common Market is the place where the impact of integration has been the most apparent and where the most thought has been given to treaty and other solutions to the international problems created by integration.

7/A.2. International Double Taxation and National Two-Tier Taxation

Integration seeks to deal with the problems raised by the taxation of income at two *levels*, the corporate level and the shareholder level. Whether integrated or not, however, most tax systems include provisions intended to deal with the problems raised by the taxation of income by two *countries*. These provisions offer unilateral relief designed to reduce or eliminate the international double taxation of foreign-source income—that is, taxation both by the country of source (from which the income is derived) and by the country of residence of the recipient of the income. This relief may take various forms: the deduction of foreign taxes, the exemption of foreign-source income, or a credit for foreign taxes, for example.

In any event, it is essential to distinguish tax provisions intended to mitigate or eliminate the burden of international double taxation from tax provisions intended to mitigate or eliminate the burden of national two-tier taxation. The two sets of provisions have different objectives. Yet they

9. Butters, "Taxation, Incentives, and Financial Capacity," 44 *American Economic Review, Papers and Proceedings* 504, 506 (1954).

10. Wheatcroft, "A Summing Up," in Canadian Tax Foundation, *Report of the Proceedings of the Twenty-Second Tax Conference* 408, 413.

sometimes overlap, and the problem of correlating them is often particularly difficult.

7/A.3. Tax Treaties

The developing countries do not yet have a network of tax treaties as comprehensive as that of the developed countries, but the number of treaties to which developing countries are parties is increasing rapidly. The process of negotiating or renegotiating tax treaties must involve some attempt to correlate different systems of integration. The "extraordinary anarchy of the systems in force"[11] in the different countries of the world is one source of difficulty in this process.

Another is that integration systems are in a state of flux and instability. Presumably because of dissatisfaction with the results of whatever systems of integration they may be using, the developed countries often change their systems; these changes, in turn, are followed by changes in their international tax treaty arrangements—changes that are not easy to make. The 1946 treaty between the United States and Great Britain was predicated on the British system of distribution relief, which at that time involved tax credits for shareholders. Great Britain replaced this system in 1965 with an unintegrated system based on the American model, and this change was followed in 1966 by a protocol that amended the treaty to take account of Britain's new system. In 1973, however, Great Britain changed back to an integrated system based on the French model (see Chapter 6), and new treaty arrangements again followed.

After Germany adopted split rates of 51% for retained profits and 15% for distributed profits, problems arising out of the existence of foreign subsidiaries in Germany required changes in many of Germany's treaties, including its treaty with the United States. In addition, France's adoption of integration in 1965 required amendments of France's treaties with Germany, Switzerland, the United States, the United Kingdom, and several other countries; indeed, France contemplates amending or renegotiating all of its tax treaties to take account of its integration scheme.

The coexistence of different systems of integration in various countries around the world, the pattern of change and flux from one system to another within individual countries, and the difficulty of amending tax treaties to take account of changing systems all threaten to distort the

11. Cardyn, "General Report: The Multiple Burden on Dividends and Shares by Taxation on Income and Capital of Both Corporations and Shareholders," 55a *Cahiers de droit fiscal international* I/39 (1970).

international flow of capital and investment. As far as treaties are concerned, the problems of arranging mutual accommodations between countries using different corporation-shareholder tax structures appear to be more difficult than those involved in working out tax treaties between countries that have unintegrated corporation and individual income taxes. In unintegrated systems, the taxation of the corporation is not related to the taxation of the shareholder. The corporation is taxed uniformly on all its profits, whether distributed or undistributed, and no adjustment is made for distributions. It is therefore immaterial whether the recipient of the distribution is a resident or a nonresident. Similarly, the shareholder is taxed on his dividend receipts, and no adjustment is made for any tax paid by the corporation. Because the shareholder receives no adjustment in any case, the residence of the corporation paying the dividend does not affect the situation. In negotiating a tax treaty between two countries with unintegrated systems, it is necessary only to correlate the tax systems so that international double taxation is avoided. It is not necessary also to correlate the two systems so that one country's corporation income tax is adjusted to the other country's individual income tax, or vice versa.

As soon as one country introduces some degree of integration (thereby relating the corporation and the individual income taxes), the situation becomes more complicated. It is then necessary to correlate the tax systems of treaty partners not only in order to avoid international double taxation but also in order to take account of the distribution relief that one or the other (or both) of them offers. Moreover, the problem of correlating the two systems in the latter respect is relatively new. Because integration has become significant only in recent years, no pattern of international accommodation has been established yet.

The draft tax treaty published in 1963 by the Fiscal Committee of the Organisation for Economic Co-operation and Development was based on the assumption that both treaty partners would be using unintegrated tax structures. The draft recognized that some countries used integrated systems but considered the resulting problems to be "special," arising out of "peculiarities" in some national tax laws.[12] Later the OECD acknowledged that integration had become more than a peculiarity of certain countries, however. After reviewing the various problems that the integration of the corporation and individual income taxes raises with regard to the free international flow of capital, the OECD made the following statement[13]:

12. Organisation for Economic Co-operation and Development, Fiscal Committee, *Draft Double Taxation Convention on Income and Capital* 104.

13. "New Emphasis on Taxation Policy: OECD Sets Up a New Committee on Fiscal Affairs," 11 *European Taxation* I/206, I/207 (1971); reprinted from *OECD Observer*, August 1971, pp. 12, 14.

> The separate system does not differentiate between residents who invest at home or abroad, since the residents get no credit or special rate treatment when they invest at home. Under other systems which give some kind of relief in respect of domestic corporation tax paid but do not extend it to foreign corporation tax, there is an a priori presumption that investment at home of residents is encouraged.
>
> In the actual world of co-existing systems, however, the disincentive to invest abroad may be reduced, removed, or even reversed as a result of the tax treatment given in the foreign country where investment takes place. If it takes place in a country with a split-rate system, the investor automatically gets the benefit of the lower rate for distributed profits, and if it takes place in a country with an imputation system he may get the benefit of the tax credit, depending upon whether or not the country is prepared to extend it to non-residents, but in any case will have to claim it.
>
> Where direct investment is concerned, the situation can differ. As regards inward direct investment the split-rate system encourages foreign firms to set up subsidiaries rather than branches and the imputation systems discourage both the setting up of branches and subsidiaries whilst the separate system appears neutral between the two. The systems as such have no effect on outward direct investment, though it may be noted in passing that outward direct investment is usually discouraged either because of the overspill problem or because of intermediary withholding taxes paid in the country of investment but not fully credited.

Three major studies of the impact of integration at the international level conclude that integration raises such acute international problems and threatens to create such interference with the free flow of investment capital that unintegrated tax systems are preferable. In a study made for the European Economic Community, Professor van den Tempel recommended that if international as well as domestic aspects were considered, an unintegrated corporation-shareholder tax structure "is the most suitable to be adopted as a harmonized system in the European Economic Communities."[14]

Although the Commission of the European Economic Community announced in November 1973 its intention of proposing to the Council (as part of the process of aligning the structure of legislation within the Common Market) that all nine member countries be required to adopt integration at the shareholder level,[15] it once stated that it could not rule out the adoption of a "classic" or unintegrated tax structure for the Common Market. To a "great extent," the Commission asserted at that time, it

14. Van den Tempel, *Corporation Tax and Individual Income Tax in the European Communities* 41.

15. Such a directive was proposed in 1975, undoubtedly because of the already increased use of integration at the shareholder level within the countries involved.

shared Professor van den Tempel's view that since any "technical complication was of a nature to restrict the movements of capital," considerations of tax technique "particularly as to international relations" should be controlling (determinant) in the choice of the Common Market's common structure of corporation and individual income taxes. The unintegrated tax structure recommended by Professor van den Tempel seemed "particularly suitable" for use within the Common Market for two equally important reasons: one, "the absence of any aspect of discrimination," and the other, its "technical simplicity."[16]

The van den Tempel study dealt only with developed countries, especially the problems of harmonizing the different systems of integration used by the Common Market countries. Nevertheless, his conclusion that the complications of integration are of a nature to restrict the movement of capital may be of particular importance to developing countries, whose development may depend, at least in part, on a flow of capital from foreign sources.

In a later survey that considers relations among developing countries as well as among developed countries, Professor Cardyn also concluded that only an unintegrated tax structure could ensure the degree of neutrality appropriate to international tax relationships.[17] He was driven to support the use of "classic" unintegrated tax systems, Professor Cardyn stated, "by experience of the sometimes insuperable distortions produced by the other methods [integration], and by the knowledge that these distortions are more serious the greater the degree of integration of the two taxes."[18]

A more recent and comprehensive study of the international implications of the integration of corporation and individual income taxes was made by two economists in the International Monetary Fund. After reviewing matters in the light of key analytical criteria—namely, world efficiency, national efficiency, and inter-country equity—they concluded[19]:

16. "Structure de l'impôt des sociétés" (Doc. 7228/XIV/70-D de la Commission des Communautés Européenes du 29 Mai 1970), ¶ 8, reprinted in 41 *La Fiscalité du Marché Commun* 93, 97 (1970) (unofficial translation from French text).

17. Cardyn, "General Report: The Multiple Burden on Dividends and Shares by Taxation on Income and Capital of Both Corporations and Shareholders," 55a *Cahiers de droit fiscal international* I/39, I/67 (1970).

18. Cardyn, "General Report: The Multiple Burden on Dividends and Shares by Taxation on Income and Capital of Both Corporations and Shareholders," 55a *Cahiers de droit fiscal international* I/39, I/66 (1970). After considering Germany's efforts to renegotiate its tax treaties to counteract the advantages given to certain nonresident shareholders by Germany's system of integration at the corporate level, another commentator said: "The complications are of such a nature that it also appears more desirable in this respect not to discriminate for tax purposes between the treatment of undistributed and distributed profits." International Bureau of Fiscal Documentation, *Annual Report, 1964*, 5–6.

19. Sato and Bird, "International Aspects of the Taxation of Corporations and Shareholders," 22 *International Monetary Fund Staff Papers* 384, 444–445 (1975).

Whatever the domestic advantages and disadvantages of the alternative systems of taxing corporations and shareholders discussed in this paper, it is clear that the different systems vary widely in their international implications. Judged by the criterion of world-wide efficient resource allocation (in an undistorted market), which has been provisionally taken as a standard of reference here, any integration system involves difficulties and complexities.

The split rate system, for example, poses serious practical problems in that the full crediting needed to achieve neutrality may be complicated by the refund problem if a low effective corporation tax rate is applied under this system—that is, if there is a high ratio of dividends to total profits. There are also technical difficulties in achieving capital-export neutrality in the case of individual portfolio investment. Full equalization of tax burdens between domestic and foreign investments would thus be difficult to achieve.

The dividend credit system, while free of some of these problems, has to integrate foreign corporation tax with domestic personal income tax in order to achieve capital-export neutrality. As evidenced by the debates in the United Kingdom, France, and Canada, this requirement presents practical difficulties for the achievement of capital-export neutrality by the capital exporter. These problems are particularly acute when the capital-importing country imposes a high corporation tax on foreign-owned investments. Extension of the dividend credit to foreign investors may serve the purpose of capital-import neutrality, but it also complicates the tax arrangements necessary to achieve capital-export neutrality in the investor's country. The problems are essentially the same, but more serious, for a full integration system. If corporate policy is assumed to be affected by the personal income tax under full integration, these difficulties are compounded by the need to equalize the personal tax burden between domestic and foreign investments. The problems to which any integration system gives rise are not significantly reduced when the corporation tax is assumed to be universally shifted.

The separate entity [unintegrated] system, however, escapes these difficulties and thus clearly a superior system in terms of capital-export neutrality. Although the system is not entirely free of problems, it appears to provide better basis for the attainment of "world efficiency"—that is, the efficient allocation of capital among countries.

7/B. Unintegrated Tax Structures

As a background to the discussion in the following sections of the impact of integration in the international area, it may be appropriate to summarize how unintegrated tax structures generally operate in the international area. The United States, France before its adoption of a shareholder dividend credit in 1965, and Sweden before its adoption of a limited dividend deduction in 1960 serve as examples.

7/B.1. Corporate Level

First, a corporation income tax is levied uniformly on all profits, retained and distributed. No distribution relief is granted, regardless of whether distributions go to residents or nonresidents.

Second, with regard to corporate profits from foreign sources, some form of relief from international double taxation is given to corporations by the country of residence to take account of taxes levied on those profits by the country of source. This relief may take the form of a credit for foreign taxes (the United States), a deduction for foreign taxes (Sweden), or an exemption (France). In any event, this relief is designed to eliminate or mitigate international double taxation; no element of integration or distribution relief is involved.

Third, if a corporation receives dividends from other resident corporations, some form of intercorporate dividend exemption is provided to the recipient corporation in order to avoid "chain taxation." Intercorporate dividend exemptions may or may not apply to dividends from nonresident corporations. If intercorporate dividend exemptions do not apply, the recipient corporation is ordinarily entitled to a foreign tax credit or some other form of relief from international double taxation in the country of residence in order to take account of any tax levied in the country of source.

7/B.2. Shareholder Level

First, a resident shareholder is subject to an individual income tax on dividends from domestic corporations. There is no integration adjustment to take account of tax paid at the corporate level. If a dividend from a domestic corporation is paid out of profits earned by a corporation abroad, relief from international double taxation which is given to the corporation on those profits generally does not spill over to the shareholder.

Second, a resident shareholder is subject to an individual income tax on dividends from nonresident corporations. There is no integration adjustment to take account of tax paid at the corporate level. Generally speaking, a resident shareholder is entitled to relief from international double taxation which takes account of any tax (ordinarily a withholding tax) levied on the dividends by the country of source.

Third, a nonresident shareholder is not subject to an individual income tax on income in the country of source. Instead, dividends are generally subject to a flat-rate withholding tax in the country of source.

7/B.3. International Implications

In its operation, an unintegrated corporation-individual tax system presents some complexity; generally, however, it is neutral and nondiscriminatory in its international impact. Because resident corporations are not entitled to distribution relief in any event, no question arises about whether to extend distribution relief to dividends going to nonresident shareholders. Because resident shareholders are not entitled to distribution relief with respect to dividends from resident corporations, no question arises about whether to provide distribution relief for dividends going to nonresident shareholders or for dividends received by resident shareholders from nonresident corporations. Although the country of residence may give some relief from international double taxation to take account of taxation by the country of source, resident shareholders pay income tax on an equal basis with respect to all dividends, whether from resident or nonresident corporations. Nonresident shareholders are ordinarily not subject to the individual income tax in the country that is the source of the dividend; but in lieu thereof, a withholding tax is applied.

Because of the nondiscriminatory and relatively simple nature of unintegrated tax structures, two countries with such structures which are at comparable stages of development find it relatively easy to agree on tax treaty clauses dealing with corporations and shareholders. Indeed, the treaties follow a relatively standard pattern, based on the principle of reciprocity. To apply that principle, the treaties need make no great changes in the pattern of corporation and shareholder taxation described above. Most treaties, however, provide a reciprocal reduction of the withholding tax levied by the country of source on dividends going to the country of residence: from 25% to 30% in the typical nontreaty case to 15% in the case of dividends to portfolio investors and 5% in the case of dividends from subsidiaries to parent corporations. In turn, on a reciprocal basis, the country of residence ordinarily agrees to take account of the withholding tax levied by the country of source, generally by giving resident shareholders a credit for that tax.

7/C. Integration at the Corporate Level

7/C.1. In General

Systems of integration at the corporate level ordinarily provide distribution relief to resident corporations for all qualifying distributions, without regard to the residence of the shareholder. Distribution relief in such systems of integration goes to the corporation; the test of eligibility for relief is the residence of the corporation, not the residence of the shareholder. In giving distribution relief for dividends paid to nonresident as well as resident shareholders, these systems of integration therefore merely reflect in the international area the pattern that they exhibit domestically. On the domestic scene, distribution relief ordinarily goes to the corporation regardless of the tax status of the shareholder (that is, whether or not the shareholder is in fact subject to the individual income tax on his dividend receipt). At the international level, distribution relief goes to the corporation even if the dividend recipient, as a nonresident, is outside the reach of the source country's individual income tax structure. The split-rate systems relied upon in the past by Germany and by Japan serve as examples. In each case, the lower rate for distributed profits was available to a resident corporation even with respect to dividends paid to nonresident shareholders.

It is precisely because distribution relief at the corporate level extends to dividends paid to nonresident as well as resident shareholders that France and Canada *rejected* integration at the corporate level. Instead, those countries chose integration at the shareholder level, which provides relief only to resident shareholders (see 7/D below).

As previously noted, integration seeks to reduce the burden of the corporation income tax on the distributed component of corporate profits. If, indeed, that is its aim, it may be argued that there is no reason to deny the benefit of that reduction to nonresident shareholders. In most cases, nonresident shareholders, though not subject to the individual income tax in the country of the source of the dividend, are subject to a withholding tax in lieu of the individual income tax. In short, if there is two-tier taxation when dividends are paid to resident shareholders, there is at least a degree of two-tier taxation when dividends are paid to nonresidents. The difference is that in the nonresident case, the second tier is flat rate (a withholding tax) rather than progressive (an income tax). The application of a withholding tax to distributions to nonresidents is also relied upon to justify the allowance to the corporation of distribution relief that extends to those distributions. In defense of the fact that integration at the corporate level would give relief to dividends paid out to foreigners, a British report asserted that the existence of Britain's withholding tax on dividends to nonresidents serves "to balance the distribution relief on those dividends."[20]

If, however, there is no withholding tax on dividends paid to nonresidents, there may be no justification for giving resident corporations distribution relief with respect to distributions to nonresidents. Sweden, for example, provides distribution relief at the corporate level by way of a deduction for "normal" dividends paid on certain new share issues.

20. United Kingdom, Chancellor of the Exchequer, *Reform of Corporation Tax* 12.

Sweden also withholds tax at the source (at a 30% rate) in the case of dividends paid to nonresidents; Swedish tax treaties generally reduce, but do not eliminate, this tax. Under this system of integration, Sweden usually allows corporations to deduct otherwise qualified dividends paid to nonresidents even if a tax treaty reduces the rate of the Swedish withholding tax, as long as some Swedish withholding tax is payable with respect to those dividends. Further, Sweden's law governing the deductibility of dividends unilaterally provides that if a Swedish tax treaty eliminates withholding entirely on dividends to shareholders in the other treaty country (that is, reduces the Swedish withholding rate to zero), the Swedish dividend-paying corporation is not to enjoy a deduction for the dividends paid to those particular nonresident shareholders.

The added administrative burden of such a rule, which denies distribution relief at the corporate level for dividends paid to those nonresidents which enjoy a zero withholding rate, is small. Most countries require the withholding of tax at the source from dividends to nonresidents, and most tax treaties reduce the normal statutory rate. Every corporation (or its dividend-paying agent) must, in any event, scrutinize all of its dividends to nonresidents and determine the withholding rate (whether determined by treaty or statute) applicable to each dividend. There is little additional burden in providing that no distribution relief will be available to a dividend-paying corporation for those dividends to which a zero treaty rate applies.

Sweden uses its own tax law to deal with the problem of distribution relief at the corporate level for distributions not subject to withholding when paid to nonresidents, but another alternative is to resort to the tax treaty device. In that case, distribution relief would apply at the corporate level in the usual manner for all dividend distributions, whether to resident or nonresident shareholders, but the country's tax treaties could seek to compensate for the relief thereby given to nonresident shareholders by increasing the withholding tax on dividends to nonresidents to a rate higher than the customary treaty rate of withholding. The Fiscal Committee of the OECD suggested this possibility "to ensure that non-resident shareholders . . . are not in a more favourable tax position than resident shareholders."[21] Yet a compensatory increase in the withholding tax on

21. Organisation for Economic Co-operation and Development, Fiscal Committee, *Draft Double Taxation Convention on Income and Capital* 105. In the United Kingdom, the bulk of investment from overseas is direct investment by U.S. parent corporations. It has been said that the United Kingdom could afford to adopt integration at the corporate level only if the United States would agree to compensate the United Kingdom by nonreciprocal withholding rates: 5%, for example, on dividends from U.S. subsidiaries to U.K. parents and 30% on dividends from U.K. subsidiaries to U.S. parents. Chown, "The Reform of Corporation Tax: Some International Factors," 1971 *British Tax Review* 215, 219.

dividends paid to nonresidents by countries using split-rate systems may be difficult to arrange (see, for example, the discussion below of the treaty between Germany and the United States).

As a general rule, though, countries that adopt integration at the corporate level give distribution relief for all distributions, whether the shareholder is a resident or a nonresident. An argument in support of this practice is that the denial of such relief increases the burden on resident corporations and resident shareholders. A split-rate system amounts to a progressive tax on corporations (see Chapter 5): the corporate tax rate increases as distributions eligible for relief decline. To the extent that distributions to nonresidents do not qualify for relief, the corporation's tax rate rises—to the detriment, presumably, of the corporation and its resident shareholders.[22]

7/C.2. Direct Investment: Dividends From Resident Subsidiaries to Nonresident Parent Corporations

A major portion of international investment is represented by direct investment rather than portfolio investment. This is true even within such highly developed countries as Germany and Sweden, in which the existence of modern stock exchanges and a network of underwriters and stockbrokers makes portfolio investment from overseas relatively simple. The predominance of foreign direct investment over foreign portfolio investment may be even greater in the developing countries. The portfolio investor from a capital-exporting country will find it difficult (in many cases, even impossible) to make a portfolio investment in a developing country. An investor from a capital-exporting country (particularly a corporate investor), however, will have little or no difficulty in making a direct investment in a developing country by establishing a subsidiary there.

The considerable quantity of international investment represented by direct investment and the fact that distribution relief at the corporate level in effect spills over to nonresident shareholders have proven to be a major cause of difficulty in the operation of systems of integration at the corporate level. Such systems appear to be nondiscriminatory because resident and nonresident shareholders alike may benefit from distribution relief. In fact, however, they introduce a new element of discrimination in favor of nonresident parent companies. The nonresident parent (to whom

22. Van den Tempel points out, moreover, that in a country providing distribution relief at the corporate level, a denial of that relief with respect to distributions to nonresidents would mean a greater tax burden for corporations with foreign ownership than for corporations owned domestically. This might constitute a violation of the nondiscrimination clauses often found in tax treaties. Van den Tempel, *Corporation Tax and Individual Income Tax in the European Communities* 25.

local distribution relief spills over) is in a position to control the dividend policy of the resident subsidiary on the basis of tax rather than business considerations. Germany, which was up to 1977 the major example of a country using a corporate-level system of integration and the country with perhaps the widest gap between its rates on retained profits (51%) and distributed profits (15%), serves as an example.[23]

As a practical matter, a publicly held German corporation seeking to take maximum advantage of the lower rate for distributed earnings but at the same time needing capital for its business operations is hardly in a position to distribute earnings to the maximum extent and then to obtain an equivalent sum from its shareholders (as loans or as contributions to capital, for example). But the German subsidiary of a foreign parent company (an American company, for example) is in a different position. The U.S. parent has far more discretion in fixing the dividend policy of its foreign subsidiary than does a German corporation that must deal directly with its own shareholders. The Germany subsidiary is virtually in a position to pay out to its parent the largest dividend that will qualify for the reduced rate of tax. Such a tax-induced dividend might exceed the amount that would be disbursed on the basis of normal business and financial considerations. Yet if the subsidiary thereafter needs funds, temporarily or permanently, to meet its operating needs, it may obtain those funds from its parent, for example, "in the form of new share capital or as a loan to the business."[24] After Germany widened the gap in its rates on retained and distributed profits to 36 percentage points, such practices became increasingly common; as a result, some foreign-owned subsidiaries in Germany were enjoying a tax advantage over German-owned corporations.[25]

23. The problem was not limited to Germany. It is emphasized in the United Kingdom, for example, that if an American or other nonresident parent corporation owns a U.K. subsidiary, "the distribution policy [of the subsidiary] can be adjusted to the tax interests of the non-resident shareholder." That is, distribution relief at the corporate level may lead to excessive distributions to foreign parent corporations, with adverse effects both on tax revenues and the balance of payments in the country in which the subsidiary is located. Chown, "The Reform of Corporation Tax: Some International Factors," 1971 *British Tax Review* 215, 218.

24. Rädler and Edwards, "The Split Rate of Corporation Income Tax in Germany—A Tax Advantage for Foreign-Owned Subsidiaries," *CCH Common Market Reports* (Transfer Binder) ¶ 9051 (1963).

25. See Wrede, "Reform of the Corporation Tax and the Trade Tax," in Great Britain, Parliament, House of Commons, *Report From the Select Committee on Corporation Tax* 203, 208. (The abandonment of integration at the corporate level and the use, in its place, of integration at the shareholder level "eliminates the privileged position of foreign groups.") See also Musgrave, "Harmonization of Direct Business Taxes: A Case Study," in Shoup (ed.), 2 *Fiscal Harmonization in Common Markets* 207, 243. (Because of the preferential rate for distributed profits at the corporate level in the country of the subsidiary's residence, a larger share of the tax base is transferred from that country to the country of the parent's residence.)

In the case of U.S. subsidiaries, the 1954 treaty between Germany and the United States fixed the withholding rate at 15% (compared to Germany's nontreaty rate of 25% and the U.S. nontreaty rate of 30%). It was the combination of (1) the reduced treaty rate of withholding on dividends to U.S. shareholders and (2) the reduced statutory rate of the corporate tax on distributions (including distributions to U.S. parent corporations) that led to the alleged tax advantage of U.S. parent corporations with subsidiaries in Germany.

If the interrelationship of the U.S. and German tax structures is taken into account, however, it is far from clear that U.S. parent corporations actually benefited from the combination of German tax reductions mentioned above. Under U.S. tax law, U.S. corporations are taxed on their world-wide income, including their dividends from foreign subsidiaries. At the same time, though, these corporations are entitled to a credit for foreign taxes. The U.S. foreign tax credit has two separate elements: (1) a direct credit for the foreign withholding tax imposed on dividends from the subsidiary and (2) an indirect credit for that portion of the corporation income tax paid by the subsidiary which is allocable to the profits from which the dividend was paid.[26] Hence, if a dividend is paid by a German subsidiary to a U.S. parent corporation, the U.S. parent receives a credit for German taxes paid. In the usual case, then, a reduction in German taxes on the subsidiary and its dividends results in a reduction in the U.S. foreign tax credit; in turn, the reduced credit results in a higher U.S. tax. The beneficiary of German distribution relief therefore appears to be the U.S. treasury rather than U.S. parent corporations. Yet this might not have been true in all cases, and it might not have been true if, for example, the German subsidiary was not owned directly by the U.S. parent, but indirectly through the intermediary of a Swiss or other third-country holding company that, in its turn, did not redistribute to the U.S. parent the dividends received from the German subsidiary. In such a case, the combination of German distribution relief, a reduced German withholding rate, and the additional element of a low level of tax in the third country might give the U.S. firm a genuine tax saving in comparison to an all-German firm. As a general proposition, however, it would seem that the German treasury's loss was the U.S. treasury's gain and that in the case of a U.S. parent and German subsidiary, the real beneficiary of German distribution relief was the U.S. treasury, rather than the U.S. parent corporation, as is commonly alleged.[27]

In the case of German subsidiaries paying dividends to German parent

26. See WTS: *United States*, 11/3.2; Owens and Ball, 1 *The Indirect Credit*.

27. The Carter Commission in Canada had been attracted to integration at the corporate level (through use of a dividend deduction) but finally rejected the idea, in part because it "would serve to increase the amount collected by foreign treasuries." Canada, Royal Commission on Taxation, 4 *Report of the Royal Commission on Taxation* 44. Because of the operation of the

corporations which the parents do not, in turn, redistribute to their shareholders (and might therefore be reinvested in the subsidiary), Germany recaptures, by statute, the distribution relief enjoyed by the subsidiaries. Recapture is accomplished by the use of an "after-tax" (*Nachsteuer*), which is levied at the rate of 36% if a subsidiary pays a dividend to a parent that does not redistribute it. This additional tax is levied only on *domestic* parent corporations, however; the German view is that such a recapture device could not practicably be applied to *foreign* parent corporations, which are for the most part outside the reach of the German tax system.

It does seem, however, that Germany probably could have dealt unilaterally with the problem of "wash" distributions by German subsidiaries to foreign parents. For example, because the German subsidiaries are within German jurisdiction, Germany might have amended its law establishing the split rate for German corporations in such a way that the preferential rate for distributions was eliminated, or increased, in the case of "wash" distributions to foreign parent corporations.[28] In short, Germany could have followed the precedent of Sweden, which uses its statutory law to deal with the problem of distributions to nonresidents enjoying an excessive tax advantage (in the Swedish case, an advantage arising because of an exemption from withholding). Germany chose instead to use the tax treaty route; although the treaty solutions may be complex, they indicate that the problem of excessive relief received by foreign parent corporations as a result of corporate-level integration is not insuperable.

To meet the problem posed by U.S. subsidiaries in Germany, Germany proposed that the German withholding rate in parent-subsidiary cases be raised to something in the neighborhood of 25%, without a reciprocal increase in the U.S. withholding rate on dividends from U.S. subsidiaries to German parent corporations. The United States rejected the German proposal, insisting that withholding rates must be reduced by treaty on a reciprocal basis.[29] In Professor Surrey's words, the United States took "the

U.S. indirect credit for foreign corporate taxes, that is, a Canadian reduction in corporate taxes through a dividend deduction would simply result in a higher U.S. tax on the U.S. parents of Canadian subsidiaries.

28. The unilateral use of domestic law to penalize "wash" distributions to foreign parent corporations might raise a question of violation of the nondiscrimination clauses in many tax treaties, as was noted above. Presumably, this problem could be solved by amending the nondiscrimination clauses so that they would not restrict German authority to act in the case of a defined tax abuse.

29. The Fiscal Committee of the OECD has taken the position, however, that a country granting distribution relief at the corporate level should be entitled to levy a higher than usual withholding tax on dividends to nonresident shareholders as compensation "for the fact that the distributed profits have not been taxed, or have been taxed at a reduced rate, in the hands of the company." Organisation for Economic Co-operation and Development, Fiscal Committee, *Draft Double Taxation Convention on Income and Capital* 105.

firm position that international withholding rates should be reciprocal and hence we cannot agree to any upward adjustment by other countries to accommodate to their internal tax policies."[30] Finally, Germany and the United States agreed in 1965 on a protocol to their tax treaty under which Germany may levy an additional 10% tax (over and above the treaty withholding rate of 15%) on tax-benefited dividends reinvested in more than nominal amounts by the U.S. parent corporation in a German subsidiary.[31]

Yet the problem created by the reinvestment of the profits of foreign-owned subsidiaries which had been distributed and borne tax at an apparently lower rate than the profits of German-owned corporations was not limited to subsidiaries owned by American parent corporations. In an effort to control the problem of "phantom dividends" to foreign parent corporations which arose out of Germany's split-rate system, Germany was forced to revise its tax treaties with a number of other countries—France, Sweden, Norway, Luxembourg, and the Netherlands, for example. The method is different in most cases, however, from the method used in the U.S. treaty. Generally speaking, German tax treaties provide that as long as the differential in Germany's rates on retained and distributed profits is at least 20 percentage points, Germany will levy its statutory withholding rate of 25% (rather than the reduced treaty rate) on dividends to parent corporations in the other treaty country.

Thus, Germany has evolved two different treaty patterns for dealing with international problems raised by its corporate-level system of integration. However different in form one German treaty may be from the next, the effort in all cases is to ensure that nonresident parent companies do not take improper advantage, at the expense of the German fisc, of Germany's lower rate at the corporate level for distributed profits. Although tax treaties may be used, as they have been by Germany, to reduce or even eliminate the tax benefit to nonresident parent corporations (or to foreign treasuries) arising out of corporate-level integration, the treaty process is difficult.[32]

30. Surrey, "The United States Tax System and International Tax Relationships," 12 *Canadian Tax Journal* 460, 463 (1964). The Carter Commission, rejecting integration at the corporate level as providing unwarranted relief to nonresident shareholders, also rejected the possibility of overcoming this by increasing the withholding tax on dividends to such shareholders. "Such a substantial withholding tax, regardless of the underlying circumstances, would obviously be unacceptable to some of the countries with which it would be necessary to renegotiate tax treaties." Canada, Royal Commission on Taxation, 4 *Report of the Royal Commission on Taxation* 44.

31. Complex rules are required to define reinvestment for this purpose and to determine when it is deemed to occur. See WTS: *Germany* (2d ed.), 11/5.8b3.

32. The German changeover from the split-rate system in 1977 was essentially intended to deny the benefit of integration to nonresident investors, especially direct investors. Germany

In considering the adoption of integration, the United Kingdom paid particular attention to the problem of U.K. subsidiaries of U.S. parent corporations. The United States is "by far the most important direct investor" in the United Kingdom. The British Board of Inland Revenue, in discussing the possible effect of the United Kingdom's adoption of a split-rate system based on the German model, estimated the loss to British tax revenues (and to the British balance of payments) which might result from the application of the integration system to U.S.-owned subsidiaries in Britain. It compared the split-rate system with integration at the shareholder level, which would not extend to nonresident shareholders (except by treaty). It estimated that if U.S. subsidiaries continued their same pattern of dividend distribution to U.S. parents, the losses would amount to £25 million per year. If, after integration, the U.S. subsidiaries distributed all of their profits to their U.S. parents, British losses would amount to between £45 million and £50 million per year. The British regarded full distribution as unlikely, however, mainly because a reduction in the U.K. tax on the subsidiary, combined with the operation of the U.S. foreign tax credit, would simply result in an increase in the U.S. tax on the parent corporation (at least in the case in which the parent owned the subsidiary directly rather than through an intermediate subsidiary in a third country, such as Switzerland). The British therefore estimated that their annual loss from the adoption of integration at the corporate level which would be attributable to the paying out of dividends from British subsidiaries to U.S. parent corporations might amount to £30 million.[33]

Problems of the kind faced by Germany (and potentially by Great Britain) in the parent-subsidiary situation are likely to arise, however, only if distribution relief at the corporate level is sizable—as it is in Germany, where the difference between the rate on retained profits (51%) and the rate on distributed profits (15%) amounts to 36 percentage points. Sweden also offers distribution relief at the corporate level, but the relief is small (see Chapter 5). Sweden's experience indicates that minor distribution relief at the corporate level is not likely to induce local subsidiaries to pay "wash" dividends to foreign parents solely in order to take advantage of Swedish distribution relief. If there is any such problem, it has not been large enough to warrant the administrative complexities of a possible solution.

had long felt that the split-rate system was exploited by foreign direct investors (or by foreign treasuries) through their manipulation of the dividend policy of the German subsidiary. The main motive of the change may be said to be Germany's resentment of a discriminatory extension of the integration benefit which is inherent in integration at the corporate level. See the Appendix for a brief description of the present German system.

33. United Kingdom, Board of Inland Revenue, "International Investment," in United Kingdom, Parliament, House of Commons, *Report From the Select Committee on Corporation Tax* 213, 214.

In any event, a country that is considering whether to adopt distribution relief at the corporate level should bear in mind that a substantial degree of distribution relief at the corporate level may lead to an excessive outflow of capital from domestic subsidiaries to foreign parent corporations. This capital may remain outside the country permanently, or it may return to the subsidiary in the guise of a "new" investment.

7/C.3. Portfolio Investment: Dividends From Resident Corporations to Nonresident Portfolio Investors

The international problems generated by distribution relief at the corporate level center around foreign direct investment; they seem not to involve foreign portfolio investment, which is probably smaller in volume than direct investment, especially in developing countries. Nonresident portfolio investors, as distinguished from the nonresident direct investors discussed in the preceding section, are not likely to be able to affect dividend policy in such a way as to take improper advantage of distribution relief at the corporate level.[34] The corporation in which the nonresident shareholder has made a portfolio investment usually does not have discretion to vary its dividend policy from year to year because of tax considerations; the practical need to maintain a reasonably steady dividend and to avoid dividend reductions from year to year is a strong restraint. Moreover, nonresident portfolio investors are ordinarily not entitled to an "indirect credit" for a portion of a foreign corporation income tax. In the case of foreign portfolio investment (as distinguished from foreign direct investment), integration at the corporate level is therefore not likely to affect local dividend policy or to result in a transfer of tax revenue to the treasury of the nonresident portfolio investor's country of residence. As a result of this combination of factors, problems with nonresident portfolio investors do not seem to arise in countries offering integration at the corporate level.

34. The British Board of Inland Revenue puts the matter bluntly in discussing the international aspects of integration: "A portfolio investor has no effective control over the policies of the company in which he has invested; a direct investor . . . does have such influence." For this purpose, the Board assumes that any foreign parent corporation with a 10% holding in a British subsidiary "has sufficient influence to warrant his investment being described as direct." United Kingdom, Board of Inland Revenue, "International Investment," in United Kingdom, Parliament, House of Commons, *Report From the Select Committee on Corporation Tax* 213.

7/C.4. Dividends From Nonresident Corporations to Resident Shareholders

Corporate-level systems of integration reduce the burden of the domestic corporation income tax on dividends paid by resident corporations, but they generally make no provision for reducing the burden of a foreign corporation income tax on dividends paid to resident shareholders by nonresident corporations. The foreign corporation income tax is considered the concern of the country of the foreign corporation's residence, not the country of the shareholder's residence. The country of the shareholder's residence may follow an outmoded schedular system based on the notion of territoriality and exempt foreign dividends as a result. In the ordinary case, however, a country providing integration at the corporate level taxes its residents uniformly on all dividends, whether they come from foreign or domestic sources.

Side by side with the integration scheme, there may be a system of relief from international double taxation which takes account of the foreign corporation income tax. For example, this system may give resident shareholders not only a direct credit for the foreign withholding tax on the dividend but also an indirect credit for the foreign corporation income tax on the profits from which the dividend was paid. Such relief from international double taxation may relieve the burden of *two* corporation income taxes, but it leaves intact the burden of one corporation income tax. To that extent, a country providing distribution relief at the corporate level gives relief in the purely domestic area (to the resident corporation and the resident shareholder) and in one sector of the international area (to the resident corporation and the nonresident shareholder) but gives no relief in another sector of the international area (to the nonresident corporation and the resident shareholder). The result is discrimination against investment by residents in foreign corporations. As far as is known, however, no country offering integration at the corporate level includes in its statutory law any measures designed to reduce or eliminate this discrimination against investment abroad. The United States, as a result, has complained that European systems of integration at the corporate level discriminate against investment by European investors in foreign (including American) corporations.[35]

7/C.5. Income of Resident Corporations From Foreign Sources

Most corporation income tax structures include special provisions for

35. Gordon, "International Fiscal Arrangements Distorted by Foreign Tax Policies; New Rules Needed," 37 *Journal of Taxation* 113 (1972).

income from foreign sources. In some countries, some or all of such income is exempt at the corporate level. Other countries apply their intercorporate dividend exemption or preference to dividends from foreign as well as domestic subsidiaries. Still others provide tax credits or other relief provisions at the corporate level for income taxed abroad.

Difficulties arise in correlating such provisions, which are aimed essentially at relieving international double taxation, with a corporate-level integration system, which is aimed essentially at relieving two-tier taxation on the domestic scene. One problem is whether a country using a split-rate system should extend its lower rate for distributed profits to distributions made (or deemed to be made) out of income from foreign sources which is either taxed at a preferential rate or exempt from tax at the corporate level.

It may be argued that the special treatment of foreign income at the corporate level seeks to mitigate international double taxation and that distribution relief has another purpose, which is to mitigate the impact of two-tier taxation. It may then be argued that there is no incompatibility between the two. According to this view, distribution relief at the corporate level should extend to distributions made out of foreign-source income.

In contrast, it may be argued that distribution relief seeks to mitigate the burden of the corporation income tax with respect to distributed income; if the country of the corporation's residence has already reduced its corporation income tax on any particular segment of income (whether because previously taxed abroad or for some other reason), then no further relief is appropriate. According to this view, relief from the corporation income tax is the concern of the country of the source of the corporation's profits rather than the country of the corporation's residence. If that position is taken and no distribution relief is to be given for distributions from income on which the corporation tax has already been reduced, it may become necessary to establish rules for determining the source of distributions or to establish a presumption that distributions come first from income not otherwise entitled to tax relief at the corporate level. Even if distribution relief is denied to the component of corporate income deemed to come from abroad, however, the very existence of nonqualifying income may result in a lower tax at the corporate level, because it may permit a greater distribution of the taxed domestic income that does qualify for distribution relief.[36]

In a discussion of corporation income tax reform which was published in 1971, the British government dealt with the problem of correlating the rules for the mitigation of international double taxation with the rules for the

36. Van den Tempel, *Corporation Tax and Individual Income Tax in the European Communities* 25.

mitigation of domestic two-tier taxation.[37] Although the government later introduced integration at the shareholder level, it indicated at that time its preference for integration at the corporate level through a split-rate system based on the German model. The government summarized its proposal for the correlation of international double taxation relief (by way of a foreign tax credit) and integration relief (by way of a split-rate system) in the following manner[38]:

> In a two-rate system operated in the United Kingdom the arrangements for relief for foreign tax would allow a company to allocate its distributions in such a way as to secure the maximum relief available within the general framework of the tax. The arrangements would permit a company to assume that so far as possible its distributions were made out of income which had not borne foreign tax [that is, domestic income], leaving [international] double taxation relief to be set against tax on retained income which would be regarded as being charged at the higher rate.

This proposed British solution would have followed the system then used by Germany.[39] It would allow two systems of tax relief to operate simultaneously in the case of integration at the corporate level. First, relief from international double taxation would be given to the corporation and would be allocated as far as possible to the retained portion of the corporation's profits. Second, distribution relief from domestic two-tier taxation would be given and would be allocated as far as possible to the distributed component of the corporation's profits. A nonresident shareholder would benefit on both counts. Insofar as a British corporation enjoyed relief from international double taxation with respect to retained profits, the nonresident shareholder (like the resident shareholder) would receive the benefit of a lower rate of tax on the corporation in which he owned shares. Insofar as a British corporation enjoyed the benefits of a lower rate of tax on distributed profits, the nonresident shareholder (again, like the resident shareholder) would benefit.[40]

7/C.6. Branches of Foreign Corporations

Countries offering distribution relief at the corporate level generally do not extend that relief to the local branches of foreign corporations. Germany, for

37. United Kingdom, Chancellor of the Exchequer, *Reform of Corporation Tax* 10, 11.
38. United Kingdom, Chancellor of the Exchequer, *Reform of Corporation Tax* 11; examples of the necessary calculations are given at 15–16.
39. WTS: *Germany* (2d ed.), 11/2.9b.
40. Great Britain decided, however, to integrate its taxes at the shareholder level rather than the corporate level, and the proposal discussed above never became law.

example, used a split-rate system with rates of 51% on retained profits and 15% on distributed profits, for resident corporations. Branches of nonresident corporations paid tax at the flat rate of 49%, however, whatever the proportions of profits retained and distributed. In a case in 1970, a French corporation with a branch in Germany claimed that it was entitled to the benefits of Germany's split rates and that its German branch profits should be taxed at the 51% and 15% rates available to German corporations, rather than at the 49% rate prescribed for branch profits. Germany's Supreme Tax Court rejected this contention, however. The court held that neither the national treatment clause nor the nondiscrimination clause of the French-German treaty supported the French corporation's contention, because the French corporation remained a nonresident of Germany despite the existence of its German branch, and the treaty did not prohibit differential taxation of residents and nonresidents.[41]

When the United Kingdom was considering the adoption of a split-rate system of integration at the corporate level, the British took the position that it would be administratively impracticable to determine what proportion of the profits of the British branch of a nonresident corporation was distributed by the home office. Hence, the United Kingdom proposed a flat rate of 50% on branch profits, and no relief was to be given by the United Kingdom for profits distributed by the home office abroad.

Norway, in contrast, took a position exactly opposite to the German position (and the proposed British position). Norway offers integration at the corporate level through a dividend deduction, rather than split rates. The Norwegian Ministry of Finance is of the view that if a tax treaty requires Norway to offer national treatment to the permanent establishments in Norway of a treaty partner, Norway should allow the establishment to deduct from its income taxable in Norway that portion of the dividends paid by the home office in the other country which was deemed to come from Norwegian-source income.[42]

The practice of taxing the local branch of a foreign corporation on the basis both of the income earned in that country and of the portion of that income deemed to have been distributed by the home office is not uncommon; it is followed by France, for example, and many other countries.[43] This practice seeks to equalize the tax position of a local branch with the tax position of a local subsidiary; the practice is generally followed in order to increase the tax on the local branch by taking account of home-office distributions, rather than to decrease that tax (as in Norway).

41. "Germany: Decision of the Supreme Tax Court ('Bundesfinanzhof') of January 13, 1970," 10 *European Taxation* II/119 (1970).

42. Arntzen and Bugge, *Doing Business in Norway* (2d ed.) 186, n. 3.

43. WTS: *France*, 11/3.7.

7/D. Integration at the Shareholder Level

7/D.1. In General

Integration, it was emphasized at the outset, causes special difficulties in the international area. On the whole, though, the difficulties may be more acute if integration is provided at the shareholder level than if it is provided at the corporate level. Shareholder-level integration systems operate, in effect, by giving the shareholder a refund of part of the corporation income tax. A country that provides integration at the shareholder level gives relief from its corporation income tax in its capacity as the country of the shareholder's residence; it does not give relief in the capacity of the country of source, the country in which the corporation's profits are earned.

Two kinds of international discrimination follow from integration at the shareholder level. First, resident shareholders in domestic corporations receive a refund of part of the domestic corporation income tax, but no refund is made to resident shareholders in foreign corporations. Second, resident shareholders in domestic corporations receive such a refund, but as a general rule, nonresident shareholders in domestic corporations do not. Of these two kinds of international tax discrimination, the latter is perhaps the more important. Countries using such systems of integration at the shareholder level even emphasize that a prime reason for the choice of the shareholder level over the corporate level is precisely to ensure that distribution relief does not operate to the benefit of nonresident shareholders (as it normally does in the case of integration at the corporate level).

In 1965, for example, France abandoned the use of an unintegrated corporation-individual tax structure and adopted integration at the shareholder level (see Chapter 6). In the process, France made it clear that the shareholder level was chosen in order to give relief only to resident shareholders and to deny relief to nonresident shareholders. Political factors were important in this decision; at the time, the French government's policy generally was hostile to investment in France by foreign interests.

To justify its tax discrimination against nonresidents, France advanced several arguments. In comparison with tax receipts before integration, integration results in revenue losses, the French Ministry of Finance said. Integration at the shareholder level has the virtue of confining the losses to those arising out of tax concessions to residents. France saw no reason to give a tax reduction to nonresidents or to suffer revenue losses in order to benefit foreigners.

Another factor in the French choice of the shareholder level was French resentment of the rising level of foreign (especially American) ownership of French corporations. Distribution relief confined to French shareholders and not extending to American (and other nonresident) shareholders would make French shares more attractive to French investors and would, at least in principle, induce French residents to buy more French shares; this, in turn, would push up the price of French shares and make their acquisition less attractive to Americans (and other foreigners).

Moreover, many French shares nominally owned by nonresidents, the French Ministry asserted, were actually owned by residents of France who had deposited their shares in nominee form in banks abroad (generally in Switzerland) in order to evade the French individual income tax (and French inheritance taxes as well). To a considerable extent, therefore, the denial of relief to nonresident shareholders meant the denial of relief to French tax evaders.

Canada has also emphasized that a prime virtue of integration at the shareholder level is that it gives no relief to nonresidents.[44] The Royal Commission that considered reform of the Canadian tax structure asserted that the "main drawback" of integration at the corporate level was that it would provide relief to nonresident shareholders. Using arguments remarkably similar to those advanced by the French only one year earlier, the Royal Commission chose distribution relief at the shareholder level because such relief would benefit only Canadian shareholders—that is, it would not spill over to the benefit of American and other nonresident investors. To give relief to nonresident shareholders is objectionable, the Royal Commission asserted, because it "would result in unwarranted revenue costs and would serve to increase the amount collected by foreign treasuries."[45]

Just as France had done, the Royal Commission emphasized the high proportion of foreign ownership (specifically, American ownership) of

44. Of the total capital employed in Canadian manufacturing, 57% is controlled by nonresidents (45% by the United States alone). In mining and petroleum, the proportion of nonresident control is higher (65% and 74%, respectively). Nonresident-controlled corporations earned 63.8% of Canadian corporate taxable income in the manufacturing sector, for example (the 1965–1968 average). Government of Canada, *Foreign Direct Investment in Canada* 20, 23 (Tables 4, 7). The report is skeptical about the efficacy or advisability of using the tax structure to change the pattern of investment in Canada. See the discussion of tax policy at 360–366.

45. Canada, Royal Commission on Taxation, 4 *Report of the Royal Commission on Taxation* 44. The assertion that distribution relief by Canada to nonresident shareholders "would serve to increase the amount collected by foreign treasuries" refers to the credit for foreign taxes given to their taxpayers by the United States and the United Kingdom, which are major investors in Canada, and by other countries. Generally speaking, the lower the Canadian tax, the lower the tax credit given by the United States or the United Kingdom and the higher the tax therefore collected by their treasuries.

Canadian corporations and the resulting desire to make Canadian shares fiscally more attractive to Canadian residents, but not to nonresidents. The White Paper issued after the Commission's report and the subsequent action of the Canadian Parliament (enlarging the pre-existing system of integration at the shareholder level) both followed the Royal Commission's principle that distribution relief should be given at the shareholder level in order not to give relief to nonresidents.[46]

7/D.2. Direct Investment: Dividends From Resident Subsidiaries to Nonresident Parent Corporations

The international problems generated by offering a substantial degree of distribution relief at the corporate level relate primarily to direct investment by nonresident parent corporations. As the German example demonstrates, nonresident parents are in a position to manipulate the dividend policy of their domestic subsidiaries for tax reasons. In the German case, however, no problems arise with nonresident portfolio investors; when the treaty between the United States and Germany had to be amended to deal with direct investment, no changes were needed with respect to portfolio investment.

In contrast, integration at the shareholder level raises problems with respect to portfolio investment by nonresidents, but it appears to raise no problems with respect to direct investment. The French experience provides an example. After France's adoption of integration at the shareholder level in 1965, complaints of discrimination against nonresident portfolio investors were filed by some of the major capital-exporting countries (the United States, Germany, and Switzerland, for example) (see the discussion in the next section). No problem arose in France with respect to dividends from French subsidiaries to nonresident parents.

The French reform in which shareholder-level integration was adopted in place of an unintegrated tax structure brought about virtually no change in tax for resident corporations, whether owned by residents or nonresidents. The rate of the French corporation income tax (a uniform rate applied to all profits, retained and distributed) was 50% both before and after integration. Manipulation of the dividend policy of French subsidiaries by nonresident parent corporations offered no tax advantages to either subsidiaries or parents. France's adoption of distribution relief for French resident shareholders seems to have been a matter of indifference to nonresident direct investors.

46. See, for example, "Canada Tax Law Is Aimed at U.S.," *The New York Times*, 27 December 1971, p. 45.

Under French domestic law, a French parent corporation does not receive a dividend credit with respect to its dividends from French subsidiaries. The dividend is almost wholly exempt from tax in the hands of the French parent corporation. The fact that French domestic law does not allow a parent corporation to claim the direct benefit of a dividend credit with respect to dividends from subsidiaries does not mean, however, that the credit is lost by the shareholders of the parent. Through a complicated process, the credit is passed through to the parent's shareholders if the dividend from the subsidiary is redistributed. To impose any comparable redistribution requirement on the nonresident parents of French subsidiaries—in order to give the parents or their shareholders a benefit comparable to that enjoyed by French parent corporations—was regarded as too complicated to be practicable. Yet no complaints seem to have followed from nonresident parent corporations. This fact suggests that a country's adoption of integration at the shareholder is not likely to affect foreign *direct* investment, even if the benefits of the system are limited to resident shareholders.

7/D.3. Portfolio Investment: Dividends From Resident Corporations to Nonresident Portfolio Investors

a. In General

France's adoption of a shareholder dividend credit, limited to resident shareholders, may have been a matter of indifference to foreign direct investors. The tax position of the French subsidiaries of foreign direct investors relative to that of French-owned corporations was no different or worse after the reform than it had been before. The new shareholder credit was not, however, a matter of indifference to nonresident portfolio investors, or at least not to those foreign governments which asserted charges of discrimination on behalf of their portfolio investors. These governments objected to the discrimination against nonresidents which is inherent in a system that grants substantial distribution relief to resident shareholders but no relief to nonresidents.

When France adopted integration at the shareholder level in 1965, it was in the process of renegotiating its tax treaties with the United States and Switzerland, both major sources of capital flowing into France. Both countries complained of discrimination and asked France to extend the benefit of French distribution relief to their residents who owned shares in French corporations. In the United States, this request was based "largely on the ground that the French tax on United States shareholders should not be heavier than on French shareholders."[47] France refused, and the treaties were signed without French distribution relief being extended to Swiss or American shareholders.

With Germany—one of France's partners in the European Economic Community—matters stood on a different footing, however. The Treaty of Rome, which established the Community, calls on the members to remove obstacles to the free movement of capital within the Community.[48] Germany argued that France's tax discrimination against German and other nonresident shareholders was such an obstacle, and the argument had considerable force. As a practical matter, moreover, the French shareholder credit had failed in one of its objectives—to raise the price of listed French shares by making such shares more attractive to French investors. Indeed, after France's adoption of integration, the price of shares on the French Bourse fell. Although the adoption of integration did not necessarily cause this fall in prices, it was nonetheless suggested in some quarters that the system's discrimination against nonresidents made French shares unattractive to nonresidents and thus contributed to the fall. In some cases, for example, the availability of the French dividend credit led French corporations to reduce their cash dividends; this action was particularly prejudicial to nonresident shareholders, who found their dividends reduced with no compensatory tax credit provided.[49]

In a press release issued on 13 September 1967, the French Ministry of Finance announced that, primarily in order to encourage nonresident investors to buy French shares, it was willing, by treaty, to extend to residents of other countries (particularly the Common Market countries) tax benefits that would be equivalent to those given by the French integration system to French residents. An agreement with Germany was announced in February of 1968.

After Switzerland and the United States demanded treatment no less favorable than that given to Germany, France reached agreements with these two countries in 1969 and 1970. Negotiations went on with other countries, and the French Finance Act of 1970 gave the government the right, by tax treaty or by amendment of an existing treaty, to extend the benefits of the

47. "Report of the Department of State on the Protocol to the 1967 Treaty With France, Signed on October 12, 1970," 1 *CCH Tax Treaties* ¶ 2839.

48. Article 67(1) of the treaty provides that "to the extent necessary to ensure the proper functioning of the common market, Member States shall progressively abolish between themselves all restrictions on the movement of capital belonging to persons resident in Member States and any discrimination based on the nationality or on the place of residence of the parties or on the place where such capital is invested."

49. Communauté Économique Européene, Commission, *Le Développement d'un marché européen des capitaux* 225.

French dividends-received credit to shareholders in other countries.[50] France has tax treaties with nearly all of the developed countries of the world and with many less developed countries. When the process of treaty amendment is complete, most of the world's investors will be entitled to benefits under the French system of integration which are equivalent to those enjoyed by French resident shareholders.

The result, in short, is a complete reversal of the 1965 French policy of using integration at the shareholder level to discriminate against nonresidents. This change in tax policy may be a reflection of a wider change in French policy; generally speaking, French policy toward inward capital movements has become somewhat more liberal since 1965. The removal of tax discrimination against nonresident shareholders was accomplished only by treaty, however; shareholders residing in a country that has no tax treaty with France still do not enjoy the distribution relief available to French resident shareholders.

b. Methods of Treaty Relief

A European journal, discussing the fact that a shareholder dividend credit leads to "barriers to the movement of capital," acknowledged that these barriers could be removed by tax treaty but added that "in practice the administrative complications could be a nightmare."[51] Although the charge of "nightmare" may be exaggerated, an analysis of France's treaties with Germany, Switzerland, and the United States indicates that it has some substance.

1. French treaty with Germany. A protocol of June 1969 amended the 1959 treaty between France and Germany so that Germany was required to give to German residents owning shares in French corporations (other than German parent corporations receiving dividends from French subsidiaries) the same dividend tax benefits as those enjoyed by a French resident owning shares in a French corporation. A German holder of a French share who receives a dividend from a French corporation is entitled to claim, against his German income tax, exactly the same credit that a French resident receiving the identical dividend would be entitled to claim against the French income tax—a credit equal to 50% of the dividend. Just as the French shareholder

50. The provision in the Finance Act was designed to relieve the government of the need to submit to Parliament for ratification every supplement or amendment for changing an existing tax treaty to provide for the extension of French distribution relief to residents of a treaty partner. In addition to its agreements with the United States, Switzerland, and Germany, France has been able to reach agreements with a number of other countries on the extension of its dividend credit to shareholders resident in those countries.

51. "Germany Changes to Tax Credits," *The Economist*, 13 November 1971, p. 80.

must, the German shareholder must gross up his French dividend by the amount of the credit. If the credit exceeds the amount of his tax, the German shareholder is entitled to a refund of the difference from the German treasury.

In the first instance, the burden of the credit falls on the German treasury. The protocol then establishes a complicated method through which the French treasury reimburses the German treasury for a portion of the tax revenue lost by Germany. The reimbursement scheme involves several steps, which are described below.

First, the French tax code requires France, in the absence of a treaty, to withhold tax at the rate of 25% from dividends paid to nonresidents. In line with normal treaty practice, the 1959 tax treaty between France and Germany reduced the French withholding rate to 15%. The 1969 protocol provides for the total elimination of the French withholding tax on all French dividends paid to German shareholders. Whether the German shareholder is a portfolio investor or a German parent corporation receiving dividends from a French subsidiary, the French government will withhold nothing from the French dividend.

Second, the French treasury must pay over annually to the German treasury a sum equivalent to the amount of tax revenue lost by Germany because of Germany's agreement to provide benefits equal to the French credit (or refund) to German holders of French shares. The payment, however, is reduced by a sum equal to 15% of the total amount of dividends involved grossed up by the amount of the German treaty credit. (In effect, the situation is the same as it would be if the 15% withholding tax under the 1959 treaty had continued but were applied to both the dividend and the credit and as if Germany had given credit for that French withholding tax.)

The result of this arrangement is that France and Germany share the burden of the credit given to German shareholders. On a French dividend of F 100 (grossed up by the amount of the credit to F 150), the French reimbursement to the German government will be reduced by 15% of F 150, or by F 22.5; F 22.5 is equal to 45% of the credit of F 50. Taking account of this reduction, France will pay the German government F 27.5 with respect to a tax credit of F 50, or a sum equal to 55% of the credit. France, that is, bears 55% of the cost of extending the tax credit to German shareholders, and Germany bears the remaining 45%.

Third, the protocol makes no change in the 1959 treaty treatment of French shareholders in German corporations. Germany continues to withhold tax at the rate of 15% on dividends to French portfolio investors and 25% on dividends to the French parents of German subsidiaries. The French holder of a German share, moreover, enjoys no credit against his German dividend equivalent to the credit he enjoys with respect to a French dividend.

The result of this arrangement, nevertheless, is that if the taxes at both the corporate and the shareholder levels and Germany's split-rate system of distribution relief at the corporate level are taken into account, a French portfolio investor has the same after-tax return on corporate-source income of German origin as he does on corporate-source income of French origin, given France's credit system of distribution relief at the shareholder level.[52] Similarly, a German portfolio investor has the same after-tax return from German shares as from French shares—if, that is, the German portfolio investor takes into account the tax due at the corporate level as well as the tax due at his own level.

2. French treaties with the United States and Switzerland. The essence of the complicated Franco-German arrangement described above is an inter-country financial arrangement. The German government gives its residents a credit against the tax due on portfolio holdings in French shares and is then reimbursed by the French government for the tax revenue lost by the credit. In France's treaties with the United States and Switzerland (and in its treaties with a number of other countries), French distribution relief takes a different form: the French government makes payments in cash, equivalent in amount to the French dividend credit, to residents of those countries who have portfolio holdings in French shares.

The protocol to the treaty between France and the United States does not extend the French dividend credit to dividends paid on the direct investments of American parent corporations in French subsidiaries. (Under U.S. tax law, U.S. parent corporations receiving dividends from French subsidiaries are entitled in any event to a direct credit for the French tax withheld from the dividends and to an indirect credit for an aliquot share of the French corporation income tax paid on the profits underlying the dividend.) The protocol extends the French dividend credit only to portfolio investors—that is, U.S. resident individuals and U.S. corporations owning less than 10% of the voting stock of the French corporation paying the dividends (and hence not entitled to the U.S. indirect tax credit). Suppose, for example, a French corporation declares a dividend of F 100 to an American portfolio shareholder. The French government must make a supplemental payment in cash to the U.S. shareholder which is equal to the tax credit that a French

52. As a practical matter, however, a French portfolio investor who receives a dividend of F 100 from a French corporation will enjoy, and will know he enjoys, the benefit of a tax credit of F 50. The same investor receiving a dividend equivalent to F 100 from a German corporation will enjoy no credit (except for the German withholding tax). It is far from clear that the French portfolio investor will consider himself enriched by the fact that the German corporation enjoyed the benefit of a lower rate on its dividend distributed to him. There would seem to be no evidence, for example, to indicate that U.S. *portfolio* investors (as distinguished from U.S. *direct* investors) prefer German shares to American shares because German corporations pay a lower rate of corporation tax on distributed profits than American corporations do.

shareholder would enjoy on a French dividend of the same amount—namely, F 50.

In principle, the scheme of the French government subsidy to U.S. portfolio investors operates in the following manner. The protocol treats the French cash payment to U.S. shareholders as equivalent to a dividend for all treaty purposes. The protocol permits France to apply the same withholding rate as before (15%) to dividends on U.S. portfolio holdings of French shares. This rate now applies both to the dividend proper (F 100) and to the cash payment in lieu of the French tax credit (F 50). The total amount withheld by France, then, is F 22.5 (15% of F 150). The U.S. shareholder receives a net total of F 127.5 for every F 100 of dividends declared by a French corporation. The total of F 127.5 is made up of a dividend proper of F 100 minus a withholding tax of 15%, or a receipt of F 85, plus a cash payment (in lieu of a dividend credit) of F 50—again minus a withholding tax of 15% or F 7.5—for a receipt of F 42.5. Total receipts are therefore F 85 plus F 42.5, or F 127.5. The U.S. shareholder has the choice, for U.S. tax purposes, of reporting a net income of F 127.5 and forgoing the tax credit or of reporting a grossed-up income of F 150 and claiming a credit of F 22.5 for the French tax withheld at the source.

In principle, this arrangement makes French shares more desirable to American portfolio investors than comparable American shares (at least from the point of view of dividend income available after tax). Consider the case of the Standard Oil Company of New Jersey ("Jersey"), a publicly held U.S. corporation. Jersey has a French affiliate, Esso de France, controlled by Jersey but listed on the Paris exchange. A considerable portion of Esso's shares are publicly held by French, American, and other portfolio investors, and shares are available at any time to any would-be purchasers. The American investor has the choice of buying shares in Jersey (the U.S. parent) or shares in Esso (the French affiliate). Both Jersey and Esso normally pay dividends. If the American investor buys shares in Jersey, and if Jersey declares a dividend of 100, the American shareholder receives 100 and no more. If, however, Esso de France declares a dividend of 100, an American shareholder will receive not merely 100 but also a supplemental cash payment of 50 from the French government (both subject to the French withholding tax of 15%, which is creditable against the U.S. tax). For example, if the American investor is in the 30% bracket, he will pay, on a Jersey dividend of 100, a tax of 30 and will have 70 remaining in after-tax income.

On an Esso dividend of 100 (supplemented by the French government's subsidy of 50), however, he will pay a French tax of 22.5 (at the 15% withholding rate) and a U.S. tax of 45 (at the 30% rate) minus his U.S. foreign tax credit (for the French withholding tax) of 22.5, or a total tax of 45. He will have after-tax income of 105. The after-tax income of the American portfolio investor, in summary, is 70 if he buys the American share and 105 if he buys the French share—a 50% difference in favor of the French share.

The U.S. Department of State said that this "may be expected to improve the French financial market by encouraging portfolio investment in corporate securities"[53]. (It did not mention the impact on the U.S. financial market.) The protocol eliminates tax discrimination between French investors buying French shares and American investors buying French shares. But the inevitable result of extending French distribution relief to shareholders in the United States, a country that provides no distribution relief, is to create a new and perhaps equally invidious tax discrimination between Americans buying American shares and Americans buying French shares. The arrangement is defended, however, on the ground that in a world in which tax structures and rates are not uniform, differential results of this kind are inevitable; the result is no different, for example, than the result that might follow if France reduced its corporation tax rate from 50% to, say, 30% while the U.S. rate remained at 48%.

The U.S. Treasury Department complains, moreover, that another form of discrimination remains. The protocol does nothing to remove the tax discrimination in France between French investors buying French shares (who will receive a tax credit) and French investors buying American shares (who will receive no tax credit).[54] The United States, for its part, made no change in the pre-existing treaty withholding rate (15%) for portfolio dividends paid to French residents.

In the case of dividends paid by subsidiaries in one country to parent corporations in the other, the withholding rate on both sides continued as it was before (5%). Nothing in the protocol made any adjustment in U.S. taxation which can be regarded as a partial absorption by the United States of the burden of making payments in lieu of credit to American shareholders which falls on the French treasury. How much that cost to the French treasury is has not been estimated, but presumably it is small. As the U.S. State Department noted, "the present volume of United States portfolio investment in France is small." Nevertheless, the Department adds, "inclusion of the credit in the convention establishes an important and desirable precedent."

Although the details of France's 1969 protocol with Switzerland differ, the treatment of portfolio dividends from French corporations to Swiss residents is essentially the same as under the U.S. protocol. The French government makes a cash payment to the Swiss shareholder which supplements the dividend proper; this payment is equal to the tax credit to which the same dividend would entitle a French shareholder (50%). The French agreements with Switzerland and the United States (and a number of other countries) in effect extend the French dividend credit to Swiss and American investors

53. "Report of the Department of State on the Protocol to the 1967 Treaty With France, Signed on October 12, 1970," 1 *CCH Tax Treaties* ¶ 2839.

54. Gordon, "International Fiscal Arrangements Distorted by Foreign Tax Policies; New Rules Needed," 37 *Journal of Taxation* 113 (1972).

who buy French shares. Neither agreement, however, extends the French credit to French investors who buy Swiss or American shares.

What lessons can a developing country draw from the French case? First, it would seem that integration at the shareholder level is not likely to have any significant effect, one way or the other, on foreign *direct* investment. Second, it would seem that integration at the shareholder level might reduce foreign *portfolio* investment. The extension by treaties of distribution relief to nonresident shareholders in order to counter that reduction is cumbersome, but not impossible.

c. Treatment of Additional Tax for Dividends Paid to Nonresident Shareholders

Chapter 6, which deals with integration at the shareholder level, pointed out that distribution relief at that level, which seeks to relieve the shareholder of part of the burden of the corporation income tax, is predicated on the assumption that the corporation income tax has been paid on the profits from which the dividend comes. A special problem arises if the dividend comes from profits on which no corporation income tax has been paid or which have been taxed at a preferential rate. Should any reduction in distribution relief be made to take account of that treatment?

The answer to this question varies from country to country. Belgium, for example, makes no adjustment and gives its residents a credit for almost one half of the basic rate of the corporation tax whether or not such tax has actually been paid. France, however, takes the opposite position. If a dividend is paid from profits on which the corporation income tax has not been paid at the full 50% rate, the shareholder receives his tax credit in the normal course, but the corporation must pay an additional tax (*précompte*) in an amount equal to the shareholder's credit. By using the device of the additional tax, France ensures that it does not give relief to shareholders for corporation taxes that have never been paid.

Consider, however, the case of a shareholder who is not a resident of France and who is therefore not entitled to any tax credit for the French corporation tax (in the absence of a tax treaty). If this shareholder is not entitled to any tax credit, there is no basis for levying an additional tax on the corporation to compensate for the credit. The French tax code makes no provision for relief in this case. Unless some remedial action is taken, the result is that a nonresident shareholder is denied the benefits of the integration scheme (the tax credit) but must share in its burden (the additional tax imposed on the corporation to compensate for the credit).

The French tax administration itself acted without awaiting corrective action by the French Parliament to amend the tax law. The administration refunds the additional tax to corporations to the extent that the additional tax arises out of dividends paid to nonresident shareholders (who are not entitled to the tax credit) who are residents of a country with which France has a tax treaty or of a country that was a French colony. The reimbursement is made only if the nonresident is not entitled to the shareholder credit; if France extends the shareholder credit by tax treaty to shareholders resident in a foreign country, then corporations paying dividends to shareholders in that country lose the right to a reimbursement for the additional tax paid with respect to those particular dividends. U.S. shareholders in French corporations, for example, are entitled to the same distribution relief as French shareholders under the protocol to the French-U.S. tax treaty discussed above; as a result, a French corporation paying a dividend to a U.S. shareholder is not entitled to be reimbursed for any additional tax paid as a consequence of that dividend.

The need for action that will correct this situation with respect to dividends paid to nonresident shareholders not entitled to a tax credit is another example of the complexities introduced into the international tax area by integration.

7/D.4. Dividends From Nonresident Corporations to Resident Shareholders

Countries that adopt integration at the shareholder level almost invariably give resident shareholders relief only in the case of dividends from resident corporations. These countries generally do not extend integration relief to dividends from nonresident corporations. In this respect, integration at the shareholder level does not differ from integration at the corporate level, which also gives no relief to the resident shareholder in a nonresident corporation.

Whatever level is chosen, therefore, integration may serve the interests of a developing country by making investment at home more attractive than investment abroad, at least as far as taxes are concerned. The extent to which this tax factor will actually influence the pattern of investment will depend on other factors, including other elements of the tax structure. Some developing countries, for example, follow a territorial principle of taxation and do not tax their residents on income from foreign sources; in such a case, integration at home is not likely to eliminate the tax advantages of investment abroad.

7/D.5. Dividends to Resident Shareholders Paid by Resident Corporations out of Foreign Income

Relief from international double taxation of income earned abroad is provided in many corporate tax structures—by exemption, for example, or by a foreign tax credit (see 7/A.2 above). Yet suppose that country *X* provides such relief to its resident corporations and at the same time provides some form of distribution relief by way of integration at the shareholder level—a dividends-received credit, for example. Suppose, further, that a resident corporation pays a dividend out of foreign-source income and that the corporation has been given relief with respect to that income in order to take account of foreign taxes thereon. Should the dividend from that foreign income be entitled to integration relief at the shareholder level?

For ease of administration at the shareholder level, most countries offering integration by way of a dividends-received credit provide a *uniform* credit for the shareholder, whatever the source of the profits from which the dividend is paid and whatever the rate of tax paid by the corporation on those profits (see Chapter 6). The question then becomes: if it is assumed that a corporation pays a dividend out of foreign profits (taxed at less than the full domestic rate because of relief for foreign taxes) and that the shareholder is entitled to a uniform credit whether the source of the dividend is domestic profits (taxed at the full domestic rate) or foreign profits (taxed at less than the full domestic rate), should any additional tax be levied on the corporation to compensate for the part of the credit attributable to the portion of the dividend coming from tax-preferred foreign income?

The argument in support of a dividends-received credit is that tax relief is necessary to reduce the burden of the corporation income tax on the distributed component of corporate profits. If that tax has not in fact been paid at the full domestic rate to the treasury of the country that provides relief to the shareholder, it may be argued that no basis exists for such relief. If, for reasons of administrative convenience, shareholder relief is given in any event, it may be argued that the corporation should pay an additional tax to country *X* to justify the shareholder's relief.

France, for example, takes the latter position. If a French corporation pays a dividend out of foreign profits (tax-preferred at the corporate level under French law), that dividend entitles a resident shareholder to the same credit as a dividend from domestic profits taxed at the full corporate tax rate. The corporation must, however, pay an additional or compensatory tax equal to the amount of the shareholder's credit.

It may be argued, though, that the additional tax serves to nullify the relief from international double taxation which is given to the corporation in the first instance. If a French corporation earns foreign profits, it receives a tax benefit; if it pays those profits out, it loses those benefits to the extent of the shareholder's tax credit.

For that reason, the Canadian law takes a position exactly opposite to the French position. The shareholder in Canada is entitled to a credit regardless of the source of the profits from which the dividend was paid or the rate of Canadian tax paid on those profits. In contrast to the French practice, no additional tax is required of a Canadian corporation if it pays dividends out of profits that have not borne full Canadian tax at the corporate level (foreign profits, for example). The Royal Commission and the White Paper recommended that Canada follow the French practice and levy a compensatory tax on the corporation. The Canadian tax law does not follow these recommendations, however, because it was felt that the compensatory tax would nullify the incentive to invest abroad given to Canadian corporations by Canada's foreign tax credit system.

In April 1973, the United Kingdom integrated its corporation and individual income taxes by the use of a shareholder dividend credit based on the French model. Because of Britain's long tradition of investment overseas, income earned abroad is particularly important to British corporations. Whether or not to extend the dividend credit to dividends paid from foreign profits was therefore a major problem in Britain. In the years before 1965, when the United Kingdom also gave shareholders a dividends-received credit, the United Kingdom had permitted its credit for foreign taxes to "spill over" to the shareholders in certain circumstances. The shareholder's credit varied from dividend to dividend, depending on the proportion of the dividend that came from foreign sources. The necessary calculations were extraordinarily complicated.[55]

When the British government revived the shareholder dividend credit in 1973, it decided to follow the French practice of giving shareholders a uniform credit for all dividends, but if dividends were paid out of foreign profits, of levying an additional tax on the corporation "to ensure that the United Kingdom Exchequer was not put in a position of having to repay to shareholders, or treat as paid on behalf of shareholders, tax which it had in fact never received."[56]

Under Britain's 1973 credit scheme, dividends are presumed in the first instance to have come from profits taxed at the full corporate rate (that is, domestic profits). If dividends are paid from profits earned abroad on which the paying corporation paid less than the normal British corporate tax rate because of relief for taxes paid abroad, the shareholder receives the same dividend credit as he would have if the dividend had come from domestic profits. The corporation, however, must compensate the tax administration for the shareholder's credit by paying, in effect, an additional tax equivalent to the French *précompte.*

The operation of the British scheme can be illustrated by assuming that a British corporation has before-tax income of £200, substantially all of

55. See WTS: *United Kingdom,* 11/2.13f, 11/2.13g.

56. United Kingdom, Chancellor of the Exchequer, *Reform of Corporation Tax* 40.

which is from foreign sources. If the rate of the British corporation income tax is 50%, the corporation will owe a corporation income tax of £100, against which it may claim a credit for foreign taxes. If the corporation chooses to pay a dividend of £100, it must withhold 30% (£30 in this case) from the dividend and pay that sum to the British treasury as "advance corporation tax" or ACT. The corporation is entitled to a credit against its corporation tax of £100 for the ACT of £30; to the extent that the corporation income tax has already been reduced or eliminated by the credit for foreign taxes, the credit for ACT is lost; no refunds of ACT are permitted. The shareholder who recieves a net dividend of £70 (£100 minus ACT of £30) must gross up that amount to £100 and report £100 as taxable income. He is entitled to a dividend credit (or refund) of £30 against the tax due from him.

For a corporation with no domestic-source income against which to credit the ACT, the ACT is lost and thus amounts to an additional tax, similar in operation and effect to the French *précompte.* Dividend-paying British corporations with substantial amounts of foreign-source income objected vigorously to the additional tax, and transitional relief on a declining scale was given to them for the first five years after the new system took effect.

The additional tax is designed to compensate the treasury for the shareholder dividend credit to the extent that the latter covers dividends paid from foreign-source profits. To avoid the additional tax, British corporations whose profits came chiefly from foreign sources and whose dividends necessarily came in whole or in part from those foreign-source profits were said to be contemplating mergers with corporations enjoying domestic profits. Suppose that a corporation whose profits are mainly from overseas (an oil company, for example) merges with a corporation whose profits are mainly from domestic sources (a retail grocery chain, for example). The merged corporation will be able to make distributions to shareholders from its domestic profits at the same time that it meets its need for retained profits by accumulating and reinvesting its profits from foreign sources. The ACT will not be lost, because it can be credited against the corporation income tax on the domestic profits while the foreign tax credit is used to offset the British tax on the foreign profits. Some "bizarre" mergers were anticipated at the time of the introduction of the new integration scheme, mergers made "for that most undesirable of all reasons, tax avoidance."[57]

57. "Corporation Tax Takeovers," *The Economist*, 17 June 1972, p. 70. See also "Imperial Shell Industries?" *The Economist*, 4 March 1972, p. 87. In one actual case, the British affiliate of a U.S. copy-machine company sought to merge with a British brewery whose profits came mostly from British sources; the copy-machine affiliate derived most of its profits from outside Britain and sought the merger "to avoid the disadvantages which will be suffered

A developing country will presumably attempt to encourage its residents to invest at home rather than abroad. In that case, the French (and the more recent British) practice of a uniform credit to residents for all dividends from domestic corporations, coupled with an additional tax on domestic corporations which would compensate the treasury for the cost of the credit if a full domestic tax has not been paid at the corporate level (because the underlying earnings came from abroad, for example), would be preferable to the pre-1965 British practice.

7/D.6. Branches of Foreign Corporations

Countries that offer distribution relief generally do not extend that relief to local branches of foreign corporations. This practice was noted in section 7/C.6 above in connection with integration at the corporate level. In the case of integration at the shareholder level, the practice is generally the same. Branch profits "return to the foreign parent and it is there that distribution takes place."[58] For that reason, the United Kingdom did not offer any distribution relief to the British branches of foreign corporations when it adopted integration by way of a shareholder dividend credit. This treatment is an example of the common view that if a branch makes a distribution, relief should be the concern of the country of the foreign parent corporation.

Some countries, however, levy two taxes on the profits of foreign branches operating in those countries. France, for example, first levies its corporation income tax on branch profits at its normal French rate. France also levies a "tax on distributions" on the branch: if the foreign corporation distributes dividends at its home office, France asserts jurisdiction to tax the portion of the home-office dividends which is presumed to derive from French-source profits.[59] Some developing countries whose tax systems are based on the French model levy a similar tax on the imputed share of overseas dividends. France's shareholder dividend credit does not extend to dividends from nonresident corporations, even if a portion of the

under the imputation tax system." "Rank Organisation: New Tax Imputations," *Investors' Chronicle* (London), 7 July 1972. (The shareholders of the British copy firm, particularly its many U.S. portfolio shareholders, objected to the proposed merger as they preferred growth to tax benefits; hence, the merger proposal was dropped.)

58. United Kingdom, Chancellor of the Exchequer, *Reform of Corporation Tax* 11.

59. The "tax on distributions" is designed to equalize the tax treatment of resident and nonresident corporations. If a French resident corporation earns profits and pays dividends, two taxes are due: (1) the corporation income tax on the profits and (2) the individual income tax on the dividends. France similarly levies two taxes on a nonresident corporation doing business in France through a branch: (1) the corporation income tax on the branch profits and (2) the tax on distributions on the dividends presumed to have been paid out of those profits. See WTS: *France*, 11/3.7.

underlying profits came from French sources and thus was subject to the French "tax on distributions." Resident shareholders in nonresident corporations, that is, do not benefit from French distribution relief. Yet to deny distribution relief to French shareholders in the foreign corporations and at the same time to impose a "tax on distributions" on the French branch profits is considered harsh. As a result, the tax on distributions is to be reduced to the extent that the foreign parent is able to show that distributions were made to shareholders resident and taxable in France.[60]

7/E. Conclusion

At the beginning of this chapter, several commentators were cited as saying that integration adds such elements of complexity, discrimination, and nonneutrality to a tax structure that, from the point of view of international investment and the free flow of capital, unintegrated tax systems are preferable. This chapter has illustrated some of those elements. The proposition was asserted, however, by authorities from developed countries, and it is far from clear that it applies with full force to the developing countries. A developing country that is considering whether to adopt integration and if so, at what level or levels, will make its choice on the basis of its own national interest, in which purely domestic considerations will ordinarily predominate. It is unlikely that the impact of integration on investment from abroad and on investment by its residents in other countries will be enough to determine the choice. That impact should nevertheless be taken into account; at the least, it may be enough to remind the developing country that there are alternatives to integration—rate reduction, for example, or retention rather than distribution allowances.

As the Common Market Commission stated, unintegrated systems have two major virtues: "technical simplicity" and the "absence of any aspect of discrimination" (7/A.3). Certainly the matter of "technical simplicity" must be a prime consideration if a developing country is considering the adoption of any integration system. In any event, if a developing country chooses integration, it must be aware of the complexities and discriminations involved (especially in the international area) and must be prepared to take such corrective measures as may be feasible—by treaty if possible and unilaterally in other cases.

60. The amendment to the French-German tax treaty which extended the French dividend credit to German shareholders also ended the imposition of the French "tax on distributions" on the French branches of German corporations. The amendment to the treaty with Switzerland did not abolish the "tax on distributions," but it reduced the rate from the ordinary 25% to 5%.

Appendix
German System Effective in 1977

The material below is reprinted with the permission of the author and the publisher from Hugh J. Ault, "International Issues in Corporate Tax Integration," 10 *Law & Policy in International Business* 461, 466–471 (1978); copyright, ©, 1978 by Law & Policy in International Business.

* * * *

1. The System in Outline

The new German imputation system[16] combines features of the previously employed split rate structure[17] with a full credit on distributions for corporate level taxes paid. The system works as follows. Retained profits are initially taxed at a rate of 56 percent[18]. When a distribution is made, the distribution results in a reduction of corporate taxes in the year of distribution equal to the difference between the rate for retained profits (56 percent) and the rate for distributed profits (36 percent).[19] Thus, the maximum profits distribution from a before-tax income of 100 is 64. This distribution is subject to a 25 percent withholding tax but carries with it a refundable credit for the 36 of corporate tax. The operation of the new system is

16. The new German system described in the text was enacted after nearly a decade of discussion and came into effect on January 1, 1977. For a translation and detailed discussion of the new German legislation see H. AULT & A. RAEDLER, THE GERMAN CORPORATION TAX REFORM LAW 1977 (1976). *See also* Ault, *Germany*: *The New Corporation Tax System*, 8 INTERTAX 262 (1976).

17. Under the pre-1977 German split rate system, retained income was taxed at a 51 percent rate and distributed income at a 15 percent rate. The special lower rate for distributions applied only if the corporate profits were distributed immediately. Since earnings must be retained to pay the tax on distributions, those earnings were in turn taxed at the higher rate for retentions. As a result, the effective rate of tax on distributions was approximately 23.5 percent. Tillinghast, *supra* note 5, at 401.

18. *Koerperschaftsteuerreformgesetz* [German Corporate Tax Reform Law], §23(1), Aug. 31, 1976, [1976] Bundesgesetzblatt [BGBl] I 2641 (W. Ger.).

19. *Id.* §27(1).

illustrated in the following example, which ignores the withholding tax, as it is not essential to the operation of the imputation system.

Income Before Tax	100
Less Tentative Corporate Tax	56
	44
Decrease in Corporate Tax on Full Distribution	20
Available for Distribution	64
Shareholder Includes:	
Distribution	64
Imputation Credit (9/16 of 64)	36
	100
Shareholder Credit or Refund	36

All distributions, no matter when made, carry out the imputation credit to the individual shareholder.[20] Intercorporate dividends are treated as taxable but carry with them the imputation credit. Thus, as long as income remains in corporate "solution," it will bear a tax of 56 percent. When the income is distributed to individual shareholders, either directly or through a chain of subsidiaries, the corporate level tax will be fully eliminated through the combination of the reduction in tax at the corporate level and the imputation credit to the individual shareholder. The effective rate of tax at the corporate level will vary from 56 percent to 36 percent depending on the level of distributions.

2. Treatment of Foreign Income

If a German corporation receives foreign source income, that income may either be tax free in Germany under a tax treaty[21] or may be fully taxed but carry with it a foreign tax credit[22] which will reduce or eliminate German corporate level tax. The foreign taxes paid on the foreign income are not taken into account in establishing the tax burden which must be borne by the German corporation's income in the context of the imputation system. In other words, the foreign taxes paid on foreign source income do not count as taxes paid for purposes of the imputation system.

20. *Einkommensteuergesetz* [German Income Tax Law] §36(2)3, Sept. 5, 1974, [1951] Bundesgesetzblatt [BGBl] I 493 (W. Ger.). The imputation credit is always nine-sixteenths of the cash distribution.

21. Germany in its tax treaties typically cedes taxing jurisdiction to the country of source and exempts the foreign source profits from taxation whether received from a foreign permanent establishment or a foreign subsidiary corporation. *See, e.g.*, Double Taxation Convention, July 22, 1954, United States-Germany, art. XV, 5 U.S.T. 2768, T.I.A.S. No. 3133, *as amended by* Protocol for the Avoidance of Double Taxation, Sept. 17, 1965, United States-Germany, art. 12, 16 U.S.T. 1875, T.I.A.S. No. 5920.

22. In the absence of a treaty, foreign profits are fully taxable but a foreign tax credit is granted for foreign income taxes paid, including underlying corporate taxes paid by foreign subsidiaries. German Corporate Tax Reform Law, *supra* note 18, §26.

When foreign source income which has not been taxed in Germany, either because of an exemption under a treaty or through the operation of the foreign tax credit, is distributed, an additional tax equal to 36 percent (the amount of credit granted at the shareholder level) must be withheld from the distribution by the corporation. If, because of the operation of foreign tax credit, the foreign income has borne some German tax but less than 36 percent, the difference must be made up on distribution.[23]

This corporate tax increase is functionally equivalent to the French *précompte*, * * *. It applies not only to foreign source income but to all income which has not borne full taxation in Germany. It ensures that all income distributions which carry a shareholder credit will have in fact borne a 36 percent tax which has been paid to the German treasury.[24] Thus, for a German corporation with foreign source profits which are taxed abroad, the tax burden at the corporate level involves both the foreign taxes and the German compensating corporate tax. To put it another way, the foreign corporate taxes are not integrated into the German imputation system but represent an additional cost of producing foreign source income. This statutory approach has been criticized as inconsistent with Germany's obligation to exempt foreign source income under its tax treaties, but the issue has not yet been resolved.[25]

The effect of the failure to integrate foreign taxes into the German imputation system is ameliorated somewhat by a tracing rule which treats fully taxed domestic profits as distributed first for purposes of the imputation system.[26] Thus, foreign profits are in effect treated as retained earnings until all fully taxed domestic profits have been distributed, and as a result, no additional corporation tax is incurred until all domestic income has been distributed. In practice, this provision makes it extremely important for German companies to have the right mix of tax-free foreign income and fully taxed domestic income in order to avoid an increase in tax on the foreign source income distributions.

23. *Id.* §27; Ault, *supra* note 16, at 264–65.

24. German Corporate Tax Reform Law, *supra* note 18, §27; Ault, *supra* note 16, at 264–65.

25. As indicated in note 21 *supra*, Germany in its treaties cedes taxing jurisdiction to the country of source and does not tax that income in Germany when received by a German corporation. However, when the income is distributed the 36 percent corporate tax increase takes place in the year of distribution and must be withheld from the dividend. *See* German Corporate Tax Reform Law, *supra* note 18, §27. For example, if a German corporation realizes profits from a foreign permanent establishment those profits are not taxed in Germany when realized but when the profits are distributed as dividends to the German corporation's individual shareholders, a corporate tax increase may be required. It has been asserted that this imposition of the corporate tax increase at the time of distribution violates Germany's agreement with its treaty partners to cede to them full jurisdiction over the taxation of income arising in their country. *See* Wohlschlegel, *Koerperschaftsteurreform mit Hindernissen: Herstellung der Ausschuettungsbelastung und Steuerbefreiungen nach Abkommenrecht*, 11 FINANZ-RUNDSCHAU 243 (1976). The point illustrates nicely the ambiguous character of corporate level taxes in an imputation system; see note 14 *supra*.

26. German Corporate Tax Reform Law, *supra* note 18, §28(2).

3. Shareholders Receiving Credit

Under German domestic legislation, the imputation credit at the shareholder level is available only to domestic taxpayers who receive distributions from domestic corporations.[27] It does not extend to foreign individual or corporate shareholders. Distributions to such shareholders bear tax at the corporate level at the 36 percent rate, calculated as indicated above, but for these shareholders that rate is final, *i.e.*, there remains a residual 36 percent tax at the corporate level after distributions have been made since the credit is not available to the shareholders. Relief is only given to foreign shareholders for the 36 percent corporate level tax where such tax has been imposed on distribution of foreign income.[28] In those cases, the foreign shareholder is entitled to a refund of the 36 percent tax. The following table summarizes the impact on a full distribution of earnings by a German subsidiary of a U.S. parent company.

U.S. Parent—Full Distribution

Income Before Tax	100
Less: Trade Tax[29]	15
	85
Corporate Tax (36%)	30.6
Income After Corporate Level Tax	54.4
Less: Withholding Tax (15%)	8.2
Income After German Taxes	46.2
German Tax Burden	53.8

The 53.8 percent tax represents a net increase of 8.3 percentage points over that applicable under the old split rate system under which the rate was about 45.5 percent.[30] * * * *

4. Treaty Policy

The legislative history of the new German enactment indicates that the impact on foreign investment of the imputation system will be handled through a modification of the 25 percent withholding rate but not by granting the imputation credit to

27. German Income Tax Law, *supra* note 20, §36(2)3.

28. German Corporate Tax Reform Law, *supra* note 18, §52. Relief is also given for distributions of profits which arose before the enactment of the new imputation system.

29. *See* note 93 *infra.*

30. For a comparison of the old and new German systems, see Ault, *supra* note 16, at 272.

foreign shareholders.[32] In its income tax treaties negotiated prior to the 1977 legislation, Germany was able to negotiate a 25 percent nonreciprocal withholding rate in connection with its earlier split rate system of corporate taxation.[33] Those treaties allowed Germany to apply unilaterally a 25 percent withholding rate in all situations in which there was a 20 percent difference between the taxation of distributed and undistributed profits in its domestic legislation. Only in the case of the United States and Canada was Germany unable to establish the higher withholding rate.[34] At present, the German position is that, given the 20 percent differential between the 56 percent rate of tax on retained profits and the 36 percent rate on distributions (even though this 36 is credited at the individual shareholder level), it is still entitled to apply the higher 25 percent withholding tax rate under its existing treaties.[35] Some reduction in the rate is anticipated in its future treaties.

As to the question of the extension of the credit to nonresident shareholders, the German argument is as follows. The reduction in tax from 56 percent to 36 percent for distributed profits benefits all shareholders, foreign and domestic. Germany cannot be required to take the further step of granting the imputation credit to the nonresident shareholders as well, since this in effect would reduce its share of tax revenues on corporate investment in Germany to the 25 percent withholding tax.[36]

* * * *

32. A resolution passed by the German Bundestag states as follows:

> [We have] discussed the effects of the reform of the German corporation tax system on foreign holders of shares in German corporations including the aspects of market competition and investment policy. [We are] of the opinion that these aspects can be taken into account in a satisfactory way by the reduced—but not refundable—corporation tax rate of 36% for distributed profits of German corporations on the one hand, and the capital yields [withholding] tax on the other, which is flexible under international rules applicable between countries.

Bundesrat-Drucksache 421/76.

33. *See* Taylor, *U.S. Tax Treaties and Common Market Corporate Tax Systems*, 28 TAX LAW. 73, 84 (1974–75).

34. Protocol for the Avoidance of Double Taxation, Sept. 17, 1965, United States-Germany, 16 U.S.T. 1875, T.I.A.S. No. 5920. Convention for the Avoidance of Double Taxation, June 4, 1956, Canada-Germany, [1957] Bundesgesetzblatt (W. Ger.) 188, 316 U.N.T.S. 231. Germany argued that it was necessary to have the higher withholding rate to compensate for the fact that the distribution relief under the split rate system was available to foreign as well as domestic shareholders. The argument was first that the higher withholding rate was appropriate in principle, and second that as a practical matter foreign corporations were taking advantage of the lower distribution rate and then reinvesting the profits in Germany in such a way that the total foreign and German tax burden was less than that borne by profits retained in German controlled enterprises. In the U.S. negotiations, the United States insisted on reciprocal withholding rates of 15 percent, but did agree to allow Germany to apply the higher 25 percent rate in cases in which profits distributed to U.S. parents were in fact reinvested. For an extensive discussion of the background and mechanics of the reinvestment question, see Tillinghast, *supra* note 5, at 404–06.

35. *See* Tillinghast, *supra* note 5, at 403. This objection fails to take the U.S. taxes (federal and state) into account. *Id.* at 404–06.

36. WORLD TAX SERIES—GERMANY 11/5.8(b)(3)(a) (1969).

Bibliography

This bibliography lists both the books and articles cited in this study (preceded by an asterisk) and other materials on integration published in more recent years.

*ARDANT, G. *Histoire de l'impôt* (2 vols.). Paris: Éditions Arthème Fayard, 1971.

*ARNTZEN, A., and BUGGE, J. *Doing Business in Norway* (2d ed.). Oslo: Den norske Creditbank, 1971.

*"Au Sénat: M. Jean Taittinger: Suppression de l'avoir fiscal ne peut être envisagée," *Le Monde*, 27 April 1972, p. 10.

AULT, H. "Germany: The New Corporation Tax System," 1976 *Intertax* 262.

AULT, H. "International Issues in Corporate Tax Integration," 10 *Law & Policy in International Business* 461 (1978).

AULT, H., and RÄDLER, A. *The German Corporation Tax Law With 1980 Amendments* (*Körperschaftsteuerreformgesetz 1977 mit Änderungen von 1980*): *Comments and Translation.* Deventer: Kluwer; and Frankfurt: Alfred Metzner, 1980.

AULT, H., and RÄDLER, A. *The German Corporation Tax Reform Law 1977* (*Körperschaftsteuerreformgesetz 1977*): *Comments and Translation.* Deventer: Kluwer; and Frankfurt: Alfred Metzner, 1976.

BARTLETT, R. "The Harmonisation of Company Taxation Within the EEC," 1977 *Journal of Business Law* 292.

*BERLE, A., and MEANS, G. *The Modern Corporation and Private Property.* New York: Commerce Clearing House, Inc., 1932.

BIRD, R. "International Aspects of Integration," 28 *National Tax Journal* 302 (1975).

*BIRD, R. *Taxation and Development*: *Lessons From Colombian Experience.* Cambridge, Mass.: Harvard University Press, 1970.

*BIRD, R., and OLDMAN, O. "Tax Research and Tax Reform in Latin America," 3-3 *Latin American Research Review* 5 (1968).

*BIRD, R., and OLDMAN, O. (eds.). *Readings on Taxation in Developing Countries.* Baltimore: The Johns Hopkins Press, 1964.

*BITTKER, B., and EUSTICE, J. *Federal Income Taxation of Corporations and Shareholders* (2d ed.). Branford, Conn.: Federal Tax Press, Inc., 1966.

*BOWEN, H. "Optional Partnership Treatment of Corporate Earnings." In: Tax Institute, *How Should Corporations Be Taxed?* 61. New York: 1947.

BRACEWELL-MILNES, B. "United Kingdom Tax Structure," 14 *European Taxation* 155 (1974).

BRANNON, G. "Dividend Relief and Tax Reform," 3-32 *Tax Notes* 3 (1975).

BREAK, G. "Integrating Corporate and Personal Income Taxes: The Carter Commission Proposals," 34 *Law & Contemporary Problems* 726 (1969).

BREAK, G. "Integration of the Corporation and Personal Income Taxes," 22 *National Tax Journal* 39 (1969).

BREAK, G., and PECHMAN, J. "Relationship Between the Individual and Cor-
Washington, D.C.: The Brookings Institution, 1976. Especially Chapter 4.

BREAK, G., and PECHMAN, J: "Relationship Between the Individual and Corporate Income Taxes," 28 *National Tax Journal* 341 (1975).

*BRITTAIN, J. *Corporate Dividend Policy.* Washington, D.C.: The Brookings Institution, 1966.

*BROWN, J. "An Overview of the White Paper." In: Canadian Tax Foundation, *Report of the Proceedings of the Twenty-Second Tax Conference* 5. Toronto: 1970.

BROWN, R. (ed.). "Canada's Expanding Tax Treaty Network and the Channelling of International Investments," 25 *Canadian Tax Journal* 637 (1977).

BROWN, R. (ed.). "U.S. Tax Reform Proposals—Threat to Canada?" 26 *Canadian Tax Journal* 68 (1978).

BROWNLEE, O. "Integrating Corporation and Individual Income Taxes," 3-35 *Tax Notes* 17 (1975).

BROWNLEE, O. *Taxing the Income From U.S. Corporation Investments Abroad.* Washington, D.C.: American Enterprise Institute, 1979.

*BUCOVETSKY, M., and BIRD, R. "Tax Reform in Canada: A Progress Report," 25 *National Tax Journal* 15 (1972).

*BUEHLER, A. *The Undistributed Profits Tax.* New York: McGraw-Hill Book Co., Inc., 1937.

BURGE, M. "The New Revamped U.K. Corporate Tax System: How It Will Operate," 37 *Journal of Taxation* 110 (1972).

BURGE, M. "New U.K. Corporate Tax May Require Changes in the Way U.S. Businesses Operate There," 37 *Journal of Taxation* 160 (1962).

BURGE, M. "New U.S.–U.K. Tax Treaty Brings Novel Approach to International Transactions," 44 *Journal of Taxation* 294 (1976).

*BUTTERS, J. "Taxation, Incentives, and Financial Capacity," 44 *American Economic Review, Papers and Proceedings* 504 (1954).

*BUTTERS, J. "Would the Complete Integration of the Corporate and Personal Income Taxes Injure Small Business?" In: National Tax Association, *1947 Proceedings of the Fortieth Annual Conference on Taxation* 189. Sacramento: 1947.

*BUTTERS, J., and LINTNER, J. *Effect of Federal Taxes on Growing Enterprises.* Boston: Harvard University, Graduate School of Business Administration, Division of Research, 1945.

*BUTTERS, J., THOMPSON, L., and BOLLINGER, L. *Effects of Taxation: Investment by Individuals*. Boston: Harvard University, Graduate School of Business Administration, Division of Research, 1953.

BYRNE, J. "Integration of Corporation and Individual Taxes No Panacea," 3-31 *Tax Notes* 3 (1975).

*CANADA, DEPARTMENT OF FINANCE. *Summary of 1971 Tax Reform Legislation*. Ottawa: 1971.

*CANADA, MINISTER OF FINANCE. *Proposals for Tax Reform*. Ottawa: Queen's Printer, 1969. The Canadian "White Paper."

CANADA, ROYAL COMMISSION ON CORPORATE CONCENTRATION. *Report of the Royal Commission on Corporate Concentration*. Ottawa: Minister of Supply and Services Canada, 1978.

*CANADA, ROYAL COMMISSION ON TAXATION. *Report of the Royal Commission on Taxation* (6 vols.). Ottawa: Queen's Printer, 1966, 1967. "Carter Commission Report."

*"Canada Tax Law Is Aimed at U.S.," *The New York Times*, 27 December 1971, p. 45.

*CARDYN, C. "General Report: The Multiple Burden on Dividends and Shares by Taxation on Income and Capital of Both Corporations and Shareholders," 55a *Cahiers de droit fiscal international*, I/39 (1970).

CARLSON, G. "International Aspects of Corporate-Shareholder Tax Integration," 11 *Case Western Reserve Journal of International Law* 535 (1979).

CASNA, R. "Another Step Forward to Tax Harmonization? The Proposed Directive on Taxation of Investment Fund Income," 18 *European Taxation* 372 (1978).

*"Chaban-Delmas' TV Speech Fails To Still Critics," *The New York Times*, 17 February 1972, p. 4.

*"Chaban-Fiscal," *The Economist*, 12 February 1972, p. 74.

*CHOMMIE, J. *The Law of Federal Income Taxation*. St. Paul: West Publishing Co., 1968.

*CHOWN, J. *The Reform of Corporation Tax*. London: Institute for Fiscal Studies, 1971.

*CHOWN, J. "The Reform of Corporation Tax: Some International Factors," 1971 *British Tax Review* 215.

CHOWN, J. "The Harmonization of Corporation Tax in the EEC," 1976 *British Tax Review* 39.

CHOWN, J., and NORMAN, R. *Corporation Tax Under the Imputation System: A Business Study*. London: The Financial Times, 1973.

CHOWN, J., and ROWLAND, P. "The Finance Bill—The Reform of Corporation Tax," 1972 *British Tax Review* 133.

CHRISTIAN, E., JR. *Integration of the Corporate Tax: Methods, Motivations, and Effects*. Washington, D.C.: American Enterprise Institute, 1977. Reprint No. 80.

COHEN, E. "Possible Solutions to Practical Problems in Integration of the Corporate and Shareholder Income Tax," 28 *National Tax Journal* 359 (1975).

COIGNARD, L. "French Corporate Tax Reform and Treatment of Dividends," 157 *The Accountant* 311 (1967).

*COLM, G. "The Corporation and the Corporate Income Tax in the American

Economy," 44 *American Economic Review, Papers and Proceedings* 486 (1954).
COMELLO, W. "Italy: Mr. Pandolfi Proposes an Imputation System," 17 *European Taxation* 273.
"A Common European System of Corporate/Shareholder Taxation?" 16 *European Taxation* 41 (1976).
*COMMUNAUTÉ ÉCONOMIQUE EUROPÉENE, COMMISSION. *Le Développement d'un marché européen des capitaux: Rapport d'un groupe d'experts constitué par la Commission de la CEE.* Brussels: 1966. "Segré Report."
"A Comparative Analysis of the Classical, Dual Rate, and Imputation Taxation Systems and an Examination of the Corporate Tax Systems in Belgium, France, Germany, Italy, the Netherlands, and the United Kingdom," 12 *European Taxation,* I/112 (1972).
"Corporate/Shareholder Tax Integration: National Meeting of the U.S.A. Branch of the International Fiscal Association (I.F.A.) on January 12, 1978, New York," 33 *Bulletin for International Fiscal Documentation* 290 (1979).
*"Corporation Tax Takeovers," *The Economist*, 17 June 1972, p. 70.
COX, J. "The Corporate Income Tax and Integration: A Summary of Positions and the Prospects for Change," 58 *Taxes* 10 (1980).
*CROCKETT, J. "Tax Pattern in Latin America," 15 *National Tax Journal* 93 (1962).

DEL GIUDICE, C. "Italy: The Imputation System and Its Implications for Foreign Shareholders," 20 *European Taxation* 309 (1980).
DOBELL, A., and WILSON, T. "The Impact of Taxation on Capital Flows and the Balance of Payments." In: F. Machlup, W. Salant, and L. Tarshis (eds.), *International Mobility and Movement of Capital* 519. New York: Columbia University Press, 1972.
DURAND, P. "A Storm in a Tea Cup: The French 'Avoir Fiscal,'" 26 *Bulletin for International Fiscal Documentation* 144 (1972).
DYHR, P. "Denmark: Introduction of an Imputation System," 16 *European Taxation* 342 (1976).

EISNER, R. "A Hard Look at Corporate Taxes," *Business Week*, 14 December 1974, p. 18.
*"European Communities: The Corporation Income Tax Split Rate Versus the Shareholders' Tax Credit As a Means of Easing the Double Taxation Burden on Corporate Distributions," 8 *European Taxation* 197 (1968).

*FANTOZZI, A. "Italy: The New Method of Taxation of Dividends: The Imputation System," 18 *European Taxation* 260 (1978).
FARRELL, M. "On the Structure of the Capital Market," 72 *Economic Journal* 830 (1962).
FELDSTEIN, M. "Corporate Tax Integration." In: United States, Congress, Senate, Committee on the Budget, *Encouraging Capital Formation Through the Tax Code: Joint Seminars Before the Task Force on Tax Policy and Tax Expenditures and the Task Force on Capital Needs and Monetary Policy* 165. Washington,

D.C.: United States Government Printing Office, 1975. Committee Print, 94th Congress, 1st Session.

FELDSTEIN, M. "Corporate Taxation and Dividend Behaviour," 37 *Review of Economic Studies* 57 (1970).

FELDSTEIN, M. "Corporate Taxation and Dividend Behaviour: A Reply and Extension," 39 *Review of Economic Studies* 415 (1972).

FELDSTEIN, M. "The Effectiveness of the British Differential Profits Tax," 77 *Economic Journal* 947 (1967).

FELDSTEIN, M. "On the Theory of Tax Reform," 6 *Journal of Public Economics* 77 (1976).

FELDSTEIN, M. "Tax Incentives, Corporate Saving and Capital Accumulation in the United States," 2 *Journal of Public Economics* 159 (1973).

FELDSTEIN, M., and FANE, G. "Taxes, Corporate Dividend Policy and Personal Savings: The British Postwar Experience," 44 *Review of Economics and Statistics* 399 (1973).

FELDSTEIN, M., and FLEMMING, J. "Tax Policy, Corporate Saving and Investment Behaviour in Britain," 38 *Review of Economic Studies* 377 (1971).

FELDSTEIN, M., and FRISCH, D. *Corporate Tax Integration: A Quantitative Comparison of Alternatives.* New York: Tax Foundation, Inc., 1977.

FELDSTEIN, M., and FRISCH, D. "Corporate Tax Integration: The Estimated Effects on Capital Accumulation and Tax Distribution of Two Integration Proposals," 30 *National Tax Journal* 37 (1977).

*FLETCHER, W. *Cyclopedia of the Law of Private Corporations* (perm. ed.). Chicago: Callaghan and Co., 1961.

*"France: A Premier Explains, or at Any Rate, Tries," *The New York Times*, 20 February 1972, §4, p. 2.

"France: Corporate Tax Reform and the Treatment of Dividends," 5 *European Taxation* 135 (1965).

"France: Corporate Tax Reform and the Treatment of Dividends: An Incentive Program," 5 *European Taxation* 101 (1965).

"France: New Treatment of Dividend Distributions Under the Tax Treaties Concluded With Germany, Switzerland and the United States—Extension of the 'Avoir Fiscal' to Nonresident Shareholders," 10 *European Taxation*, I/228 (1970).

"France: The New Provisions Concerning Intercorporate Dividends," 5 *European Taxation* 288 (1965).

*"France: Yes, But Should It Be Like That?" *The Economist*, 19 February 1972, p. 37.

*"French Premier Denies Tax Fraud; Chaban, on T.V., Sees Charge As 'Political Maneuver,'" *The New York Times*, 16 February 1972, p. 1.

FROMM, G. (ed.). *Effect of Investment Tax Credit and Accelerated Depreciation on the Level of Interest.* Washington, D.C.: The Brookings Institution, 1970.

GABINET, L., and COFFEY, R. "The Implications of the Economic Concept of Income for Corporation-Shareholder Income Tax Systems," 27 *Case Western Reserve Law Review* 895 (1977).

*"Germany Changes to Tax Credits," *The Economist*, 13 November 1971, pp. 79, 80.

*"Germany: Decision of the Supreme Tax Court ('Bundesfinanzhof') of January 13, 1970," 10 *European Taxation*, II/119 (1970).

GIBSON, R. "Imputation Tax Systems in France, Italy, West Germany and the United Kingdom: Wave of the Future?" 27 *Canadian Tax Journal* 347 (1979).

*"Giscard Lets the Hounds Slip," *The Economist*, 5 February 1972, p. 34.

*GOODE, R. *The Corporation Income Tax*. New York: John Wiley & Sons, Inc., 1951.

*GOODE, R. "Corporation Income Tax Rates." In: United States, Congress, House of Representatives, Committee on Ways and Means, 3 *Tax Revision Compendium* 2280. Washington, D.C.: United States Government Printing Office, 1959.

GOODE, R. "The Postwar Corporation Tax Structure." In: R. Blakey *et al.*, *How Should Corporations Be Taxed?* 46. New York: Tax Institute, Inc., 1946.

*GOODE, R. *The Postwar Corporation Tax Structure*. Washington, D.C.: United States Treasury Department, Divison of Tax Research, 1946.

*GORDON, N. "International Fiscal Arrangements Distorted by Foreign Tax Policies; New Rules Needed," 37 *Journal of Taxation* 113 (1972).

GOUREVITCH, H. "Corporate Tax Integration," 31 *Tax Lawyer* 65 (1977–1978).

GOUREVITCH, H. "Integration of Corporate and Shareholder Taxes on Income: The European Experience." In: Fund for Public Policy Research, 2 *Studies in Taxation, Public Finance and Related Subjects—A Compendium* 1. Washington, D.C.: 1978.

GRAETZ, M. "Dividend Relief Via Shareholder Credits: Tax Preferences Under Chairman Ullman's Proposal," 7 *Tax Notes* 667 (1978).

GRIFFIN, J. "The Effect on U.S. Foreign Direct Investment of the Integration of the Corporate and Personal Income Taxes." In: United States Department of the Treasury, Assistant Secretary for Tax Policy, Office of Tax Analysis, 1 *Compilation of OTA Papers*. Washington, D.C.: United States Government Printing Office, 1978. OTA Paper 22, March 1974.

*GREAT BRITAIN, CHANCELLOR OF THE EXCHEQUER. "Budget Statement," *Hansard*, 6 April 1965, col. 265.

*GROVES, H. "Equity and Expediency in Business Taxation." In: Tax Policy League, *How Shall Business Be Taxed?* 33. New York: 1937.

HAMMER, R. "The Taxation of Income From Corporate Shareholders: Review of Present Systems in Canada, France, Germany, Japan, and the U.K.," 28 *National Tax Journal* 315 (1975).

*HARBERGER, A. "Corporation Income Taxes," 15 *International Encyclopedia of the Social Sciences* 538 (1968).

*HARBERGER, A. "Issues of Tax Reform in Latin America." In: Joint Tax Program of the Organization of American States, Inter-American Development Bank, and Economic Commission for Latin America, *Fiscal Policy for Economic Growth in Latin America* 110. Baltimore: The Johns Hopkins Press, 1965.

HARBERGER, A. "A Landmark in the Annals of Taxation," 1 *Canadian Journal of Economics* 183 (1968).

*HARBRECHT, P. "The Modern Corporation Revisited," 64 *Columbia Law Review* 1410 (1964).

*HARVARD LAW SCHOOL INTERNATIONAL PROGRAM IN TAXATION. World Tax Series: *Taxation in Italy*. Prepared by C. Cobb, Jr., and F. Forte. Chicago: Commerce Clearing House, Inc., 1964. Cited: WTS: *Italy*.

*HARVARD LAW SCHOOL INTERNATIONAL PROGRAM IN TAXATION. World Tax Series: *Taxation in Sweden*. Prepared by M. Norr, F. Duffy, and H. Sterner. Boston: Little, Brown and Company, 1959. Cited: WTS: *Sweden*.

*HARVARD LAW SCHOOL INTERNATIONAL PROGRAM IN TAXATION. World Tax Series: *Taxation in the Federal Republic of Germany*. Prepared by H. Gumpel and C. Boettcher. Chicago: Commerce Clearing House, Inc., 1963. Cited: WTS: *Germany*.

*HARVARD LAW SCHOOL INTERNATIONAL PROGRAM IN TAXATION. World Tax Series: *Taxation in the United Kingdom*. Prepared by W. Brudno and F. Bower. Boston: Little, Brown and Company, 1957. Cited: WTS: *United Kingdom*.

*HARVARD LAW SCHOOL INTERNATIONAL TAX PROGRAM. World Tax Series: *Taxation in France*. Prepared by M. Norr and P. Kerlan. Chicago: Commerce Clearing House, Inc., 1966. Cited: WTS: *France*.

*HARVARD LAW SCHOOL INTERNATIONAL TAX PROGRAM. World Tax Series: *Taxation in the Federal Republic of Germany* (2d ed.). Prepared by H. Gumpel. Chicago: Commerce Clearing House, Inc., loose-leaf, 1969—. Cited: WTS: *Germany* (2d).

*HARVARD LAW SCHOOL INTERNATIONAL TAX PROGRAM. World Tax Series: *Taxation in the United States*. Prepared by M. Chirelstein, L. Day, E. Owens, and S. Surrey. Chicago: Commerce Clearing House, Inc., 1963; Supplement, 1965. Cited: WTS: *United States*.

*HÄUSER, K. "West Germany." In: National Bureau of Economic Research, *Foreign Tax Policies and Economic Growth* 97. New York: Columbia University Press, 1966.

HEINING, A. "The Domestic and International Consequences of the German Corporation Tax Split Rate," 158 *The Accountant* 339 (1968).

HELLIWELL, J. "Proposals for Tax Reform: A Review of the 'White Paper,'" 3 *Canadian Journal of Economics* 487 (1970).

HOLDSTOCK, P. "The U.K. Imputation System: The Peculiarities of the ACT," *Price Waterhouse International News*, May–June 1978, p. 24.

HOLLAND, D. "Some Observations on Full Integration," 28 *National Tax Journal* 353 (1975).

*HOLLAND, D. "Stockholder Differential Taxation and Tax Relief." In: United States, Congress, House of Representatives, Committee on Ways and Means, 3 *Tax Revision Compendium* 1551, 1572. Washington, D.C.: United States Government Printing Office, 1959.

"How the EEC Commission Proposes to Harmonize the Systems of Corporation Taxation and of Withholding Taxes on Dividends," 16 *European Taxation* 52 (1976).

HUFBAUER, G., and FOSTER, D. "U.S. Taxation of the Undistributed Income of Controlled Foreign Corporations in Tax Policy." In: United States Department of the Treasury, *Essays in International Taxation: 1976*, 1. Washington, D.C.: United States Government Printing Office, 1976.

HUFBAUER, G., SCHMIDT, W., TURE, N., BROWNLEE, O., and SMITH, D. *U.S. Taxation of American Business Abroad: An Exchange of Views.* Washington, D.C.: American Enterprise Institute, 1975.

*"Imperial Shell Industries?" *The Economist*, 4 March 1972, p. 87.

*INFORMATION CANADA. *Foreign Direct Investment in Canada.* Ottawa: 1972. "Gray Report."

INGLIS, A., and BROWN, R. "The Road Not Taken: Trends in the Relief of Corporate Double Taxation in the United Kingdom and Canada," 19 *Canadian Tax Journal* 259 (1971).

INSTITUTE FOR FISCAL STUDIES. *Conference on Proposals for a Tax-Credit System.* London: 1973.

*INTERNATIONAL BUREAU OF FISCAL DOCUMENTATION. *Annual Report, 1964.* Amsterdam: 1965.

INTERNATIONAL FISCAL ASSOCIATION, 15th Congress, Second Subject. "The Taxation of Interconnected Companies," 45 *Cahiers de droit fiscal international* 1 (1961).

INTERNATIONAL FISCAL ASSOCIATION, 18th Congress, Second Subject. "The Delimitation Between the Country of Residence and Other Countries of the Power To Tax Corporations and/or Their Shareholders," 49b *Cahiers de droit fiscal international* 1 (1964); 49c *Cahiers de droit fiscal international* 114 (1964). Especially S. Ross (U.S. Reporter), 49b *Cahiers de droit fiscal international* 184 (1964).

*JAPAN, MINISTRY OF FINANCE, TAX BUREAU. *An Outline of Japanese Taxes 1971.* Tokyo: 1971.

*JOINT TAX PROGRAM OF THE ORGANIZATION OF AMERICAN STATES AND INTER-AMERICAN DEVELOPMENT BANK. *Fiscal Survey of Colombia.* Baltimore: The Johns Hopkins Press, 1965.

JONES, D. "Corporations, Double Taxation and the Theory of Integration," 27 *Canadian Tax Journal* 405 (1979).

*JOULOS, J., and KLIMOWSKY, E. "National Report, Israel: The Multiple Burden on Dividends and Shares by Taxation on Income and Capital by Both Corporations and Shareholders," 55a *Cahiers de droit fiscal international*, II/171 (1970).

JUDGE, N. "Ireland: New System of Corporation Tax," 16 *European Taxation* 138 (1976).

*KALDOR, N. "The Economic Effects of Alternative Systems of Corporation Tax." In: United Kingdom, Parliament, House of Commons, *Report From the Select Committee on Corporation Tax* 248. London: H.M. Stationery Office, 1971.

KALDOR, N. *An Expenditure Tax.* London: Allen & Unwin, 1955.

*KALDOR, N. *Indian Tax Reform.* New Delhi: Government of India, Ministry of Finance, Department of Economic Affairs, 1956.

*KEITH, E. "Flat Rate Corporation Tax Versus Present Tax." In: Tax Institute, *Reappraisal of Business Taxation* 175. Princeton, N.J.: 1962.

KERLAN, P. "The French Imputation System: The 'Avoir Fiscal,'" 33 *Bulletin for International Fiscal Documentation* 459 (1979).

KESSELMAN, J. *General Equilibrium Appraisal of Corporate Tax Integration: Potential and Limitations.* Vancouver: University of British Columbia, Department of Economics, 1978.

KING, M. "Corporate Taxation and Dividend Behaviour: A Comment," 38 *Review of Economic Studies* 377 (1971).

KING, M. "Corporate Taxation and Dividend Behaviour: A Further Comment," 39 *Review of Economic Studies* 231 (1972).

*KING, M. "Memorandum." In: United Kingdom, Parliament, House of Commons, *Report From the Select Committee on Corporation Tax* 231. London: H.M. Stationery Office, 1971.

KINGSON, C., and SCHOENBLUM, J. "Derivative Foreign Tax Credit and U.K. ACT: Dealing With an Integrated Tax System," 45 *Journal of Taxation* 266 (1976).

KITENDAUGH, G. "Taxation and Economic Policy," 43 *Taxes* 111 (1965).

KRZYZANIAK, M. (ed.). *Effects of Corporation Income Tax.* Detroit: Wayne State University Press, 1966.

KUIPER, W. "Federal Republic of Germany: Corporate Income Tax Reform Law: Disguised Profits Distributions," 16 *European Taxation* 418 (1976).

LAMP, W. "Dividend Provisions of Proposed U.S.-U.K. Income Tax Treaty," 55 *Taxes* 300 (1977).

LAMP, W. "U.S.-U.K. Tax Treaty Proposal: New Look at Dividends," 64-3 *Financial Executive* 14 (1976).

*LINDBECK, A. "Theories and Problems in Swedish Economic Policy in the Post-War Period," 58 *American Economic Review, Supplement* 1 (1968).

LINTNER, J. "Distribution of Incomes of Corporations Among Dividends, Retained Earnings and Taxes," 46 *American Economic Review, Papers and Proceedings* 97 (1956).

LUBICK, D. "Statement of Donald C. Lubick, Acting Secretary for Tax Policy, Treasury Department." In: United States, Congress, House of Representatives, Committee on Ways and Means, *The President's 1978 Tax Reduction and Reform Proposals: Hearings on the President's 1978 Tax Program* 6244. Washington, D.C.: United States Government Printing Office, 1978. Serial 95-78, 95th Congress, 2d Session.

"Luxembourg: The 1967 Income Tax Reform," 8 *European Taxation* 104 (1968).

*MASON, E. "Corporation," 3 *International Encyclopedia of the Social Sciences* 396 (1968).

*MASON, E. (ed.). *The Corporation in Modern Society.* Cambridge, Mass.: Harvard University Press, 1959.

MCDANIEL, P., and AULT, H. *Introduction to United States International Taxation.* Deventer: Kluwer, 1977.

McLure, C., Jr. "The Case for Integrating the Income Taxes," 28 *National Tax Journal* 257 (1975).

McLure, C., Jr. "Integrating the Income Taxes: How To Do It Right," 5-36 *Tax Notes* 3 (1977).

McLure, C., Jr. "Integration of the Income Taxes: Why and How," 2 *Journal of Corporate Taxation* 429 (1975–1976).

*McLure, C., Jr. "Integration of the Personal and Corporate Income Taxes: The Missing Element in Recent Tax Reform Proposals," 88 *Harvard Law Review* 532 (1975).

McLure, C., Jr. *Must Corporate Income Be Taxed Twice*? Washington, D.C.: The Brookings Institution, 1979.

McLure, C., Jr. "A Status Report on Tax Integration in the United States," 31 *National Tax Journal* 313 (1978).

McLure, C., Jr., and Surrey, S. "Integration of Income Taxes: Issues for Debate," 55-5 *Harvard Business Review* 169 (1977).

Mieszkowski, P. "Carter on the Taxation of International Income Flows," 22 *National Tax Journal* 97 (1969).

*Miller, M. "The Corporation Income Tax and Corporate Financial Policies." In: Commission on Money and Credit, *Stabilization Policies* 381. Englewood Cliffs, N.J.: Prentice-Hall, Inc., 1963.

Miller, N. "The Corporation Tax in the United Kingdom: Some Implications for U.S. Investors," 43 *Taxes* 678 (1965).

*Mitchell, C. "Corporate-Source Income Under the Tax Reform Bill," 19 *Canadian Tax Journal* 379 (1971).

Mittendorff-Snaas, I. "Federal Republic of Germany: Introduction of a Total Imputation System," 16 *European Taxation* 348 (1976).

*Moore, M. "The Carter Report: Some Misgivings," 1 *Canadian Journal of Economics* 195 (1968).

*Musgrave, P. "Harmonization of Direct Business Taxes: A Case Study." In: C. Shoup (ed.), 2 *Fiscal Harmonization in Common Markets*. New York: Columbia University Press, 1967.

*Musgrave, P. "International Aspects—II." In: Canadian Tax Foundation, *Report of the Proceedings of the Twenty-Second Tax Conference* 308. Toronto: 1970.

*Musgrave, R. "The Carter Commission Report," 1 *Canadian Journal of Economics* 159 (1968).

*Musgrave, R. "Growth With Equity," 53 *American Economic Review, Papers and Proceedings* 323 (1963).

*Musgrave, R. "Taxation of Corporations." In: Canadian Tax Foundation, *Report of the Proceedings of the Twenty-Second Tax Conference* 124. Toronto: 1970.

*Musgrave, R., and Gillis, M. *Fiscal Reform for Colombia: Final Report and Staff Papers of the Colombian Commission on Tax Reform*. Cambridge, Mass.: Harvard Law School International Tax Program, 1971.

*Musgrave, R., and Musgrave, P. *Public Finance in Theory and Practice.* New York: McGraw-Hill Book Company, 1973.

*"New Emphasis on Taxation Policy: OECD Sets Up a New Committee on Fiscal

Affairs," 11 *European Taxation*, I/206 (1971). Reprinted from *OECD Observer*, August 1971, p. 12.

NEW YORK STATE BAR ASSOCIATION, TAX SECTION, COMMITTEE ON CORPORATIONS. "Report on the Integration of Corporate and Individual Income Taxes," 31 *Tax Lawyer* 37 (1977–1978).

NOBES, C. "EEC Imputation Systems of Corporation Tax and the Proposal for a Directive on Harmonisation," 1979 *Journal of Business Law* 306.

*NORR, M. "The French Reform of Dividend Taxation and Common Market Tax Harmonization," 44 *Taxes* 320 (1966).

*NORR, M. *Reserves for Future Investment: A Swedish Tax Incentive.* Amsterdam: International Bureau of Fiscal Documentation, 1974.

*OLDMAN, O. "Tax Reform in El Salvador," 6 *Inter-American Law Review* 379 (1964).

*OLDMAN, O., and OWENS, E. "The International Tax Program," 14 *Canadian Tax Journal* 444 (1966).

ORGANISATION FOR ECONOMIC CO-OPERATION AND DEVELOPMENT. *Company Tax Systems in OECD Member Countries.* Paris: 1973.

ORGANISATION FOR ECONOMIC CO-OPERATION AND DEVELOPMENT. *Theoretical and Empirical Aspects of Corporate Taxation.* Paris: 1974.

*ORGANISATION FOR ECONOMIC CO-OPERATION AND DEVELOPMENT, FISCAL COMMITTEE. *Draft Double Taxation Convention on Income and Capital: Report of the OECD Fiscal Committee.* Paris: 1963.

*OWENS, E., and BALL, G. *The Indirect Credit* (2 vols.). Cambridge, Mass.: Harvard Law School International Tax Program, vol. I, 1975; vol. II, 1979.

PARKER, J. "Evaluating Proposals for Eliminating Double Taxation in the U.S.," 30 *Tax Executive* 210 (1977–1978).

PATRICK, R., JR. "Simplifying the Taxation of Foreign Source Income," 30 *National Tax Journal* 321 (1977).

*PAUL, R. *Taxation in the United States.* Boston: Little, Brown and Company, 1954.

*PECHMAN, J. *Federal Tax Policy.* Washington, D.C.: The Brookings Institution, 1966.

*PECHMAN, J. *Federal Tax Policy* (rev. ed.). Washington, D.C.: The Brookings Institution, 1971.

*PECHMAN, J. "Taxation: Personal Income Tax," 15 *International Encyclopedia of the Social Sciences* 529 (1968).

*PETRIE, J. *The Taxation of Corporate Income in Canada.* Toronto: University of Toronto Press, 1952.

PICKERILL, R. "European Attempts To Achieve Equity in Corporate Taxes," 30 *Tax Executive* 211 (1977–1978).

PLASSCHAERT, S. "First Principles About Schedular and Global Frames of Income Taxation," 30 *Bulletin for International Fiscal Documentation* 99 (1976).

POOL, W. "Reply to the Special Issue on the Harmonisation of Systems of Company Taxation and of Withholding Taxes," 16 *European Taxation* 334 (1976).

*POPKIN, W. *The Deduction for Business Expenses and Losses*. Cambridge, Mass.: Harvard Law School International Tax Program, 1973.

*"Premier's Tax Avoidance Stirs French," *The New York Times*, 7 February 1972, p. 7.

*PREST, A. "Corporate Income Taxation in Latin America." In: Joint Tax Program of the Organization of American States, Inter-American Development Bank, and Economic Commission for Latin America, *Fiscal Policy for Economic Growth in Latin America* 234. Baltimore: The Johns Hopkins Press, 1965.

*PREST, A. "Minutes of Evidence Taken 6 July 1971." In: United Kingdom, Parliament, House of Commons, *Report From the Select Committee on Corporation Tax* 110. London: H.M. Stationery Office, 1971.

*PREST, A. "The Select Committee on Corporation Tax," 1972 *British Tax Review* 15.

*"Proposed Directive for the Harmonisation of Systems of Company Taxation and of Withholding Taxes on Dividends," 16 *European Taxation* 52 (1976).

*RÄDLER, A. "Corporate Income Taxation in the European Economic Community," 19 *Canadian Tax Journal* 277 (1971).

RÄDLER, A. "The German Imputation System: Model Computation of Tax Burden of a German Subsidiary or Branch," 33 *Bulletin for International Fiscal Documentation* 317 (1979).

*RÄDLER, A. "International Aspects—II." In: Canadian Tax Foundation, *Report of the Proceedings of the Twenty-Second Tax Conference* 299. Toronto: 1970.

RÄDLER, A. "International Capital Markets and Taxation," 13-6 *Management International Review* 65 (1973).

*RÄDLER, A., and EDWARDS, R. "The Split Rate of Corporation Income Tax in Germany—A Tax Advantage for Foreign-Owned Subsidiaries," *CCH Common Market Reports* (Transfer Binder) ¶ 9051 (1963).

*"Rank Organisation: New Tax Imputations," *Investors' Chronicle* [London], 7 July 1972, p. 24.

*RÉAMONN, S. *The Philosophy of the Corporate Tax*. Dublin: Institute of Public Administration, 1970.

"Relation Between the Corporation and Individual Income Taxes." In: J. Pechman and G. Break, *Federal Tax Reform: The Impossible Dream?* 90. Washington, D.C.: The Brookings Institution, 1975.

*"Report of the Department of State on the Protocol to the 1967 Treaty With France, Signed on October 12, 1970," 1 *CCH Tax Treaties* ¶ 2839.

*ROBERTS, S., *et al.* "A Report on Complexity and the Income Tax," 27 *Tax Law Review* 325 (1971–1972).

RUBNER, A. "The Irrelevancy of the British Differential Profits Tax," 74 *Economic Journal* 347 (1964).

*SAMUELSON, P. *Economics* (10th ed.). New York: McGraw-Hill Book Company, 1976.

SANDEN, B. T. "Taxation of Income From Corporate Shareholding," 28 *National Tax Journal* 255 (1975).

SATO, M. "International Aspects of Integration of the Corporate and Personal

Income Taxes," 8 *Georgia Journal of International and Comparative Law* 779 (1978).

*SATO, M. "The Tax Treatment of Partnerships." Unpublished, International Monetary Fund, Washington, D.C., 1 May 1973. DM/73/30.

*SATO, M., and BIRD, R. "International Aspects of the Taxation of Corporations and Shareholders," 22 *International Monetary Fund Staff Papers* 384 (1975).

*SCHLESINGER, E. "Tax Policy Recommendations of Technical Assistance Missions: Evaluation, Pattern, and Interpretation." In: Joint Tax Program of the Organization of American States, Inter-American Development Bank, and Economic Commission for Latin America, *Fiscal Policy for Economic Growth in Latin America* 425. Baltimore: The Johns Hopkins Press, 1965.

*SCHUMPETER, J. *Business Cycles* (2 vols.). New York: McGraw-Hill Book Company, Inc., 1939.

SEVERIENS, J. "Does a Dividend Tax Credit Work?" 54 *Taxes* 17 (1976).

SEVERIENS, J. "The Imputation Tax System: A Re-Appraisal," 30 *Bulletin for International Fiscal Documentation* 143 (1976).

*SHOUP, C. *Public Finance.* Chicago: Aldine Publishing Co., 1969.

*SHOUP, C., *et al. The Fiscal System of Venezuela: A Report.* Baltimore: The Johns Hopkins Press, 1959.

SIVAPRAKASAM, C. "Proposals for Harmonisation of Company and Dividend Taxation Among E.E.C. Countries," 16 *European Taxation* 328 (1976).

SKINNER, R. "Problems Involved in Alternative Proposals for Integration or Reduction in U.S. Tax: Implementation," 28 *National Tax Journal* 368 (1975).

*SLITOR, R. "The Corporate Income Tax: A Re-Evaluation," 5 *National Tax Journal* 289 (1952).

*SLITOR, R. "Reform of the Business Tax Structure: Analysis of Problems and Alternative Remedial Proposals." In: R. Musgrave and M. Gillis, *Fiscal Reform for Colombia: Final Report and Staff Papers of the Colombian Commission on Tax Reform* 463. Cambridge, Mass.: Harvard Law School International Tax Program, 1971.

SLITOR, R. "The Role of Corporate Income Taxation," 7 *National Tax Journal* 227 (1954).

SMITH, D. "Relief From Double Taxation of Dividend Income," 55-1 *Harvard Business Review* 87 (1977).

SOLDATI, M. "Taxing Corporate Income: European Harmonization and the Italian Experience," 24 *American Journal of Comparative Law* 273 (1976).

"Special Issue on the Harmonisation of Systems of Company Taxation and of Withholding Taxes on Dividends (E.E.C.-Commission Proposal of 23 July 1975)," 16 *European Taxation* 39 (1976).

STONE, R. "Debt-Equity Distinctions in the Tax Treatment of the Corporation and Its Shareholders," 42 *Tulane Law Review* 251 (1968).

*"Structure de l'impôt des sociétés" (Doc. 7228/XIV/70-D de la Commission des Communautés Européenes du 29 Mai 1970), ¶ 8, reprinted in 41 *La Fiscalité du Marché Commun* 93 (1970).

SUNLEY, E. "Effective Corporate Tax Rates and Integration," 3-34 *Tax Notes* 3 (1975).

*SURREY, S. "Income Tax Problems of Corporations and Shareholders: American

Law Institute Tax Project—American Bar Association Committee Study on Legislative Revision," 14 *Tax Law Review* 1 (1958–1959).

SURREY, S. "Reflections on 'Integration' of Corporation and Individual Income Taxes," 28 *National Tax Journal* 335 (1975).

*SURREY, S. "Statement by Assistant Secretary of the Treasury Surrey, April 21, 1966, at the School of Law of the State University of New York [at Buffalo], on Federal Tax Policy in the 1960's." In: United States Treasury Department, *Annual Report of the Secretary of the Treasury on the State of Finances for the Fiscal Year Ended June 30, 1966*, 366. Washington, D.C.: United States Government Printing Office, 1967. Reprinted in W. Hellmuth and O. Oldman (eds.), *Tax Policy and Tax Reform: 1961–1969—Selected Speeches and Testimony of Stanley S. Surrey* 115. Chicago: Commerce Clearing House, Inc., 1973.

*SURREY, S. "The United States Tax System and International Relationships—Current Developments, 1965–6," 20 *Bulletin for International Fiscal Documentation* 45 (1966).

*SURREY, S. "The United States Tax System and International Tax Relationships," 12 *Canadian Tax Journal* 460 (1964).

SURREY, S. "The United States Tax System and International Tax Relationships—Current Developments, 1967," 2 *CCH Tax Treaties* ¶ 9970. Address before the National Foreign Trade Council Convention, New York, 1 November 1967.

SURREY, S. "The United States Tax System and International Tax Relationships—Perspective in 1964." In: W. Hellmuth and O. Oldman (eds.), *Tax Policy and Tax Reform: 1961–1969—Selected Speeches and Testimony of Stanley S. Surrey* 329. Chicago: Commerce Clearing House, Inc., 1973.

SURREY, S., and MCLURE, C., JR. "Integration of Income Taxes: Issues for Debate," 55-5 *Harvard Business Review* 169 (1977).

*SUTHERLAND, W. "A Brief Description of Federal Taxes on Corporations Since 1861," 7 *Law & Contemporary Problems* 266 (1940).

TASK FORCE ON TAX POLICY AND TAX EXPENDITURES. "Tax Expenditures: Briefing Paper on Tax Incentives for Business Investment." In: United States, Congress, Senate, Committee on the Budget, *Encouraging Capital Formation Through the Tax Code: Joint Seminars Before the Task Force on Tax Policy and Tax Expenditures and the Task Force on Capital Needs and Monetary Policy* 223, at 236. Washington, D.C.: United States Government Printing Office, 1975. Committee Print, 94th Congress, 1st Session.

TAYLOR, W. "U.S. Tax Treaties and Common Market Corporate Tax Systems," 28 *Tax Lawyer* 73 (1974–1975).

TELKAMP, H. "The Effects of the 1977 German Corporation Tax Reform on the Sale of Shares Between Domestic and Foreign Taxpayers," 1978 *Intertax* 19.

*THOM, S. "The Individual and the Family in Tax Reform." In: Canadian Tax Foundation, *Report of the Proceedings of the Twenty-Second Tax Conference* 14. Toronto: 1970.

*UEMATSU, M. "Computation of Income in Japanese Income Tax Administration: A Study in the Adjustment of Theory to Reality." In: A. von Mehren (ed.), *Law* *in Japan*: *The Legal Order in a Changing Society* 567. Cambridge, Mass.: Harvard University Press, 1963.

"The UK Retaliatory Strike—The ACT Concession," *International Tax Report*, 29 August 1977, p. 4.

*UNITED KINGDOM, BOARD OF INLAND REVENUE. "International Investment." In: United Kingdom, Parliament, House of Commons, *Report From the Select Comittee on Corporation Tax* 213. London: H.M. Stationery Office, 1971.

*UNITED KINGDOM, CHANCELLOR OF THE EXCHEQUER. *Reform of Corporation Tax.* London: H.M. Stationery Office, 1971. Cmnd. 4630. "Green Paper."

*UNITED KINGDOM, INCOME TAX CODIFICATION COMMITTEE. *Report* (2 vols.). London: H.M. Stationery Office, 1936. Cmd. 5131, 5132.

UNITED KINGDOM, PARLIAMENT, HOUSE OF COMMONS. *Report From the Select Committee on Corporation Tax.* London: H.M. Stationery Office, 1971.

*UNITED KINGDOM, ROYAL COMMISSION ON THE TAXATION OF PROFITS AND INCOME. *Final Report.* London: H.M. Stationery Office, 1955. Cmd. 9474.

*UNITED NATIONS, ECONOMIC AND SOCIAL COUNCIL, FISCAL COMMISSION. *Comparative Approach to National and International Corporate Tax Problems.* U.N. Doc. No. E/CN.8/55, 3 May 1951.

*UNITED NATIONS, ECONOMIC AND SOCIAL COUNCIL, FISCAL COMMISSION. *Corporate Tax Problems.* New York: 1952. U.N. Doc. No. E/CN.8/66.

*UNITED STATES, CONGRESS, HOUSE OF REPRESENTATIVES, COMMITTEE ON WAYS AND MEANS. *President's 1961 Tax Recommendations—Hearings* (4 vols.). Washington, D.C.: United States Government Printing Office, 1961. 87th Congress, 1st Session.

UNITED STATES, CONGRESS, JOINT COMMITTEE ON TAXATION. *Tax Policy and Capital Formation*: *Prepared for the Use of the Task Force on Capital Formation of the Committee on Ways and Means.* Washington, D.C.: United States Government Printing Office, 1977. Committee Print, 95th Congress, 1st Session. Especially pp. 9–17.

*UNITED STATES, CONGRESS, SENATE, COMMITTEE ON FINANCE. *Technical Amendments Act of 1958*: *Report To Accompany H.R. 8381.* Washington, D.C.: United States Government Printing Office, 1958. S. Rep. No. 1983, 85th Congress, 2d Session.

UNITED STATES, DEPARTMENT OF THE TREASURY. *Blueprints for Basic Tax Reform.* Washington, D.C.: United States Government Printing Office, 1977. Especially pp. 68–75, 194–200.

*UNITED STATES, DEPARTMENT OF THE TREASURY, INTERNAL REVENUE SERVICE. *Statistics of Income—1970, Corporation Income Tax Returns.* Washington, D.C.: United States Government Printing Office, 1974.

*U.S. TAX MISSION TO JAPAN (Shoup Mission). *Report on Japanese Taxation* (4 vols.). Tokyo: General Headquarters, Supreme Commander for the Allied Powers, 1949.

*VAN DEN TEMPEL, A. *Corporation Tax and Individual Income Tax in the European Communities.* Brussels: Commission of the European Communities, 1970. Competition: Approximation of Legislation Series, Study No. 15.

VAN RAFELGHEM, C., and VAN WAARDENBURG, D. "The Impact of the 1973 Income Tax Reform on Dividend Taxation," 14 *European Taxation* 41 (1974).

VAN ROOIJEN, M. "Interrelationship of Corporation Tax and Income Tax of Shareholders," 31 *Bulletin for International Fiscal Documentation* 64 (1977).

WARREN, A. "The Corporate Interest Reduction: A Policy Evaluation," 83 *Yale Law Journal* 1585 (1974).

WARREN, A. "The Relation and Integration of Individual and Corporate Income Taxes," 94 *Harvard Law Review* 721 (1980–1981).

*WATKIN, V. *Taxes and Tax Harmonization in Central America.* Cambridge, Mass.: Harvard Law School International Tax Program, 1967.

*WHEATCROFT, G. "A Summing Up." In: Canadian Tax Foundation, *Report of the Proceedings of the Twenty-Second Tax Conference* 408. Toronto: 1970.

WOLFMAN, B. "Integration of Corporate and Individual Income Taxes in the United States," 33 *Bulletin for International Fiscal Documentation* 305 (1979).

WOODWORTH, L. "Statement of Assistant Secretary of the Treasury Laurence N. Woodworth Before the Senate Foreign Relations Committee on Pending Income Tax Treaties With the U.K., Korea, and the Philippines," 1977–8 *Tax Management International Journal* 13.

*WREDE, F. "Reform of the Corporation Tax and the Trade Tax." In: United Kingdom, Parliament, House of Commons, *Report From the Select Committee on Corporation Tax* 203. London: H.M. Stationery Office, 1971.

YORIO, E. (ed.). *International Taxation and Transfer Pricing: Annual Proceedings of the Fordham Corporate Law Institute.* New York: Matthew Bender, 1977.

*YUDKIN, L. *A Legal Structure for Effective Income Tax Administration.* Cambridge, Mass.: Harvard Law School International Tax Program, 1971.